The Edge of Knowing

The Edge of Knowing

DREAMS, HISTORY, AND REALISM IN MODERN CHINESE LITERATURE

Roy Bing Chan

A Robert B. Heilman Book

UNIVERSITY OF WASHINGTON PRESS *Seattle and London*

the modern language initiative

THIS BOOK IS MADE POSSIBLE BY A COLLABORATIVE GRANT FROM THE ANDREW W. MELLON FOUNDATION.

The Edge of Knowing is published with support from a generous bequest established by Robert B. Heilman, distinguished scholar and chair of the University of Washington English Department from 1948 to 1971. The Heilman Book Fund assists in the publication of books in the humanities.

Printed and bound in the United States of America

21 20 19 18 17 5 4 3 2 1

University of Washington Press

www.washington.edu/uwpress

Cataloging information is on file with the Library of Congress.

ISBN 978-0-295-99899-2

The paper used in this publication is acid-free and meets the minimum requirements of American National Standard for Information Sciences—Permanence of Paper for Printed Library Materials, ANSI Z39.48–1984. ∞

For my mother, the bravest dreamer
I have ever known

CONTENTS

ACKNOWLEDGMENTS

I thank Andrew F. Jones, my mentor, whose generous care and devotion sustained me, especially during moments of doubt. It is a debt I have no chance of ever repaying. In addition, I express deep gratitude to Irina Aronovna Paperno and Barbara Spackman for their formative intellectual influence. Irina Aronovna taught me almost all I know about what to do with literature. Barbara expanded my theoretical horizons and consistently championed me. Theodore Huters generously mentored me, and I consider myself lucky to be his student although I never took a class from him. Eric Naiman and William Schaefer also offered great support and advice throughout the years. Willis Konick, Galya Diment, Gordana Crnkovic, James West, Henry Staten, and Nikolai Popov inspired me to pursue the study of literature at the University of Washington. Any remaining errors in the book are mine.

I thank my editor, Lorri Hagman, of the University of Washington Press for providing this manuscript a welcoming home, for providing salient critique, and for pushing me to produce a better, much improved manuscript. The Modern Language Initiative, funded by the Andrew W. Mellon Foundation and established by the late Helen Tartar, provided key subvention support. The University of Oregon Underrepresented Minority Recruitment Program also provided support. I thank these programs for making publication possible.

Material from Chapters 2 and 5 has appeared as articles: "Dreaming as Representation: *Wild Grass* and Realism's Responsibility," *Journal of Modern Literature in Chinese* 11, no. 2 (Spring 2014): 13–38; "Occupied Dream: Politico-Affective Space and the Collective in Zong Pu's Fiction," *Modern Chinese Literature and Culture* 25, no. 2 (Fall 2013): 21–50. I thank the editors of these journals for their gracious cooperation.

The Institution of International Education Fulbright Award and Harvard University Fairbank Center for Chinese Studies An Wang Postdoctoral Fellowship offered support that allowed me to travel, research, and write this book. Professors Wang Zhongchen, Xie Zhixi, and Wang Hui made study at Tsinghua University possible. The libraries at the University of California, Berkeley, the University of Oregon, Harvard University, Tsinghua University, the Beijing National Library, and Shanghai Library provided indispensable research support.

I thank the various interlocutors who provided such valuable critique of and support for this manuscript. They include Nick Admussen, Tie Xiao, Anup Grewal, Charles Laughlin, Enhua Zhang, Nick Kaldis, Eileen Cheng, Tom Mullaney, Jason McGrath, Haiyan Lee, Kirk Denton, Wendy Larson, Bryna Goodman, Richard King, and Ying Qian. Thank you all for your inspiration.

Countless friends at UC Berkeley, the College of William and Mary, and the University of Oregon offered fellowship in the original sense of the term. They include Andrew Leong, Anastasia Kayiatos, Amanda Buster, Evelyn Shih, Albert Wu, Juan Caballero, Michael Cronin, Nicholas Medevielle, Arthur Knight, Anita Angelone, Sergio Ferrarese, Jorge Terukina, Mark Quigley, Mayra Bottaro, Jenifer Presto, Katya Hokanson, and Susanna Lim, as well as my current colleagues in the Department of East Asian Languages and Literatures. Special thanks are due to Maram Epstein, who successfully applied for an Underrepresented Minority Recruitment Program fellowship on my behalf.

My best friend, Susan Kas, offered unstinting support in a friendship that has now lasted over fifteen years. I feel lucky to be a part of her family (including Josh, Jennie, Drew, Evee, Sylvia, and now Jonah). I look forward to running countless marathons together. As the marathon of writing this book approached the end, Cameron Mulder's warm companionship inspired me to cross the finish line.

I am tremendously grateful for my family, who supported me as I dared to wade into academic life. Without their unconditional support, a working-class kid like me would not have lasted long in the ivory tower. My brothers Ron and Rick have been stalwart champions. My parents, Bing-man Chan and Choi-yuk Tam Chan, who immigrated to this country with little education and spent all their lives as manual laborers, demonstrated the value of love, acceptance, and sacrifice. My mother, in particular, taught me that everyone deserves an equal shot at a decent life. We continue to recount our dreams to each other, sometimes strange, sometimes sad, oftentimes silly. My parents dreamed the best for all of us, and I can only hope that what I have done so far goes some way toward fulfilling their wishes.

The Edge of Knowing

Introduction

In the novel *The New Story of the Stone* (Xin shitou ji, 1905), Wu Jianren's (1866–1910) science-fiction sequel to the renowned eighteenth-century classic *Dream of the Red Chamber* (Hong lou meng; also known as *The Story of the Stone* [Shitou ji]), the protagonist Jia Baoyu, after a vague period of self-imposed exile, suddenly finds himself in contemporary twentieth-century China. In a dilapidated temple he reunites with his valet, Beiming, who has been searching for his master ever since the first novel concluded. Recounting his arduous search to find Baoyu, Beiming describes entering a mysterious and enchanted temple, where he encounters a group of Daoists. They invite him to stay the night and he consents, only to wake up suddenly reunited with Baoyu in the rundown temple. As Beiming notes, "I didn't know that once I fell asleep I would sleep right into this time, and right into this place. I am truly at a loss."[1] Baoyu is similarly at a loss, unsure of where he is and what era he inhabits. In the old temple they locate an item they have never seen before: a modern daily newspaper, Shanghai's *Shenbao*. Baoyu tries to make sense of the text; what most perplexes him, however, are the dates inscribed on the header: "The X month and X day of the twenty-sixth year of the Guangxu reign, equivalent on the Western calendar to 1901, X month and X day, Sunday. [Baoyu] gasped in shock."[2]

Other late Qing novels also feature emphasis on sleeping and dreaming as ways of figuring modernity's trauma. In the beginning of Liu E's (1857–1909) *The Travels of Lao Can* (Lao Can youji, 1903–5), the eponymous hero dreams of a steamship cast adrift in turbulent waters, filled with desperate people. Lao Can sails toward the ship in a small fishing boat, trying to offer assistance. Unable to unite (*tuanti*) for their collective rescue, the panicked passengers instead try to sink the fishing boat. The forlorn steamship unable to save itself is an obvious allegory for China's predicament.[3]

In these novels we can see how Chinese writers in the early twentieth century were framing the challenge, and even trauma, of modernity in terms of an abrupt awakening from a dream. Not only did the somatic transition from sleep to awakening suggest how global capitalist modernity was to be framed in terms of alertness; the past itself was now suddenly understood to have been a dreamy enchantment. The trope of sleeping and awakening also captured the profound sense of disorientation, even dizziness, that people emerging from a deep sleep have often experienced. How did we suddenly wake up in "this time" and in "this place"? How can we understand the reality of our present when still under the foggy spell of our dreams? Chinese writers have figuratively understood modernity not simply under the familiar terms of progress and rejuvenation but also enmeshed within a more visceral web of figures: sleeping, awakening, hallucination, and, most important, dreaming.

Dreams have long played a role in traditional Chinese culture and belief, and often were considered an occasion when communications from the numinous realm arrived to people during sleep. Dreams were an important component in both court and folk divination. They are also a prominent motif in Chinese philosophy. *The Analects* (Lun yu), a compilation of sayings attributed to Confucius (sixth century BCE), record the sage regularly dreaming of the Duke of Zhou, one of the mythical founders of Chinese civilization.[4] Many are familiar with the passage in the "Inner Chapter" of the *Zhuangzi* titled "Discussion on Making All Things Equal" (Qi wu lun) in which the philosopher muses on whether he dreamed of being a butterfly or is actually a butterfly that dreamed of Zhuangzi.[5] This parable illustrates the constant flux and instability of reality. In Buddhism, dream is often used as a metaphor for the illusoriness of the phenomenal world, thus underscoring the necessity of letting go of one's attachments. Traditional Chinese literature has often made use of dreams as a narrative device that allows characters to enter alternate worlds or convene with gods and spirits. It also often features as a narrative conceit through which characters learn to recognize life's ephemerality.

In standard Chinese (Mandarin), *dream* is *meng*. The word has spawned a large number of related words, each displaying a different shade of meaning. Nightmares are *emeng*. One can have a dream (*zuomeng*) or see within a dream (*mengjian*). A dream world is a *mengjing*. *Mengxiang* denotes dreams that are more akin to deeply held ideals or wishes than a somatic experience, while *menghuan* denotes illusory fancy. In any case, whether referring to the actual physical experience of dreaming in sleep or as a figure for desire, all the various terms have in common an interest on modes of existence and being that are fundamentally different from extant reality. While cultures do differ in their particular understandings of dreams, it is safe to say that most cultures invest in dreams a deep symbolic value that expresses an interest in possible worlds beyond the present. They express a common human interest in imagining alternate spaces and temporalities.

Through the late nineteenth and twentieth centuries, the rhetoric of dreams constituted an important discursive frame through which to imagine and represent the monumental changes in Chinese history. The language of dreams was appropriate for describing modernity's disorienting effects. Dreams and their associated rhetoric played a prominent role in twentieth-century Chinese intellectual culture and modern literature. They also complicated conventional understandings of historical knowledge and realist literary practice. Dream discourse in realist literature was a site through which hidden tensions between empiricism and desire, between social critique and utopian aspiration, and between the world and language became apparent. These antinomies in turn animated an intellectual and literary field dominated by a scientistic framework. During the May Fourth Movement, a campaign to remake and modernize Chinese culture that began in 1919, intellectuals identified dream itself as an exciting new area of scientific research, one buttressed by the arrival of psychoanalytic theories into China. However, the language and poetics of dream discourse were not transparent and abstract but polyvalent, expressive, and allusively dense. The formal materiality and semiotic richness of dream discourse and hermeneutics, one that drew upon a large indigenous heritage of dream lore, complicated simple referential notions of language and narrative. Examining dream discourse thus suggests ways in which realist narrative grappled with, on one hand, the mercurial desire and emotionality inherent within language and fiction and, on the other, a premodern literary and cultural heritage that had to be either disavowed or rendered appropriate for contemporary times.

Some readers may wonder if what is being emphasized here is the physical experience of dreaming or dream as a kind of figurative discourse about fantasy in general. Any comprehensive conception of dream should encompass both the physical and symbolic connotations. From the somatic point of view, dreams are phenomena by which we, in sleep, engender symbolic landscapes of unconscious experience that are simultaneously baffling as well as pregnant with possible, portentous significance. Dreams are thus somatic occasions whereby the body itself seemingly generates meaning. From the symbolic standpoint, dreams are figurative of desire, often utopian in nature, that carries within it the implication of an alternative embodiment, of a being "other than" that is wished for over and above one's present existence. By foregrounding their own difficult interpretation, dreams also point to the materiality of signification itself. Dreams thus engage the affective resources of the signifier and encourage the subject to engage with the creation of meaning in a seemingly tactile manner. "Dream" cannot be confined merely to a physical experience, a metaphor, or a metapragmatic discursive gesture but instead designates a dynamic conceptual matrix that encompasses all of these notions. As these various usages are related to each other, dreaming both as an experience and as metaphor will be explored.

Consideration of dreams facilitates a revised exploration of literary realism that focuses less on its narrative ontology or its sociopolitical end goals and more on its very "management" of multiple modes of representation, some more empirical, others more fantastic. In turn, these multiple modes of representation articulate a utopian desire for the real, a category that is itself constantly shifting in different literary, cultural, and political contexts. Dream is not an escape from proper historical consciousness but a supplemental mode to such consciousness. While dreams may convey a fantastic or distorted reflection of historical reality, we should also take note of the indexical relation between the form of the dream and the historical reality to which it responds. Such an emphasis on the dream's production under the pressure of historic circumstances allows us to see how dream registers the felt effects of a cataclysmic history on dreamers and their discourse.

This book examines a wide array of works, including both canonical and lesser-known texts that deserve more critical attention. These texts span China's revolutionary century, and the chapters take the reader from the early May Fourth period through the end of the Cultural Revolution in the late 1970s. Lu Xun and Mao Dun are the main foci of the chapters that deal with the Republican era (1911–49). Then a number of authors from the Mao era (1949–76), including Yang Mo, Wang Wenshi, and Li Zhun, are considered. The final chapter examines Zong Pu's post–Cultural Revolution fiction. While this work features in-depth research on dream in intellectual and literary discourse, it is not a "genealogy" of dream in modern China. Rather, it takes a cue from the long tradition of dream hermeneutics: the analysis does not merely note the presence of dream tropes in a wide array of literary works but also contextualizes close readings of dreams against a full treatment of the texts in which they appear. Only through such sustained and holistic readings can we incisively demonstrate how the examination of dreams compels us to reconsider the totality of the written text in question. Thus analysis here is not conceived merely as an identification of such and such tropes in a work but as a hermeneutic inquiry that precipitates a critical "working out" of the various tensions in the text as a whole. As such, this work relies on engaged close reading. While close formal analysis is the methodological center of the work, this textual critique is reinforced by a wide variety of theoretical approaches, including Russian Formalism, semiotics, psychoanalysis, Marxism, and affect studies. It is hoped that students and other lovers of literature will find an engaged model of formal textual analysis.

The complicated dreamwork of the long revolutionary period seems, in some ways, to have been undercut by some thirty-odd years of market reforms. State-orchestrated free enterprise could do what the previous thirty years of centralized planning could not: produce greater personal wealth, spur rapid urban and industrial development, encourage integration into a global culture, and create a vast consumer middle class, among other achievements. As a way of showcasing these accomplishments, the Chinese capital, Beijing, was awarded the 2008 Olympic Games. This book had its start when I was in Beijing during the summer of 2005 and thinking about researching the interplay of dreams and reality in modern Chinese culture. During that time the organizing committee of the Beijing Olympics unveiled their slogan: "One World, One Dream" (Tong yi ge shijie, Tong yi ge mengxiang). It seemed intriguing that the state was retrieving this old rhetoric of dreams to promote the vision of a "harmonious" Chinese society working in concert with a globalized, capitalist world, and how such a unified "dream" both co-opted and elided other visions of a possible world. There was something immediately trite and clichéd about the slogan, but this was perhaps deliberate. The tight, even glib, parallelism through which the sameness of *tong yi* was reproduced in the formal structure of the couplet, as well as the conflation of world and dream, embodied a sentimental, folksy desire for a unified realm that is hard to oppose but even harder to substantively define. The slogan was a brilliant elaboration of Michel Foucault's early formulation of dream as *idios kosmos*, a world unto itself, lying in the very bosom of PRC power.[6] This slogan, accompanied by winsome, childlike anthropomorphized mascots, basked in mass sentimentality. However, the media campaign's melodramatic contortions and its exhaustive efforts to be "cute" betrayed the hard edge of authoritarian power. When I returned to China in 2007 for a year of research, this "dream" was proclaimed everywhere on Olympic banners and advertisements hanging from school walls, factories, and subway billboards. Most people, whatever their grievances about the current state of affairs, were swept up in a wave of national pride and enthusiasm, and endorsed, if with some reservation, this dream. It was simply too cute to resist.

The Opening Ceremonies of the Beijing Games, held at 8:08 p.m. (on the eighth second) on the eighth day of the eighth month of the eighth year of the second millennium, was a dazzling and spectacular manifestation of this "dream." Through his theurgic direction, the filmmaker Zhang Yimou summoned a dream vision of China that inspired both awe and fear among viewers the world over.[7] The exacting attention paid to symbolism, numerology, synchronic precision, and so forth testified to how China was portrayed as pure aesthetic form, a universe completely immanent unto itself. Unlike Jia Baoyu's confusion about time described earlier, the careful orchestration of the Opening Ceremonies suggested that China could now demonstrate mastery over time itself.

Caught up in a mode of triumphant nationalist celebration, few anticipated the subsequent crisis of global capitalism that struck China particularly hard merely a month after the supposed achievement of the "dream." This crisis revealed and further exacerbated long-simmering inequities between rich and poor, the urban and the migrant. It has also led many to question the destructive effects of unchecked development on China's environment and natural resources and the dismantling of a state welfare system for those left behind by such growth. These problems were always there, and only became steadily worse, but were treated as short-term dilemmas that would resolve themselves once the invisible hand got around to lifting everyone up. To question the excesses of unbridled economic liberalization was to declare oneself an enemy of reform, an unrepentant stalwart of the destructive legacy of the Cultural Revolution. It seems clearer, however, that China had predicated its economic and political stability on an exaggerated rate of growth that was likely unsustainable. The central government has responded to the crisis through a massive injection of capital liquidity into banks and a speculative housing boom, thus softening for the meantime the immediate blow to masses of workers. While in some ways the state has been successful at lessening the brunt of the crisis upon its populace, it has also tried to prevent a political crisis engendered by economic difficulties through increasingly authoritarian and repressive restrictions on political activity and expression. As revolutionary movements swept through whole swaths of the Middle East, and as Western nations confronted the largest popular challenge to global capital in decades in the form of the Occupy movement, the Chinese state has rushed to lock down the restless territories of Tibet and Xinjiang, as well as compelled Hong Kong toward more submissive compliance to the Mainland. It has drummed up nationalist fervor over barely known islands in the South China Sea in order to direct popular discontent elsewhere. After thirty years of free-market dogma and the demise of state socialism, and faced with the lingering, unresolved consequences of the greatest economic crisis since the Great Depression, it might be possible again at this critical historic juncture to refresh our thinking about China's and, ultimately, the world's political, economic, and cultural future. While "One World, One Dream" was always a hackneyed slogan, it seems that a new vision of a transfigured world is precisely what is needed should we want to survive long in our new century.[8]

This study of the dreamwork of past writers ranging from the May Fourth Movement to the beginning of the Reform period thus presents itself with an eye to China's future, and the world's as well. Perhaps we should salvage dream from its relegation to idle fantasy or irrational wishful thinking and assert that the dream performs important and necessary ideological labor.[9] Dreams shake up our ways of understanding our relationship to history and offer other avenues of examining our historic situation in ways not beholden to conventional narrative logic, whether in the form of novels or in the form of political economic "development." Dreams force us to contend with the discursive materiality that limns our social existence and to examine how such materiality affects the way we relate to others. Dreams can bring us back to the very heart of historic experience itself. What follows is a tribute to both those from the past who dreamed about China and those in the present who continue to dream.

CHAPTER 1

Sleeping through Catastrophe

Dreams, Cataclysmic Modernity, and the Promises of Literary Realism

China's struggle to achieve modernity in the late nineteenth and twentieth centuries has often been framed in terms of a nation's "awakening" from the sleep of tradition. Chinese nationalists and intellectuals insisted that the nation arise from its despondent slumber. The metaphorical commonplace in Chinese discourse about the "sleeping dragon" drew from Western metaphors about post-Enlightenment nationalism; this rhetoric, in turn, circulated in discourse and imagery through myriad forms of Chinese press culture.[1] The historic transition into global modernity was rhetorically framed within the somatic logic of sleeping, dreaming, and awakening; this resulted in a complicated and intriguing proliferation of rhetoric that would draw analogous parallels between historic time and the body's rhythms. It also ensured that the modern Chinese discourse of dreams was always linked to concerns about China's fraught and complicated journey to join global modernity.

The rhetoric of sleep, awakening, and dreaming inevitably touches upon the myriad ways people the world over sought to cognitively and intuitively grasp the transformation of time under the rise of capitalist modernity. In particular, this historic transition seemed to reorganize the boundaries between day and night, and this change had plenty of symbolic and ideological ramifications. Recent scholars have explored the transformation of night under capitalist modernity and, concomitant with it, the realignment of a temporal logic that accommodated the trajectory of capital accumulation.[2] Capitalism and imperialism served as backgrounds for new Enlightenment and post-Enlightenment notions of time and history, revealing a temporal logic moving ever forward. As advances in lamp technology, street lighting, and electricity sustained longer-lasting (and less dangerous) forms of artificial light, the night itself became a temporal territory that could be far more easily colonized and made useful. Historian Craig Koslofsky has coined the term "nocturnalization" to describe the "the ongoing expansion of the legitimate social and symbolic uses of the night."[3] He contends that the rise of a bourgeois public sphere in modern Europe can be traced to the popularity of coffeehouses that mostly operated during the evening, enjoyed by men who debated issues of the day while sustained by coffee and tea; these in turn were some of the most in-demand commodities of capitalist maritime trade.[4]

In modernity time itself became rationalized, given a more precise measurement and standardization that grew to be universal in scale. Capitalism achieved the synchronization of the entire globe under one system of time, emanating from the bosom of the British Empire, in Greenwich, London. The rationalization and quantification of time grew alongside a refined calculation of capitalist value itself—wage labor, determined by hours worked, became the dominant mode of value extraction (with the significant exception of colonial slavery). Stock markets around the world synchronized their clocks, opening and closing their markets at precise moments. The move to rationalize time even further has not abated to the present day, with satellites and atomic clocks allowing for even more precision and virtual technologies allowing for business meetings to be conducted across time zones. Time was increasingly seen as something to be conquered, controlled, and made to serve humans' material needs and desires.

Modernity's progress has thus often been figured as an extension of the day against a night that houses superstition, epistemic darkness, and stagnancy. It was the early European moderns who declared the period following the Roman Empire the "dark ages," thus implying that modernity entailed a forward trajectory toward light. Capitalist liberal democracy draws its values from the Enlightenment and sees history as an ever-expanding struggle for liberty. Socialists also claim the Enlightenment's mantle but insist that its ideals can only ever be truly and universally realized when capitalism is overcome.

The Chinese assimilated many of these assumptions regarding time and awakened modernity. The anxieties that surrounded a feeling of historic belatedness added to a profound sense of existential urgency;

while the rest of the world had woken up, the Chinese were still mired in both historic and somatic nighttime. While Chinese nationalists hoped to adopt Western historical linearity, their efforts to do so were hampered by both internal instability and the obstacles of imperialism. It is tempting to assume that China could also pass through the necessary historical stages of modernization and become "just like the West," just as it is equally tempting to assume that capitalist development proceeds in the same way in all places, divorced from the context of geopolitics and global history. However, capitalism in its imperialist form distorted the linear trajectory of modern development in those lands whose political sovereignty was eroded. Ironic is the fact that while imperial China supplied Britain with massive quantities of tea that aided them in not only creating a vibrant, vital, and alert civil society but also forging a global empire where the sun never set, Britain in return offered boatloads of opium, harvested in India, that sank China even deeper into its slumber. The discussion in Chapter 3 of Mao Dun's *Midnight* will explore how homegrown capitalists hoped to develop "national industry" and thus usher in capitalist modernity; but a political situation of national sovereign crisis could only reduce their noble ambitions as nothing more than a dream. However, for all of the ways in which the chronology of modernization became contorted, the Chinese still aimed to wake up from the nightmare of domestic crisis and imperial pressure and regain their own place in the sun.

The utopian linearity of modern time fostered in its wake embodied frictions, tensions, and even crises in how humans experienced time. While the master temporal trope of modernity is one of linearity, of ever-increasing daylight, humans, like most animals, nevertheless live bound by biological circadian rhythms that have adapted to the diurnal cycle. The imperative to squeeze every ounce of value from every second that can be counted (an imperative that harassed socialists as much as capitalists) came into direct conflict with a body that demanded, and begged for, rest. Writing about the meaning of insomnia in early modern Europe, one scholar argues that the economic demands of global trade (one that, in its early development, was to a large degree dependent on slavery) had two effects on the way Europeans approached sleep. On one hand, the need to constantly monitor trade transactions and flows of capital and credit elicited great anxieties that kept many traders and businessmen up late at night, ever vigilant to possible risk. On the other, the need to stay awake further redoubled the desire for such commodities as coffee and tea.[5] Thus insomnia and global trade reinforced each other in a vicious cycle.

Modern temporal linearity comes into conflict with somatic temporal circularity. Of course, the line between the two is far blurrier; after all, we still count time based on a twenty-four-hour clock that repeats itself, and we understand that years are based on the time it takes the Earth to orbit the sun. However, modernity continues to apply pressure on our need for cyclical stability. Night and its accompanying activities—rest, dreaming, sex, reflection—continue to be either denigrated or ignored as a drain on productivity. As Karl Marx pointed out, rest and sleep were essential to the reproduction of a worker's labor power, something that capitalists continued to violate even with the passage of laws in England designed to keep rest safe.[6] As another scholar notes, "Modernity devalues dark knowledge and operations, naming them backward, primitive, irrational."[7]

It helps to focus on the persistent presence of this "dark knowledge" during a time of progressive enlightenment. The lingering fascination with dreams in Chinese intellectual and literary discourse betrays a suspicion that historic modernity is not a process of immanent unfolding and development but instead a chaotic and turbulent zigzag filled with reversals and catastrophes, a trajectory ridden with fervent hopes and tragic disappointments. Philosopher Walter Benjamin noted the prominence of dreams in traditional Chinese literature as one that highlights an emphasis on change as an experience of sudden reversal rather than gradual progress: "There is a wholly unique experience of dialectic. The compelling—the drastic—experience, which refutes everything 'gradual' about becoming and shows all seeming 'development' to be dialectical reversal, eminently and thoroughly composed, is the awakening from dream."[8] As Chinese thinkers sought to bring notions of dream into the modern world via the illuminations of science, the persistence of dreams as embodying what Benjamin described as the "drastic" experience of "dialectical reversal" countered the hope that modernity might proceed as a form of gradual development. In fact, the complex rhetoric of dreams gives witness to two intertwining forms of dialectical movement operating in Chinese intellectual discourse. One is the notion of immanent unfolding and development, the steady and sober march of progress from darkness to light. The other is the unpredictable, unsettling, but also exhilarating notion of change as revolutionary reversal.

The May Fourth Movement (1919) was sparked by the unequal terms of the Treaty of Versailles that handed Chinese territory from German colonial hands to Japanese ones, a severe blow to Chinese sovereignty and a betrayal of China's alliance with the victors. However, the movement was also a response to decades of being cowed into de facto submission by relentless colonial aggression, the failure of the 1911 revolution to produce meaningful state reform and progress, and the profound fear that Chinese civilization might disintegrate. Moreover, intellectuals faced a new world that not only seemed to have gotten ahead of them but also was using its technological, scientific, and epistemological leverage to thoroughly unseat Chinese sovereignty. For Chinese intellectuals, it was not merely an issue of trying to salvage meaning from this slow and painful cataclysm but also one of seeking to interpret and decode this new world for the sake of surviving in modernity.[9]

The May Fourth Movement intensified the desire for a more thorough social revolution, one that would not merely replace the figurehead of government but would also radically change cultural attitudes. It became clear that no meaningful transformation of the state and nation was possible without the transformation of social consciousness. Such revolutionary utopianism seemed to persist even more doggedly as China faced wave after wave of attack and calamity. Dream as a trope for revolutionary utopianism became a common feature in public discourse, even as dream was also associated with a traditional temporality that had to be canceled. As an illustration of the power of this trope, the subsequent three chapters of this book all refer in one way or another to a remarkable 1933 issue of *Eastern Miscellany* (Dongfang zazhi), the main intellectual journal of Republican China and a strong advocate for social reform (of course, references to dreams as utopia appear well before the 1930s). After the abrupt stop to *Eastern Miscellany*'s run because of the 1932 Japanese invasion of Shanghai, the editors produced a special New Year's issue that featured "dreams" for a new China from its readership, and to which many of the major literary and cultural figures (as well as politicians and bankers) contributed and/or critiqued. Dreaming seemed to capture two intimately linked aspects of revolutionary utopia. On one hand, the power of a dream experience and the desire to manifest such a dream as reality captured the urgency and necessity of realizing revolutionary desire. On the other, the fragility and evanescence of dreams bespoke the difficulty, if not impossibility, of realizing such utopian yearnings in a time of crisis. For May Fourth intellectuals, dreams thus embodied both the sense of insurrectionary excitement and the despair of disillusionment, a clarion call to agitation on one hand and a warning of the dangers of misguided adventurism on the other.

FORMS OF POLITICAL IMAGINATION: DREAM AS EXPERIENCE, INDEX, AND PALIMPSEST

The preponderance of dream lore and belief in traditional Chinese culture has been well noted. Ideas about dreams were rich, varied, and sometimes contradictory, and as one scholar suggests, there was no homogeneous philosophy of dreams in premodern China.[10] Dreams had both practical and philosophical uses and implications. Divination through dreams was an important tool in statecraft and thus a special vehicle for political knowledge. Another scholar reminds us of traditional notions that claimed the entire universe, and all phenomena occurring within it, was pregnant with meaning and significance; the cosmos was not random but a deliberate, organized latticework of signs. Gleaning such significance from nature's divine portents was a task of great intellectual and spiritual esteem, and among all of the various hermeneutic operations, "the interpretation of dreams reigned supreme."[11] In premodern China, dreaming was not merely a private reverie; in certain contexts, it could have important political uses and ramifications.

Why do dreams constitute such an intriguing form of personal and collective imagination? Dreams and their rhetoric encompass such a vast matrix of meanings (some of which conflict with each other) that it is next to impossible to summarize them neatly. But what dreams tend to illuminate are the complex ways we attempt to make both sense and meaning of the world we inhabit. They reveal multiple strategies in comprehending a reality that is far too inchoate to grasp, and they exploit different ways of carrying meaning across. Dreaming acknowledges the difficulty in coming to terms with the world around us and affirms that knowledge of this world in constant flux is never transparent or self-evident. In what follows, three ways of thinking about dreams will be explored: dreams as a special form of experience, as an index to a troubled and conflicted reality, and as a dramatization of the ways in which language and signification contort themselves in trying to make sense of the world.

Dreaming as a privileged form of envisioning a hoped-for future has long been a powerful form of political thinking and experiential imagination. While people have long reported having dreams of an idealized world, there are many fantasies that have no basis in the somatic activity of sleep. Nevertheless, even such visions framed as "dreams" draw upon a deep intimate resonance with the sensate body. Such visions troped as "dreams" remind us of the intense emotional and physical experience of dreaming. Early in his career, Michel Foucault wrote that dreaming should be considered an independent realm of experience.[12] Commenting on the work of psychologist Ludwig Binswanger, Foucault argued that one should see dreams as an autonomous form of existence and experience on par with waking life itself. By this understanding, dreams are not a faulty, fleeting imitation of a world but the modular form through which we can come to know any world at all: "[To] dream is not another way of experiencing another world, it is for the dreaming subject the radical way of experiencing its own world."[13]

Approaching dreams as a sensory experience in its own right would enjoin us to take seriously its phenomenological qualities; dreams and dream rhetoric encourage us to not only visit an "alternate" world, they often help us explore the dimensions and parameters of what it might mean to inhabit any world. In this sense, dreams are not simply an alternative to reality but a vital supplement that helps give shape to reality itself. The absorptive experience of dreams has broad parallels with the experience of art and, in particular, with narrative forms that lift us almost seamlessly into other worlds. Both art and dreams have an uncanny relationship with reality itself; while on the one hand they are unreal fabrications, on the other, they help us make sense of the inchoate reality we inhabit. Disavowed by reality, dreams and art at the same time allow us deeper insight into it.

While the rhetoric of dreaming implies a form of sensuous, alternate experience, it also gestures and points to a rift within reality itself, a conflict left unresolved. Dreams in this vein "index" a certain friction in reality. According to Freudian psychoanalysis, dreams derive from unconscious thoughts and desires that are repressed and that can only reappear in dream form. But beyond the confines of psychoanalysis, dreams have long been thought of as responding to a certain dissatisfaction or sense of lack with reality. So while a dream can envision an ideal future, it can also simultaneously indict inequities of the present. Thus at the same time a dream can represent or manifest a certain other world "out there," it can also critically point back at reality over here. This "indexical" function illuminates dreaming's pragmatic aspect. Dream rhetoric authorizes a particular way of imagining and speaking that may be read as tentatively, or even subversively, political; utopian fantasies can thus backhandedly function as political critiques of an unjust present.

The idea that dream rhetoric may indexically point to a historic crisis is borne out in traditional Chinese letters. Zhang Dai's (1597–1689) impressive set of nostalgic recollections composed after the catastrophic fall of the Ming dynasty, *Dream Reminiscences of Tao'an* (Tao'an meng yi) and *Searching for West Lake in Dream* (Xihu meng xun, preface 1671), provides us with an example of how historic collapse can evoke an aesthetic response.[14] While products of the traumatic fall of the Ming, neither collection references in its content that great historic rupture in any sustained way. And yet the use of the word "dream" in both of these titles alludes to the evanescence of past delights, swept into dust by the chaos of history itself. By framing his recollections under the rhetoric of dreaming, Zhang Dai suggests the crisis of knowledge after catastrophe, the inability to recognize the world within the conventions to which one had grown accustomed. The world has become a semiotic paradox, a hard Gordian knot that he finds himself unable to untie. That Zhang Dai employs dreams as the discursive frame through which he situates his memories suggests that dreams themselves are the very product formed by the failure of history to come to terms with itself.

While dreams offer a seemingly unmediated experience of a world, they can also offer a unique experience of language as well. The issue of a dream's interpretation, in both premodern and modern guises, not only foregrounds dreams' hermeneutic impulse but also displays their resistance to such interpretation. Dreams undo the transparency of language to convey our world and reveal language's often confusing and multilayered texture. Freud's account of how the symbolism of dreams employs condensation, displacement, and considerations of representation speaks to the dense materiality of signification that must be untangled. More often than not, the sticky, difficult knots in which signs weave themselves are a response to a historic trauma so profound that it confounds any attempt to render it into words. As such, how dreams seem to straddle the edge between meaning and meaninglessness is often a token of how the world itself resists the conventional terms by which we would seek to know it; this, in turn, often coincides with moments of dramatic, even sudden, historic transformation that renders conventional reality suddenly unknowable.

"Palimpsest" may be used to describe how dreams make visible this complex materiality of signification.[15] As a metaphor for a dream's operations, the word is attractive for two reasons. First, it conveys how underneath an apparently flat surface there are hidden depths; beneath the visible script of the dream lie obscured texts that adumbrate the dream's meaning. Second, a palimpsest helps describe how both the spectacular imagery of dream along with its discursive pragmatics can combine into unitary structure. In a palimpsest, we see not just what the words project but how the words themselves are arrayed in overlapping spatial relation to each other. Dream thus reorients and defamiliarizes our conventional approach to language and exhorts us to see it from different angles.

Moving from dreams as conveying an intense, immediate experience to dreams as expressions of language's tactile contortions, we can see how dreams make palpable the complex divide between experience and language. They seem to arise when the edges of experience and language do not match neatly but instead overlap. When the texture of language proves jagged, or when experience seems insufficient or unsatisfactory, dream rhetoric can provide a critical heuristic, one that expresses a dialectical impulse to see beyond reality's conventions. The critical, sometimes even transgressive, impulse of dreams made it a convenient trope for Chinese thinkers and writers attempting to capture a reality that eluded their abilities of description.

THE DANCE OF REASON AND DESIRE: DREAMS, SCIENCE, AND UTOPIAN MODERNITY

May Fourth thinkers understood the need for sober, critical reflection and analysis to act as a check against overly exuberant revolutionary enthusiasm. While it was well and good to be able to imagine an emancipated future, equally important were the steps to be taken in order to get there. Science, in all of its various manifestations, was at the intellectual heart of cultural and philosophical reform. "Science and democracy" was the watchword of the May Fourth Movement; there was a conscious and profound linkage between epistemological and civic reform, one that could be traced from the late Qing era. The rise of science went hand in hand with modern nation-state building, as science promoted an objective recognition of citizens that overlooked their religious, ethnic, or regional ties.[16] Science thus had a "social" value as well as a technological one in building and organizing the nation-state and its modern subjects. The culturalist turn of the May Fourth Movement was a response to the stultifying and confusing national politics between warlords and would-be restorers of the monarchy. The May Fourth exhortation for China's youth to rise up and take the nation's matters in their own hands was symptomatic of the need to produce a new political subjectivity that could successfully do the work of reimagining the state in a way that the veterans of 1911 were helpless in achieving. Rather than engage in Realpolitik, May Fourth intellectuals advocated a "spiritual politics," the need to build new political subjectivities by emphasizing culture and art. The values of scientific thinking were upheld within the broader field of culture; the "discursive community of science" championed scientific ideas and values outside the strict boundaries of scientific research.[17] The "spirit" of science, its liberation from dogma and tradition, its emphasis on individual investigation, and its focus on practical application, became incorporated within the cultural ethos of the May Fourth Movement.[18]

In the May Fourth frenzy of knowledge importation from the West, dreams became part of an intellectual fascination with psychology and psychoanalysis. While psychoanalysis of the Freudian type was not the dominant school among Chinese psychologists (behaviorism being by far the most popular), it flourished in intellectual and popular discourse through journal discussions and translations of introductory monographs into Chinese.[19] Few actually read Freud's work in the original, and *The Interpretation of Dreams* was not translated until 1932.[20] Nevertheless, the Chinese reading public was already well aware of Freudian dream theory in the early 1920s, and Freud "was considered to be the first person to try to offer a scientific explanation for dreams. Freud's way of interpreting dreams was the best known part of his theory and drew a great deal of attention from Chinese intellectuals."[21] Dreams, not surprisingly, mirrored the fate of literature in this revolutionary period: at once upheld as a vehicle of self-expression, they were also seen as a quasi-scientific, if distorted, mirror to reality and itself subject to empirical examination.

The interest in dreams within the relatively young discipline of psychology was motivated in part by the need to modernize outdated, traditional notions of dream and dream-lore that were seen as superstitious. The claims of access to divine knowledge betrayed a cosmos that was alien to scientific inquiry. Moreover, dream rhetoric was often associated with Buddhist and Daoist philosophy and metaphysics; texts ranging from the *Zhuangzi* to the *Diamond Sutra* exhorted skepticism about the substance and permanence of phenomenal reality. These notions encouraged adherents to break their attachment to the phenomenal world by seeing it as merely a dream. The hesitance to attach oneself to phenomenal reality was seen by twentieth-century intellectuals as a form of mystification that impeded proper empirical inquiry. For Chinese thinkers of the late nineteenth and twentieth centuries, the timeless wisdom of the past was precisely the kind of feudal, unempirical claptrap that had to be dispelled should China ever surpass its sense of belatedness in regards to modernity. To see the world as an evanescent dream was to escape seeing reality as it was and to inhibit any possibility of changing it.

An example of this "modernizing" urge can be seen in a curious book. In 1927 renowned pedagogue Shu Xincheng (1893–1960) produced a volume for the publisher Zhonghua Shuju's introductory series of scientific, historical, and cultural topics known as "The Series of Common Knowledge" (Changshi congshu). Topics included evolution, exercise and hygiene, and the cultural history of European antiquity. Shu Xincheng offered three tomes to this series: a general introduction to psychology (*Xinlixue da yi*, 1926), a description of the Dalton System of pedagogy (*Dao'erdun zhi jianshuo*, 1932), and a volume titled, simply, *Dream* (Meng, 1927). In his memoirs *Education and Me* (Wo he jiaoyu), published in the 1940s, he explained that he wrote *Dream* as a kind of intellectual excursus during a summer so hot that his more usual work on pedagogy was impossible.[22] His purpose in publishing the work was as follows:

> I wanted to urge my readers to treat [dream] as a natural phenomenon and use the methods of analysis and synthesis to study it, analyze it through the lens of common knowledge and philosophy, and to search out its origins and effects in order to treat [dream] as the material for moral cultivation and self reflection. Moreover, they can study psychoanalysis's method of dream interpretation in order to cure mental illness. In the end I exhorted my readers, "Friends! Let everyone seriously use the common knowledge and methods of science to break superstition and create a new life!"[23]

Shu Xincheng thus linked two reigning ideas of Republican-era reform: the need for scientific method and knowledge, and the creation of a new moral life. Wrestling dream from the vagaries of superstition, he hoped to use dream as a pedagogical tool for moral improvement.

He opened his treatise by recording a folk song he heard being performed in Nanjing that exhorted its audience to see "life as a dream" and all worldly things as "but smoke passing across one's eyes."[24] Known as *daoqing*, this genre was a sort of ballad originally associated with proselytizing Daoist monks but then became a common folk entertainment distilling moral truths about the Way (Dao). Identifying the song's skepticism of the phenomenal world as Buddhist in origin, Shu Xincheng expressed his uneasiness with this rather commonplace idea: "But if you say that life is like a dream, you will cause people to live their life within a dream; regarding dream and waking consciousness as being on the same level—I have always felt this was very unstable, and thus thought about the importance of writing an explanation of dream phenomena."[25]

Ultimately Shu Xincheng saw this rich dream culture as inevitably mired within outdated forms of superstition, symptomatic of China's epistemic belatedness. Indulgence in dream not only demonstrated China's inability to reconcile itself with modern time, it also implied that all traditional forms of culture and philosophy were stained with a dreamy illusoriness. His focus on an outdated oral tradition (*daoqing*) that spread outdated information shows that what needed updating was not only informational content but the very cultural and philosophic forms that conveyed this knowledge. One gets the sense that for Chinese intellectuals, the entirety of the premodern cultural heritage started to take on the quality of a reverie that had to be finally dispelled.

The importance for Freud of dream analysis in establishing the presence and function of the unconscious is well known. Dissatisfied with explanations for dream phenomena rooted in physiology, Freud pointed to another source in the mind as the generator of dream thoughts. Dreams pointed to a reality separate from external, material reality, one that could not be directly represented but whose basic contours and function could be inferred:

> The unconscious is the true psychical reality; *in its innermost nature it is as much unknown to us as the reality of the external world, and it is as incompletely presented by the data of consciousness as is the external world by the communications of our sense organs.*[26]
>
> If we look at unconscious wishes reduced to their most fundamental and truest shape, we shall have to conclude, no doubt, that

> *psychical* reality is a particular form of existence not to be confused with *material* reality.[27]

In this last section of *The Interpretation of Dreams*, after painstakingly examining dream phenomena and their mechanisms, Freud triumphantly presented his vision of the unconscious, and the primary and secondary processes. Moreover, what Freud demonstrated was the existence of a new "reality" that transcended the material and physiological senses of the word. His "discovery" and articulation of the unconscious can be read as his contribution to the post-Enlightenment discourse on reality. Dreams, for Freud, played a far more important role than merely as a diagnostic tool for identifying his patients' psychic maladies; dreams were the heuristic vehicle through which he could produce a new body of scientific knowledge.

In the nascent field of Republican-era Chinese psychology, dreams were widely recognized as a source of scientific knowledge. By 1922 the *Journal of Psychology* (Xinli zazhi) had already been established (one editor boasted that they created such a journal one year before the Japanese formed their own) and featured articles by prominent scholars who popularized key topics.[28] Editor and contributor Zhang Yaoxiang wrote that the original impetus for the journal was to "propagate the newest science."[29] While Freud was a major interlocutor, so were other psychologists such as Carl Jung, Havelock Ellis, and Isador Coriat. A number of articles were devoted to dreams, and they tried to wrest dreams from traditional practices of prognostication, declaring these as mere "absurdity" and "superstition"; these articles promoted using the tools of scientific analysis to discover the real unconscious and somatic sources of dream phenomena.[30] This new scholarship on dreams was a repudiation of the past cultural heritage of dreams and an effort to extract true knowledge from the superstitious non-knowledge in which dreams had been mired. However, in addition to this paradigm shift from traditional to modern perceptions of dreams, scholars were also aware of the need to suggest a bridge between the past and modernity by finding resonances between new Western conceptions and native canonical sources. Thus affirmative references to the *Zhuangzi*, the Buddhist canon, Tang-dynasty romances, and so on abound as well.

Inspired by the scientific approaches to dreams they read about in the West, Chinese psychologists conducted their own "empirical surveys" (*shiji diaocha*).[31] Du Yuanzai, for example, had fifty-four university students, male and female, fill out a questionnaire asking what they dreamed about the night before. He divided the recorded dreams into various subject categories, and each dream was designated as "happy" or "unhappy." Thirty-eight of the fifty-four dreams were unhappy ones, and the two topics that claimed the largest share were "examinations" and "fear" (each subject claimed twelve respondents), perhaps not surprising for college students in a time of national crisis.[32] Only four students recorded sexual dreams; one student speciously claimed to have had intercourse with a sow and described their congress as "truly exuberant." His dream was declared a "happy" one. Another student described a dream in which he struggled in tears to fulfill his oedipal desire to sleep with his mother, only to be rebuffed and then fall into a deep melancholy upon waking. His dream was declared "unhappy."[33] Despite the scintillating variety of dreams collected, Du Yuanzai's final conclusions to his investigation were somewhat tepid: most dreams were unhappy, the fact that examination dreams claimed a plurality was surely connected to the students' immediate and long-term professional situations, and the vast majority of dreams seemed to emanate from a powerful emotive source.[34] However, what was significant about this kind of survey was the treatment of dreams as an empirical source of psychological and sociological knowledge. To be sure, premodern Chinese scholars such as the Ming polymath Chen Shiyuan (1516–95) compiled dream encyclopedias that rival modern attempts in sophistication and comprehensiveness.[35] Nevertheless, the attempt to empirically and statistically analyze actual dreams bespoke the psychologists' adherence to a Western scientific paradigm of knowledge production that relied upon statistics, facts, and calculation.[36]

The intellectual, scientific, and aesthetic interest in dreams during the May Fourth era was thus itself split into an unresolvable antinomy. In seeking to modernize traditional notions of dream and bring it under the intellectual frame of science, they sought to demystify dream phenomena and divorce them from metaphysical notions of the divine. Dreams were now a source of modern knowledge, not timeless wisdom. Dreams allowed Chinese psychologists deeper insights into the workings of the mind; as nation-building entailed the transformation of human personality into citizenship, such probing investigation into the psyche was not out of place. And yet, writers recognized the compelling rhetorical and affective power of dreams. They never quite lost their power of enchantment; in being subsumed into scientific knowledge, this only revealed how science and reason themselves became secular sources of wonder.

LITERARY REALISM AND ITS MANAGEMENT OF DESIRE

The promotion of realism in Chinese literature was part of the May Fourth cultural wellspring. Realism represented simultaneously two cultural trends that were otherwise separate in western Europe: the power to objectively represent social reality and the ability to critique the modern world. It thus combined two seemingly "mutually exclusive tendencies": the "critical spirit of the modern" and "a supreme faith in the powers of representation."[37] "Criticism" and "faith" were the contradictory tendencies within the Chinese realist mode: on one hand a utopian desire to model the world into discourse and thus make it intelligible and, better, changeable, on the other a contrarian spirit that otherwise dispenses with wishful thinking. The entire "discursive community of science" was vexed by the productive tension between "positivist method" and "metaphysical characteristics and totalism."[38]

The new scientific orientation of literature, carrying both its critical and utopian functions, also inaugurated a new relationship between literature and history. Realism coincided with a view of history that saw the historical process as "the mass experience of hundreds of thousands, of millions" rather than "isolated and mostly adventurous-minded individuals."[39] In 1917 Chen Duxiu, frustrated by political stagnation, advocated the "plain, expressive literature of the people" as opposed to the "ornate, sycophantic literature of the aristocracy" as one way of renewing Chinese culture.[40] Literature was not only supposed to be "blind" to status but to expressly take up the cause of representing the majority, those who had been left behind from previous literature and history. Moreover, realism was charged with the task of illuminating the relationship between individual experience and historic totality. Realist narrative, in its careful attention to the flow of temporal experience, also modeled for its readers a modern sense of time.

The discussion of literary realism naturally begs the question of its definition. One runs the risk of allowing far too capacious a designation that will admit everything and thus mean nothing. But to confine "realism" to only "transparency" or "mimesis" starkly forecloses the many legitimate concerns in which realism is invested, as well as a sense of the historical conditions from which it sprung. Ludwig Wittgenstein's concept of "family resemblances" may help in trying to define a kinship of elements that belong to the category "realist."[41] Works may exhibit one, several, or all such elements and still be usefully regarded as being a "realist" kin. What follows is an attempt to outline these elements.

Realism relies upon the conceit of a truth claim upon the external world—more often than not the focus is on the social, historical world over the natural, cosmological one. The time and space in which this world exists operate under scientific principles. The realist work thus approaches the ontological status of "human document" that attests to the world and allies itself closely with the intellectual fields of history, social science, and life sciences. The presentation of a world as governed by principles of reason also entails an epistemological reorientation of consciousness that is equally governed by principles of skepticism and critique.

Realism disavows the formality of its own literary discourse and seeks discursive transparency all the while that it depends on such formal structure. It rejects a nominalist view whereby only discourse exists over an unintelligible universe. As such, realism tends to obscure the materiality of the signifier (all the while relying upon it). Realism tends to favor metonymy over metaphor and a syntagmatic organization of literary text over a paradigmatic one. Its language strives for a documentary quality rather than ornamental one.

Realism displays a particular interest in representing and illuminating the vicissitudes of and tensions among social relations, sometimes to such an extent that realism itself can be characterized as an intervention in helping reshape such social relations and marked by a certain degree of ethical and affective "commitment." This commitment can range from conservative moralism (Honoré de Balzac) to liberal contemplation (Ivan Turgenev), or even radical agitation (Mao Dun) and outright utopianism (Nikolai Chernyshevsky).

These three elements may be described as the ontological/epistemic, discursive, and pragmatic axes upon which realism operates. There is one feature that is inherent to all texts that we call "realist" but that is not so much an element of definition as it is one of condition. This is the historical context from which realism sprang. One cannot speak of a realist work without gesturing to realism's etiological origins in the global ascent of European capitalism, the industrial revolution, and the rise of the sciences, both natural and social.[42]

Recent scholarship on Chinese realism firmly situates the rise of a modern Chinese aesthetic, and in particular realism, within China's interpellation into global capitalism.[43]

The majority of realist works engage all three of the definitional elements outlined above, although they tend to emphasize one axis over the other. And of course, all three axes are often intertwined with one another (e.g., plain, referential discourse is conducive to creating the impression of unmediated ontological truth). A work like Lev Tolstoy's *War and Peace* emphasizes the importance of historical verisimilitude, while Gustave Flaubert is notable for the elegance and exactness of his prose (one thinks of the legend about Vladimir Nabokov's exam question about the color of Madame Bovary's arsenic bottle).[44] Nikolai Chernyshevsky's *What Is to Be Done* is a bold call to action that sought (and succeeded) in forging bonds of revolutionary solidarity.

When we examine the rise of Chinese realism in the May Fourth era, we find that it engaged deeply with the ontological/epistemic, discursive, and pragmatic axes. Realists were committed to a regime of truth embedded in the sciences, including biology, sociology, and history.[45] They sought new forms of literary language, in particular rooted in the *baihua* vernacular, in order to create a fictional discourse free from premodern allusion and ornamentalism. And they hoped that their work would be conducive to affective nation-building through creating a patriotic populace committed to ideals of justice and egalitarianism. Moreover, realist writers felt they were responding to the challenge of colonial modernity, and realism thus offered a cultural program and technology by which they could mount a resistance against colonial modernity while at the same time subsuming it within their own national development.

The three axes outlined above are not by any means static, or remained unchallenged, even within realist texts themselves. Each has its own utopian doppelgänger that acts as the disavowed possibility that haunts each element's iteration. While realism sought to replicate and convey an ontology built on the epistemic principles of science, it also nevertheless dreamed of utopian ways of being and knowing that went beyond what was scientifically established. While realism sought a language free from ornament and artifice, realist texts nevertheless gestured toward older forms of dense literary language that restored a sense of semantic lyricism and depth. And finally, while realism exposed a society built upon brutal relations of exploitation, it also espoused a hope for a rejuvenated sociality founded upon principles of justice and equality. Each of these utopian "others" is symptomatic of the hidden utopianism within the realist mode itself; they appear to be external to realism but in fact have their root in the desire immanently embedded in the very search for the real. Realism's pragmatic social program, especially as articulated within the context of Chinese nationalism, displayed most prominently its utopian sheen.

The critical orientation of realism, couched in scientific discourse, also aligned itself with a utopian impulse for aesthetic creation. Realism mediated between these two conflicting tendencies. It is not enough simply to negate the past; what is also needed is "the invention of a new life—not only the construction of a new social reality in which our utopian dreams would be realized, but the (re)construction of those dreams themselves."[46] This conflict between critique and faith is not realism's death knell but in fact the very radical hope that brings realism to being, a mode that thrives on a seemingly untenable contradiction between critical knowledge and fantastic nonknowledge. One should approach thinking about the real in terms of a dynamic and critical movement of thought and feeling, one that always seeks to transcend its own bounds. This perpetual movement, the sheer dynamism implied by the concept of the real, is fueled by a utopian epistemological desire; achieving knowledge not only is a step toward eventual liberation and modernization but is in itself a conceptual figure and model for freedom and utopia.

The desire that motivates realism's workings in China is inseparable from the historic conditions of global capitalist modernity. The translingual origins of the word for reality (*xianshi*) are derived from a Japanese loanword (*genjitsu*), which in turn was the Japanese translation for a key concept of the Western enlightenment.[47] Thus we can see the real, as embodied by *xianshi*, as an epistemic desire that spans the historic and geographic space of modernity. This contrasts with premodern terms for the "real," in particular *zhen*, which emphasized moral truth and authenticity over the more scientific, empiric thrust of *xianshi*. These reverse neologisms carry within their lexical genealogy the very historic trajectory of modernity along which China traveled. We can see reality, and realism, that literary mode which sought to give access to knowledge of reality, as orientations toward knowledge itself that were conditioned by the sense of historical, temporal, and geographic belatedness, the "gap-in-knowledge" that so beguiled Chinese thinkers as they faced a "superior" but hostile West.

Expanding on this motif of movement in terms of thinking about the real, Roman Jakobson's work is useful in elucidating realism not as a static artistic mode but rather as a contingent stance taken by an artist and an observer in relation to the prevailing aesthetic codes. He sought to bring "the extreme relativity of the concept of 'realism' into sharp relief."[48] Rebels against the dominant aesthetic ideology will recognize works that defy convention as more realistic, while "conservatives" will maintain that only those works that follow the established rules are faithful to reality.[49] Even when a particular, localized set of conventions from "one specific artistic current of the nineteenth century" proclaimed itself as Realism, artists within the mode immediately sought to identify their own work as exhibiting a "higher" realism in relation to that of their fellow practitioners.[50] Moreover, certain modes of writing can alternately be seen as more realistic in relation to its context; thus, figuration and euphemism may be seen as realistic precisely because "[they] sound more impressive" in contrast to descriptive denotation.[51] Jakobson was arguing against certain pieties of nineteenth-century Realism as a mode that claimed a higher ontological ground by showing how all practitioners of art, regardless of school, have appealed to the real. As such, Jakobson rejected a historical definition in favor of a Formalist one based on the immanent methodology of his own discipline.[52] However, what remains particularly striking in Jakobson's essay is the way he ascribes both a relationality and motility to the concept of realism; "extremely relative" but also irrepressibly dynamic.

We should thus take note of realism's epistemic dynamism; while on one hand realism denotes a certain set of conventions imported from Europe (the narrator-observer, the appeal to empiricism and social science, the exposé of the lower classes, the use of vernacular registers, the analogy between fictional and historiographical modes, etc.), it also implies how knowledge itself moves along an open-ended vector. Realism relies on a notion of scientific empiricism but can also transcend such an ontology when necessary.[53] For May Fourth intellectuals, even more important than the truth claims that science expounded was what scientific thinking contributed to critical insight, an indispensable tool that was essential in trying to think through the national and historic crisis.

The real has often been seen as an "agent of demystification" that unmasks (and thus arrests) desire and forces the observer/reader to confront reason.[54] However, while reality and literary realism, with its narrative roots in objective, empiric observation, have appealed to dispassionate science for legitimacy of their claim to truth, the very drive toward the real is undeniably in itself a desire. Desire lurks within reason's very structure, a volatile potential that cannot be completely contained by the reality principle or by realist convention. In this sense, then, realism would seem to carry within it an unconscious, a utopian impulse that brings the mode into being but must be effaced in the narrative. In this deformative slippage within realism, moments of maximum tension are apparent when texts lay bare the utopian desire that informs their pursuit of knowledge.

Realism was not only meant to introduce a radical epistemic change; alongside its emphasis on epistemology and ontology was a concomitant transformation in one's affective relation to society. Realism collaborated with the May Fourth endeavor to create knowledge about society. But the endeavor to "know society" went much further than an epistemic reflection of it: intellectuals sought to create and mold forms of sociality among the populace. They wanted to forge affective bonds among Chinese citizens that would give them the sensorial, psychological, and experiential reserves from which, as a collective, the Chinese could confront the challenge of global modernity. In that sense, the desire that motivates the realist search for truth is, in large extent, a desire for society itself. Too often we think of mass literacy as simply basic knowledge acquisition for a modern populace; we ignore how the promotion of mass literacy creates bonds of affiliation between readers and writers. Creating a "republic of letters" was thus essential in developing the affective ties of nationhood, solidarity, and collective resistance. Thus realism's address to the reader was both epistemic and affective all at once, and sought to transform the bonds of sociality among the populace for the sake of nation-building.

An instructive example of realism's affective concerns is Ba Jin's 1931 novel *Family* (Jia), which details the struggles of three brothers in dealing with their degenerate gentry family. The novel describes the brothers' search for new, inspired forms of affiliation that will replace the moribund bonds of kinship that entrap them. Domestic life is thus seen as a dark, cavernous dungeon of superstition and ritual, and the novel constantly describes its demoralized denizens as stuck in a dream state (the word "dream" shows up over and over again). All three brothers, Juexin, Juehui, and Juemin, share the character *jue*, or "awakening," in their names. The most idealistic of the brothers, Juehui, pours his efforts in a youth magazine titled *Dawn*; the cooperation among the editorial staff coupled with the interactions between the editors and readership (characterized by "the many letters from people [Juehui] had never met")[55] create ideal forms of national affiliation and bonding. The novel's high level of melodrama, one that has condemned the book to endless opprobrium from Western scholars, is in keeping with its emphasis on emotion, intimacy, alternative kinship, and the transformation of sociality.

Chinese realism's commitment to rejuvenating sociality finds instructive parallels with and drew probable inspiration from its Russian predecessors and models. Vissarion Belinsky, the literary critic and early standard-bearer for realism, argued in 1846 that "only in the sphere of our literature do we cease to be Johns and Peters and become simply people dealing and associating with people."[56] For Belinsky, literature was instrumental not only in reforming society but in society's very creation out of the antagonistic ruins of the feudal estates. Belinsky was fond of the term *sotsial'nost'* as denoting a certain affective sympathy and solidarity among men that could be fostered through education and literature. As he wrote in a letter to Russian essayist and friend Vasily Botkin in 1841, "Sociality, sociality—or death! This is my motto. What is it to me that most live while a single individual suffers? What is it to me that the genius upon earth lives in the clouds, while the mass flails about in filth?"[57] Realism's affective work in creating not only the new man but also the network of social relations in which this man was embedded was inherently intertwined with realism's epistemic project.

Realism thus resists static definition; it can be better understood as a flexible matrix of elements that are historically conditioned by global capitalist modernity. Realism also frequently runs up against an obscured or disavowed utopian other that exceeds the limits of critical reason. As a modal impulse, it also exerts its force on texts that are not conventional realist novels: prose poetry, socialist realism, and texts that seek to combine "revolutionary realism" alongside "revolutionary romanticism." With such a dynamic, shifting, and protean mode, how does one go about literary interpretation? We should approach the operations of literary realism as a form of narrative *management*. The term "management" is meant to highlight a specific kind of temporality when talking about these texts; rather than viewing the text as a finished, completed entity that either succeeds as "realist" or not, one should observe how such texts in fact involve dynamic, open-ended, and tactical management of competing narrative desires and imperatives. By viewing realist texts in the imperfect tense, we can see how such texts must constantly juggle between different forms of representational modalities in order to sustain the text's ultimate totality and commitment to truth.[58] That is to say, a discussion of realism cannot be confined to mere mimetic transparency, typology, historicity, or any of a number of conventional, categorical features, although these dominant traits do carry important modal signals. Instead, taking stock of realism requires a dynamic process of seeking out a radical vision of truth, one that is ever changing and embedded within the phenomenal, historical world. One scholar has noted how European realism sought to model a radical new vision of truth and link it with a world subject to principles of time and change. As such, truth was not to be found in some "timeless" realm but within the ever-changing phenomenal world, and perceived by a consciousness that is also structured temporally.[59]

Realism involves a compact between text and reader whereby the latter is asked to suspend consciousness of formal mediation in return for the immediate revelation that the text is supposed to offer. However, this sense of "immediate" revelation is in turn motivated by formal conventions that the text seeks to disavow. But when such revelation itself becomes stultified, static, in itself *formalized*, and thus impervious to dialectical insight, the text can try to salvage its claim to truth by reflecting upon its own formality and symbolic mediation. In these moments of transvaluation, whereby the pencil lines suddenly come into view, the realist text finds an avenue to re-create a new space of revelation. In this sense, realism's relation to knowledge is fetishistic; it very well knows that reality is conventionally constructed, but all the same it will operate as if this were not the case. However, when the aim of the fetishistic practice becomes infeasible, when knowledge becomes reified contemplation, then the fetishistic enchantment is revealed, and new forms are pursued. Realism thus involves both a conscious forgetting and strategic, recuperative recollection of form that happens in a dynamic, open-ended trajectory.

In pursuing an analysis of realism that attends to both its muted ruptures and dramatic oscillations, realism's *mimetic crisis* and the management thereof constitute a central, though obscured, constitutive aesthetic component of the mode.[60] Precisely because of realist narrative's desire to directly access reality, the mode cannot avoid running into moments of epistemic and formal crisis. But it is this crisis itself that fuels realism's aesthetic elaborations; in other words, realism is aesthetically important because it must encounter such dichotomous polarities and work through them. Peter Button is sharply critical of contemporary Western-based scholars, including Xiaobing Tang, Marston Anderson, and David Der-wei Wang, for retroactively projecting a poststructuralist aversion to the referential claims of realist discourse upon Chinese realism itself, thus revealing its pretensions to speak and narrate the "real" as hopelessly broken from the start.[61] This overemphasis on semiotics and the "play of the signifier" obscures the proper aesthetic and philosophical context in which Chinese realism was forged. Reading David Wang's critique of Lu Xun, Button questions the ultimate motive in Wang's appropriation of semiotic theory: "What is troubling is that a poststructuralist theory of the sign is affirmed only to the degree that it might reveal some irrevocable contradiction in the 'discursive paradigm' of Lu Xun's realist project. The break between 'signifier and signified' is meaningful only to this very limited degree."[62]

Button critiques a poststructuralist critical impulse that in the end transforms into a contrarian coup de grâce that reveals realist texts and their authors to be guilty of the most incredulous bad faith. Button points out that such criticisms are anachronistic and fail to take into account the proper historical and intellectual contexts in which realist writers were embedded. This book's own emphasis on crisis, the texture of the signifier, and the role of desire in realism may just as easily open itself to similar charges of applying retroactively a postmodern fashion for irony on a cultural phenomenon to which it is not appropriate. But it is difficult to imagine any hermeneutic enterprise that does not admit some degree of temporal incommensurability between the time of interpretation and the time of the text's immediate reception. However, an exploration of mimetic crisis and semiotic materiality within realist texts is not an attempt to unravel or deconstruct the realist project; rather, it aims to illuminate further how realism *is made*, and makes itself. In that vein this book's reading of realism is essentially a sympathetic one, even as it emphasizes substantial, but also productive, aesthetic and ideological antinomies within the mode. Moreover, realist texts themselves often betray a self-awareness of the "gaps" between text and world, and find ways to resolve and manage these conflicts. To point out that a literary mode structures crisis within its very formal structure does not condemn it to immediate failure; it may be a crucial avenue in understanding the realist text as a dynamic process rather than a reified, always belated object. Employing theories of the "fetish," whereby knowledge and non-knowledge coexist in order to structure lived reality, is more an enthusiastic acknowledgment of how fantasy inheres in the ways we perceive and make sense of reality; dispelling this element of fantasy in effect evacuates any useful and practical sense of reality. Semiotics derives as much from poststructuralist paeans to the "play of the signifier" as it does to Soviet structuralism and the Bakhtin circle; for the latter, the fact of language's polysemy was not evidence that referential language was congenitally defunct but in fact constituted the very material manifestation of social difference and mediation.[63]

Having described the complex dynamics of realism as mode and impulse, this study seeks to juxtapose dream rhetoric and realism in a dialogic relationship. By doing so, it aims to lay bare the utopian desire that forms realism's kernel. Within realist narratives, the dream's liminal and multifunctional formal presence allows readers to examine how the text's contradictory impulses cleave together. At once the description of a character's inner fantasy, as well as a mode of expression of the text's broader desires, the dream becomes a vital supplement to the realist text, both excluded from the wakened narrative and yet necessary in suggesting the text's gesture toward a hoped-for reality. Dreams also figure suggestively as an ontological doppelgänger of the realist text: at once a totality, a world unto itself, while simultaneously a fleeting fiction, an ephemeral discursive creation. As such, it ironically lays bare the fictionality that attends our suspension of disbelief when reading. That literary realism employed dream discourse could be read as in keeping with the mode's interest in science in all its forms. But dreams in realist texts offer a form of knowledge that is different from the rational knowledge of empiric mimesis. Dreams' ability to be inscribed within a scientific discourse guarantees their legitimacy; however, their insight also pushes the bounds of what is intelligible within the principles of reason.

Dreams are a site where two contending, contradictory impulses in realism intersect. On one hand we have the fact that realism must convey reality in multiple modalities. Just as Freud sought to demonstrate that dreams point to a hidden "psychic reality," so may dreams within a realist text point to an obscured epistemic reality of utopian desire. On the other hand is the fact that what announces itself as "real" does so through an act of prohibition against other ontologies that may claim the mantle of reality for themselves. For realism to lift all prohibitions would be to accept an "everything is permitted" state of chaos that would be completely unable to signify anything other than itself. Thus the status of dream as ultimately unreal betrays realism's febrile need to delimit the legitimate parameters of the ontological space it seeks to claim.

While May Fourth writers for the most part had only mediated access to Western works of psychology, they were nonetheless familiar with their basic ideas and terms. This popular interest in the new discourse in dreams produced a literary effect: dream as a narrative trope starts to become more apparent in May Fourth writing. Fictional texts from the very first decades of the twentieth century featured longer and more elaborate dreams of their characters, a trend that was likely influenced by Lin Shu's translations of Western novels.[64] However, such dreams still engaged with the native discourse of the supernatural and predestination. By the 1920s and 1930s, literary dreams were more psychological in nature and revealed engagement with the Western psychological discourse that was rapidly gaining intellectual currency in China.

It is against this vibrant intellectual background that we will explore the relationship between dreams and realism and, more broadly, the dialectic between dreams, reality, and history in modern Chinese literature. While Chinese thinkers and writers of the twentieth century sought to disavow metaphysical notions of dreaming that cast phenomenal existence into doubt, their lingering interest in dreams, however modernized and made legitimate through the framework of science, nevertheless betrayed the complexity and difficulty of accessing reality through literary form. Moreover, dreams offer a glimpse into the utopian yearning that lies at the heart of the realist impulse, yet they are often marginalized in the form of seemingly trivial or fantastic reveries. The rhetoric of dreaming thus gestures toward a utopian historic horizon that transcends the immediacy of the realist present.

Dream rhetoric thus engages with each of the three axes of realism that I defined earlier. In terms of the ontological/epistemic axis, dreams imagine a world other than the "real" mimetic one, and not governed by laws of reason and science. Moreover, dreams model a temporality that runs counter to that of either realist narrative or historiography; the time of dream refuses linearity and, more often than not, follows a circuitous logic. Dreams conflate the present "now" with the archaic past and the fantastic future and encourage us to imagine alternate temporalities.[65] Dreams thus present an experience of time and space that fundamentally transcends realism's mimetic chronotope. They encourage an epistemology fueled more by desire, yearning, and faith than critical acumen. Moreover, dream affirms the status of literature itself as an allegorical and emancipatory "common space" that does not merely reflect a fallen world but offers a temporary refuge from it, and which is accessible to all.

In terms of the discursive axis, dreams carry a powerful critical formal perspective that is brought to bear upon the realist mode. Dreams function to reveal the materiality of discourse itself, the looming weight of language that persists despite realism's attempt to transcend discourse and promise an immediate view of reality. In what ways do dreams disrupt the circuit between text and world and force us to contend with the materiality of text alongside the world it seeks to convey? Dreams, as the fictive foil of realist narrative, highlight the discursiveness of realist texts themselves, how they compel us to reflect critically about modes of representation and the presence of language that both constructs and conveys social reality. In this vein, dreams highlight the spectral, yet barely tangible, presence of language, at moments transparent, an immediate vehicle for the "blood and tears"[66] of sociality that realist literature is supposed to transmit. At other moments language appears as a constantly shifting corporeality, one to be considered alongside the human bodies that are the mode's ostensible subjects. It is language's fundamental instability, its fungible nature, that dreams so vividly capture, and it is this constant semantic shape-shifting that brings into relief language's texture, its presence as a social *thing* that resists immediate comprehension through our faculties of cognition.[67] Dreams in and around realist texts are symptomatic of a broader aesthetic-ideological anxiety over language's competing claims to reality and to itself. Dreams act as a site where we can examine realism's bipolar relation to language. On one hand, as the very medium of mass sociality and communication, language is indispensable in the forging of social bonds and solidarity. On the other hand, excessive attention to discursive form may detract from its effective address to the social. However, a relation to sociality that is unmediated risks becoming stultified and unable to transform itself when necessary.

Following upon this discussion on sociality, we elaborate more on dream's relation to realism's pragmatic axis. Realism reveals a social world marked by tension, competing interests, exploitation, and violence. Its characters are marked by an individualism that is on one hand liberating but on the other deeply dissatisfying and atomized. Dreams thus seek to remove the distance between individuals and foster a radical intersubjectivity. It is a common experience while dreaming to inhabit a certain persona and then suddenly observe the same persona as if from outside. It is as if the first and third persons ("I" and "he/she") blur. This is a good example of how dreams model this penetrative intersubjectivity. Whereas capitalist modernity reifies humans into identities of class, race, gender, sexuality, and so on, dreams defy the power of reification and affirm the universality of our species-being.

Dreams within realist texts foreground the perennial crisis that afflicts the very heart of representation; if dreams function as an allegory of the illusive nature of fictional narrative itself, then can such representation be truly believed? Can such representation bear meaning if it is but a dream? But alongside fears about fiction's failure to truly convey a sense of reality lies an always persistent utopian hope of language's semiotic possibility; its ability to signify, however tenuous, is itself allegorical of redemption. The disruptions that dreams cause for the realist mode are not meant to subvert it through contradiction; rather, this is part of realism's compact, its ability to radically correct itself at moments of mimetic distress. What dreams imply is that even the seeming meaninglessness within the crisis of representation is itself meaningful, a harbinger of a revelation that might perhaps transcend mimesis altogether. Dreams bring the reader to the very edge of what is knowable.

The following chapters explore realism and dreams in Chinese texts spanning most of the twentieth century. By pursuing a reading of realism as a form of aesthetically productive crisis, these analyses mitigate against evaluations of Chinese realism as a kind of "stillbirth"[68] that was unable to attain western European standards. Instead, realism constituted a constant grappling with competing narrative, political, and social desires that was consonant with a politico-historical reality rife with endemic crises. As a semicolonized country, China long served as a geopolitical space where western European powers sought to defer their own crises of capitalist accumulation.[69] Whereas western Europe and America could project an image of mature civil society propped up by moderate bourgeois constraint (one that often veiled and suppressed the many crises lurking underneath the surface), China was hardly allowed that luxury (although there were certainly attempts).

The mimetic crises that so often float to the surface of Chinese literary texts thus correlate with the very apparent collective crises that have plagued modern Chinese history. But in that Chinese national crises are sometimes dialectically, sometimes directly, related to global ones, the problematic symptoms of Chinese realism can be extrapolated to world literature, and world politics, as a whole. In this sense, Chinese realism allows us perspective into more volatile, dynamic aspects of the realist project itself. In seeking to represent a reality whose very frames of intelligibility were subject to sudden change and transvaluation, the authors examined here were valiantly wrestling with the hope and despair of creating a literary modernity that could testify to China's tumultuous world-historical experience. In that sense, these authors and their works speak to all of humanity, particularly in relation to the dreams we make and the worlds we desire.

CHAPTER 2

Dreaming as Representation

Lu Xun's Wild Grass *and Realism's Social Address*

The writing of Lu Xun (born Zhou Shuren, 1881–1936) touches upon the relationship between social bodies and the literary forms that seek to capture them. He exhibited a remarkable ability to depict the throes of human suffering with a combination of tragedy, empathy, and no small dose of mordant irony. His early innovations in the use of *baihua* vernacular revealed the creative potential of this new literary language to become a living, pulsating aesthetic force. Throughout his literary work one detects an abiding concern about how literature and the social world can be made to correlate with each other. This endeavor, as both Lu Xun and many scholars have recognized, is fraught with hazards; what if literature fails to obtain the affective and moral purchase it solicits from its readers in its depiction of social reality? What if, instead of compassion and moral reflection, literature's mimetic capture of social others elicits only contempt, mockery, or mere indifference? Worse still, what if it also elicited a sanctimonious sense of moral satisfaction in those who feel they have made a significant ethical effort merely by reading? The stubborn presence of an immanent disconnect between language and sociality lies at the heart of realism's quandary, one examined with great insight by Marston Anderson. Anderson argued that the ontological hierarchy between observer and observed in realist fiction constituted a formal obstacle to any real compassion or solidarity between the two: "The realist narrative," Anderson wrote, "by imitating at a formal level the relation of oppressor to oppressed, is captive to the logic of that oppression and ends by merely reproducing it."[1]

We are thus left with a most frustrating paradox. As we are immanently social beings constituted throughout by discursive and pragmatic conventions, literature should thus be able to capture and relay our reality. On the other hand, literature often ends up stuck in its conventions, calcifying what we already assume to know and blocking room for new revelation. Lu Xun was fully aware of literature's tendency to tell the same stories in the same ways and how a reader's sense of empathy can easily wane into annoyance and irritation. According to Lu Xun's own youthful literary aspirations, as recounted in his famous 1922 preface to *Call to Arms* (Nahan), he hoped literature would help mitigate his compatriots' sense of "numbness" (*mamu*) in the presence of injustice; literature might reinject into otherwise "meaningless" (*hao wu yiyi*) bodies of suffering a sense of moral significance and urgency.[2] However, the sheer brevity of his literary career, albeit an impressive and compressed one, and his later preference for a more direct essayistic style (*zawen*) betray the real difficulties in achieving literature's social address.

Lu Xun's dissatisfaction with realist narrative led to an abandonment of the form. His collection of prose poetry, *Wild Grass* (Yecao), constituted an apparent rejection of realism's pretenses to social revelation and transformation through its very aesthetic form, one far more akin to modernist experimentation. *Wild Grass* is a collection of twenty-three prose poems (*sanwen shi*) that Lu Xun wrote between 1924 and 1926 and published serially in the literary journal *Threads of Language* (Yusi). It was published as a book with a preface from the author in 1927. The contents defy easy description, but the pieces, ranging from impressionistic vignettes to poems and skits, evoke highly visual and sensual mindscapes and often dwell in intense emotional territory. Seven of the pieces explicitly take the form of a dream, although the collection as a whole can be read as a sort of nocturnal fantasia.

Critics have argued that *Wild Grass* constitutes a rejection of realism and an embrace of modernism, romanticism, symbolism, or a mixture of all three. It is frequently read as a highly personal work that expresses Lu Xun's inner turmoil, one that cannot be reduced to political concerns.[3] One critic has argued that *Wild Grass* expresses disillusionment with language and representation, constituting a collection of "allegorical ruins."[4] In this reading, the work instead stages the very "breakdown of the subject"[5] and expresses the inability of self and language to be commensurate with each other.

Wild Grass's apparent revelation of a more modernist Lu Xun runs parallel with other scholarship that has dismantled the widely held notion of Lu Xun as a politically engaged realist who earnestly believed in literature's ability to effect social change. One critic argues that Lu Xun's fictional work exhibits elements of a nascent Chinese modernism; Lu Xun's focus on the concept of "madness" (*kuang*) in "Diary of a Madman" (Kuangren riji) reveals the affinities between Lu Xun's writing and that of a global modernism.[6] Another scholar has noted that Lu Xun's work exhibits not only modernist qualities but aspects of postmodernism as well. Lu Xun's refusal to adhere to any stable convention and generic form, particularly in *Wild Grass*, suggests a postmodern aesthetic sensibility.[7] Given this preponderance of scholarship that has disavowed the notion of Lu Xun as committed realist, any attempt to note a residual engagement with realism might seem to be a stubborn subscription to the conception of Lu Xun as an ideological combatant. However, Lu Xun's aesthetic experimentation was not only confined to the features of modernism and postmodernism but also constituted at times a critical reflection on realism and its limits and, in certain cases, a wistful attempt to dream a solution to realism's own paradoxes.

Despite *Wild Grass*'s apparent break with Lu Xun's previous engagement with realist form, the notion of a complete formal separation is far more complicated. Even in this highly symbolic and formally complex text, realism reappears as residual traces. However, these realist *revenants* are inevitably transformed and twisted by the new formal landscapes they haunt. The radical recontextualizations of these realist tropes in fact furtively suggest utopian solutions to realist narrative's own ethical contradictions; at times it seems as if *Wild Grass* occasionally dreams up formal solutions to realism's own quandaries. These dreams are of course not a real solution; they can never constitute more than a utopian allegory of what an effective realist social address might be.

The aim here is not to recategorize *Wild Grass* as "realist"; faced with such a relentlessly hybridized text as *Wild Grass*, mere categorization fails to be adequate or fruitful to serious critical discussion. But there should be a broader discussion of genre and mode that goes beyond stringent categorization and historicization and instead examines ways in which generic and modal fields, replete with their particular repertoire of signals, can and do intertwine.[8] *Wild Grass*'s occasional polemicized engagement with realist convention and its epistemic premises thus invites a nuanced discussion of both *Wild Grass* and realism within the same critical frame.

Despite the apparent sense that *Wild Grass* is ultimately concerned about poetic interiority, the text deeply engages with the representation of sociality, one constituted by both its corporeal and intersubjective aspects. One of the most notable things about *Wild Grass* is its emphasis on bodily representation.[9] It is easy to insist on the autonomy and value of the body "as is" over social and textual/formal considerations of corporeality; however, *Wild Grass*'s treatment of such corporeality is always linked to questions of the representation of sociality. This paradoxical engagement of the social via the intimately personal suggests ways in which the conventional realist concern for the social lingers on in what seems at first blush to be intensely private reflections.

Wild Grass invites us to rethink the process of mimetic representation by re-embodying the affective premises and spatial parameters of such representation. *Wild Grass*'s dream form is essential to representation's reorientation for two reasons.[10] The first is the deep, visceral production deployed in dream representation, involving a sleeping body that creates images from the depths of its being. Instead of the aloof, seemingly invisible author who creates characters, we have instead a figure, trapped in a bed, psychosomatically conjuring new bodies; but none of these bodies, including the one in bed, has the stable, self-assured subjectivity granted to an author. *Wild Grass*'s narrator often comments on the terror of being in bed, dreaming up characters that unsettlingly press themselves upon him. In other words, the dream form turns the vertical, hierarchical vector of representation between observer and observed in realism to one that is horizontal, a relation whereby both positions are equally vulnerable to one another. Against the strict separation and implied hierarchy between observer and observed, the dreamscape more freely allows for the observer to become the observed. The bodies the dreamer sees are simultaneously other bodies as well as his own.[11] Dreaming thus removes the distance between subject and object and brings the two into direct contact; subject-object relations are transformed into a bewildering contiguity. The familiar comforts of hierarchy are replaced by an unsettling adjacency. The dreamed becomes an essential part of the dreamer himself.

Running alongside the heavy emphasis on dream, *Wild Grass* also underscores the constant somatic orientation of the narrator. Taken as a whole, *Wild Grass* suggests a narrative arc of sleeping: in the first piece after the preface, "Autumn Night" (Qiuye), the narrator ponders the beauty of nature in the evening, noting that the flowers and leaves around him are "dreaming."[12] At the end of the piece, he yawns and drags on his cigarette. In the second piece, "The Shadow's Leave-Taking" (Ying de gaobie), the narrator discusses how his shadow appears to him and bids farewell at the exact moment he is about to enter sleep.[13] The order of the pieces suggests a narrative logic wherein the following poems can be interpreted as visions occurring in sleep. The last piece, "The Awakening" (Yijue), features the narrator again smoking a cigarette, having a "long dream," but then suddenly waking up.[14] The few explicit dream sequences are unique in their thematization of the somatic conditions of sleep, including the physical position of the narrator in bed and his body's visceral reaction to a dream. Dreaming is not, as it were, a spiritual flight from the confines of the corporeal into the wide expanses of the ethereal. It instead constitutes a radical re-embodiment, an approach to the body that is reframed and reoriented.

Only seven of the twenty-three prose poems explicitly mention the narrator actually dreaming; it is plausible to interpret the other pieces as simply prose poems and not as dream visions. Nevertheless, the work as a whole is bookended by the narrator's emphasis on nocturnal imaginings. The strong presence of dreams in the work as a whole invites us to consider the book as operating, to a certain extent, under the dream's sign and logic. The reader of *Wild Grass* is invited to discard waking, rational, and cerebral thought in favor of a more sleepy and sensual experience.

Wild Grass's nearly exclusive use of first-person narration has often been interpreted as a window to Lu Xun's own psyche and inner demons. But other critics have warned against reading the ostensibly personal self-reference as transparent.[15] *Wild Grass*'s intricate formalism invites us to ponder the discursive pragmatics by which we announce and address ourselves to each other. Sociolinguists have noted how the use of "I," even in everyday speech, is governed by both linguistic and social conventions; the "I" should be read as a persona adopted by a speaking subject for a particular social purpose.[16] In regards to *Wild Grass*'s first-person address, a formalist approach that refuses to immediately conflate the narrative "I" with the historic "I" yields important insights.

Wild Grass's "I," this sensuous, intimate, and nocturnal subject, is not merely an index for a tortured authorial soul but also a response to the conflicts of narrative authority in Lu Xun's early and concurrent realist fiction in both its third- and first-person narrative modes. The first conflict is the gap between an omniscient, third-person narrator's formal and moral ascendancy over its objects of observation and its ostensible mission to record the lives of others objectively and dispassionately. The second is the gap between a first-person narrator that is meant to embody sympathy for the lives he observes and the fact that he simply cannot relate, respond, or sympathize with those abject characters, instead responding with silence. *Wild Grass*'s "I" is fashioned so as to illuminate these limitations but also suggest their fantastic transcendence. He bridges both an inner world and an outer, oneiric landscape. This "I" that dreams the world and all within it is an attempt to produce a literary subject that can transcend the confines of realist narration.

The genre of prose-poetry, with its ambiguous position between narrative and lyric, also complicates how we should consider issues of subjectivity. Literary theorist Käte Hamburger has proposed that fiction and lyric comprise two very different kinds of literature: fiction is primarily mimetic. It is not "reality" but instead a contrived simulation of such reality, an imitation.[17] The first-person narrator of a fictional text, then, can only be a "fictive-I," a simulation that appears to be a first-person speaker.[18] The lyric, however, is no mere "simulation" of reality; lyric comprises statements enunciated by a speaker taken to be real. The lyric-I, rather than some contrived persona or a fictive character, is a "statement-subject" or, alternatively, a "linguistic function"[19] that makes real utterances. However, this lyric-I, while understood to be non-fictive, is not necessarily congruous with the historic poet, nor are this subject's statements necessarily oriented to an extant objective reality.[20]

The question of how to take the "I" in *Wild Grass* is irresolvable; clearly the work's orientation toward the lyric would suggest a "real" enunciating subject, one too often conflated with the historic Lu Xun. On the other hand, the contrived narrative and dream situations that appear in the collection seem to suggest that the "I" still has clear affinities with the fictive-"I" of Lu Xun's narratives. The dream form complicates questions of the "I's" authenticity furthermore; is the "I" of the dream that from which the dream emanates, or is that "I" created by the dream itself? The hybrid generic nature of *Wild Grass* suggests an oscillating representational instability of the speaking self.

This instability, however, suggests a formal flexibility that enhances the work's power.

The second reason for the dream's significance in our rethinking of realism lies in its self-reflexive approach to literary form. Dreaming transforms narrative materiality into a doubled form; it seems as if the main narrative has generated a new one within its borders. Dreaming thus rejects the transparency a realist narrative seeks to achieve; it calls attention to the very edges of the narrative suddenly made visible. Philosopher Slavoj Žižek has noted how, in following the Freudian method of dream interpretation, we tend to read the manifest content (what happens in a dream) as mere ciphers for the latent content (the underlying unconscious thoughts and desires that lie behind the dream). However, Žižek insists that the "secret" of the dream lies not within the obscured latent content but instead in how that latent content is "wrapped up" in the manifest content. Rather than seeing through the dream image to access its "deeper" significance, one would do well to pay attention to the surface.[21] For Žižek, the discovery of the dream's unconscious desire only occurs through a careful analysis of the dream's formal elaborations. Dream narratives thus invite a large degree of self-reflexivity (it seems that one never recounts a dream without beginning with the formula "I dreamed"). But, in contrast to other narratives, this is precisely the tragedy of dream-narrative; once dream becomes accessible to knowledge, it has already lost its ability to enchant. One is made aware that a dream is but a play of surfaces, and this revelation of artifice would seem to subtract from the pleasures of immersion that other narratives offer. Whereas most narratives appeal to a desire for absorptive pleasure, dreams appeal to a desire for critical insight.

Herein lies the brilliant paradox of the dream form: its ability to put into suspension, on one hand, unparalleled intimacy between self and other and, on the other hand, a vital ironic distance between representation and reality. The dream form thus illuminates twin concerns of the realist mode: the imperative toward social empathy and solidarity as well as the need for critical insight into social reality. Lu Xun's frequent interest in dreams bespeaks not so much a resistance to approaching and conveying social reality but rather a desire to use multiple representative strategies to dialectically unfold reality in its many forms.

THE USEFULNESS OF DREAMS

Lu Xun's interest in the rhetoric of dreams as a way to probe the edges of reality and shake up our approach to knowing it is attested to often in his written work. Two examples of how Lu Xun employs dream rhetoric will help provide context to his treatment of dreams in *Wild Grass*. The first piece, a preface to a volume of translations by the blind Russian anarchist writer Vasily Eroshenko (1890–1952), is contemporaneous with the publication of his first volume of short stories, *Call to Arms* (Nahan, 1923). The second was written twelve years after, and not long after Lu Xun began to adopt Marxism and class analyses in earnest. While in both cases Lu Xun plays with ideas of dream so as to arrive to a more complex, trenchant understanding of reality, in the later essay, he arrives at a deeper understanding of how dream rhetoric pushes the limits of politically acceptable discourse.

In his preface to the Eroshenko volume, Lu Xun comments on the preponderance of dream narratives in the author's work:

> I felt that what [Eroshenko] wanted to announce to humanity was the tragedy of those who were not loved even though there was no one in the world unworthy of such love. But what I discovered was his child-like, beautiful, and yet realistic dream. Is this perhaps nothing other than the veil with which the writer concealed tragedy? If that is so then perhaps I have also dreamed the dream too deeply (*guoyu meng meng le*), but I wish for the author to never abandon this dream of child-like beauty, and moreover, for him to call on others to enter this dream, to see for themselves the real rainbow, [and thereby realize] we are not merely *somnambulists*.[22]

Lu Xun's enthusiasm for a writer seemingly cut from such a vastly different cloth, a man who professed anarchist politics and wrote children's tales and fables where animals talk and dream beside their human counterparts, is striking. Lu Xun veers between belief and skepticism, between incredulousness at the innocence and idealism of Eroshenko's work and yet his enthrallment by the sheer beauty of the blind Eroshenko's prophetic vision. The preface in the original Chinese is tough to read, full of hesitations, double negatives, and disjunctive particles, evidence of the epistemic difficulty inherent in trying to come to terms with the reality of Eroshenko's dreams. It betrays a tension between skepticism of and faith in utopia, and in particular, his locutions "realistic dream" and the dream's "real rainbow" are problematic. In order to transform his skepticism of Eroshenko's beautiful visions into belief, Lu Xun offers a brilliant twist:

to dismiss Eroshenko's dream as simply a veil that covers up the tragedy that lurks in his tales is not an act of demystification but, instead, of further mystification, of sinking into an even deeper dream.

The "dream" and the "real" are intertwined in a symbiotic pair. Lu Xun refuses to disavow the dream's existence, regarding it as a necessary supplement to reality itself. The complicated dance between these two words, to see the "real rainbow" within a dream, to approach a "realistic dream," suggests how Lu Xun is trying to push the limits of what we understand to be reality at any given moment. "Real" suggests a reality outside of language. It points to a truth that words cannot contain and thus gestures outside the bounds of language. "Dream," however, implies that one has entered a reality that is not, and the term indexes the discursivity of language and narrative itself, revealing that our reality is but another reverie. "Dream" points right back to the materiality of language itself. Both terms serve the functions of enchantment and disenchantment, and they both affirm and disavow each other. Lu Xun's dynamic and complex view of "reality" comes into view. It is not a static ontology but a complex form of critical thought that constantly questions itself. This reality resists its own reification, sometimes relying on paradox to break out of epistemic complacency.

Furthermore, Lu Xun rejects the notion that Eroshenko's dreams are merely private expression. As befitting a prophecy, such a vision belongs to all, a phantasmatic commons through which the masses can invest their utopian desires. Lu Xun calls on others to enter the dream and catch a glimpse of that "real rainbow." Such people are not "sleepwalkers," or merely travelers within a dream, but people bestowed with a special vision of reality. Therefore, Eroshenko's dreams are not a blanket over an uglier reality but a necessary lens through which reality can be better ascertained.

In 1933 Lu Xun composed an essay titled "Ting shuo meng," a response to the New Year's publication of *Eastern Miscellany* (Dongfang zazhi), an important intellectual journal published in Shanghai. The editors had sent out a call for readers to submit their "dreams" for both China's future and their own personal lives. At least 140 submissions were received, and they were published in the magazine under the heading "Dreams of the New Year." The title of Lu Xun's piece, "Ting shuo meng," is somewhat difficult to translate. Should it be "On Hearing Dreams," thus taking the *tingshuo* as a single semantic unit ("to hear"), or should we see the *ting* (hear) and the *shuo* (speak) as separate, and read it as "On Hearing and Speaking of Dreams"? Lu Xun's virtuoso word play is demonstrated to even greater effect when we discover yet a third reading: "On hearing of the article titled 'Shuo Meng,'" a reference to the title of the editors' commentary printed in *Eastern Miscellany*. Lu Xun also seems to be referencing the idiom "the crazy man speaks in dreams" (*chi ren shuo meng*). In any case, what remains clear is that Lu Xun's concern is with "dreaming" as a pragmatic linguistic act, a form of speech that involves both our "hearing" and "speaking." This emphasis on the issue of dreaming as discourse is made clear in the very first sentence: "The act of having dreams is free, but speaking these dreams is not free. When we have dreams, we have real dreams, but when we speak those dreams, it is hard to avoid speaking lies."[23]

Lu Xun's emphasis on "speaking dreams" rather than "having dreams," that is, on the discursive pragmatics of the dreams themselves, stems from his realization that an acquaintance's submission to the journal was altered because of its political content. The dreams submitted to *Eastern Miscellany*'s editors, then, were subject to the same kind of "censorship" as dream thoughts themselves are altered by the unconscious's own mechanisms of censorship, a parallel that Lu Xun himself notes.[24] What concerns Lu Xun are not the ostensibly unvarnished dreams one has upon sleeping but the problem of articulating such dreams as speech. Dream-speech is potentially subversive speech that must be controlled, altered, or otherwise made more amenable to structures of power. But such dream-speech, as Lu Xun notes, always stands at a tentative remove from politics as such: "I understand the reporters' great hardship. As there is no freedom of speech in the first place, one might as well speak in dreams. Rather than speak of the so-called falsity within truth, one might as well chat a bit about the truth in dreams. I happily turned the pages [of *Eastern Miscellany*], only to find out that the reporters had miserably failed in their task."[25] The apparent innocuousness of dream-speech against the background of vast censorship accounts for the potential reading of dream-speech as political speech. Dream-speech is able to hold in suspension both illusion and truth, fantasy and critique, and this slipperiness cannot help but provoke the anxiety of those who wish to contain the flow and interpretation of language. *Eastern Miscellany*'s editors seemed anxious that their call for dreams might potentially act as a conduit for seditious speech and thus invite unwanted scrutiny. In response they not only purportedly altered or discarded submissions that were deemed too critical, they also appended a commentary (the "Shuo meng" Lu Xun referred to in his article) that sought to explain that political criticisms and outright expressions of utopian visions were not "authentic" dreams at all but instead mere daydreams.

In the *Eastern Miscellany* commentary, the editors criticized those who submitted pieces that were too political in content. They argued that, according to Freud's theory of dreams, such propagandistic dreams were only instances of "daydreaming" and did not fit the "authentic" model of dreams. "Authentic," or "orthodox" (*zhengzong*), dreams were those that "express what is intently on the mind" (*yan zhi*), a classical definition of poetry. The reporter described political dreams as those that "carry forward the Way" (*zai Dao*), a reference to the classical slogan "the purpose of literature is to carry forward the Way" (*wen yi zai Dao*), a phrase that came to embody a utilitarian, social purpose to literature. Zhou Zuoren, Lu Xun's brother and a well-known critic, popularized these two slogans in literary debates as a form of shorthand denoting utilitarian (that which "carries the way") and expressive (that which "expresses intent") literature. According to the editors, only the dreams of the latter, those that express personal, individual wishes, can truly be considered "authentic" dreams, whereas the other more political dreams were forced and inauthentic.

The editors' lecture on "real" and "false" dreams seems to suggest editorial disarray. After all, in their call for submissions issued just a few months earlier, they explicitly asked readers to express not only their "individual" dreams but their dreams for China as well. That they seemingly reversed position and felt moved to remind their audience that political dreams about the nation did not count seems to indicate a sense of unease, an anxiety that they were being watched from above. Their insistence that dreams were simply the innocuous expression of private desires seemed to confirm just how potentially dangerous they were.

Lu Xun's divide between the dreams that one has versus the dreams one speaks, and the editors' demarcation between "authentic" personal dreams and "inauthentic" political ones, may be elided or at least made more problematic if we turn to Ludwig Wittgenstein's thoughts on dreams in his *Philosophical Investigations*. Wittgenstein wonders whether or not we can ever verify, through the accounting of dreaming alone, whether the dream phenomenon actually occurred:

> People who on waking tell us certain incidents (that they have been in such-and-such places, and so forth). Then we teach them the expression "I dreamt", which is followed by the narrative. Afterwards, I sometimes ask them, "Did you dream anything last night?" and am answered Yes or No, sometimes with a dream narrative, sometimes not. That is the language-game. . . .
>
> Now must I make an assumption about whether these people are deceived by their memories or not, whether they really had such images while they slept, or whether it merely seems so to them on waking? And what sense does this question have?—And what interest?! . . .
>
> Does this mean that it is nonsense ever to raise the question of whether dreams really take place during sleep, or are a memory phenomenon of the awakened? It will depend on how the question is used.[26]

As is wont with Wittgenstein's elliptical style, he provides few answers, mostly questions. But what his musings suggest is that when it comes to the issue of dreams' authenticity, we are pragmatically confined to what people report as their dreams. What constitutes dreams and the ways in which we communicate such dreams are subject to conventions and standards of usage with a particular social situation, what Wittgenstein terms "language-games." When we enter the language-game of dream-speech, we operate upon an assumption (ultimately impossible to verify within the parameters of our language-game) that what a person accounts as his dream is very possibly what he experienced. By taking part in this game, we accept such an experience "happened." By engaging in dream-speech, we performatively assume the presence of interiority that such discourse would suggest. On the level of linguistic ontology, little differentiates between an "actual" report of a dream and a narration metaphorically styled as one. To try to parse out which is a "real" neurological occurrence, and which is merely discursive fancy, takes us into a different language-game, a different social context with another aim in mind. Unconscious interiority would be something that we try to neither prove nor disprove but instead ritually assume within a particular social situation.

By focusing on dream-speech as a unique language-game, one that consists of a set of rules and a set of players, we can see the importance of such rhetoric in creating the assumptions of both interior experience (my private dream) and collective, national desire (our public dream). Moreover, we can see how such rhetoric performatively instantiated the presumed presence of individual and nation, and, more important, assumed an organic linkage between the two.

Dreams thus constituted a popular rhetorical device in the May Fourth era. On one hand, by indexing the fantastic, it created an indirect avenue toward political critique at a moment when political discourse still proved fledgling. On the other hand, the discourse of dreams seemed to promise a visceral connection between intimate experience and collective transformation. Dream-speech as language-game allowed its players to engage in a discourse of political possibility that united both individual and public concerns.

When the editors of *Eastern Miscellany* issued their call for dreams, they were inviting their readers to take part in a language-game. The response from readers, as they themselves noted, was overwhelming—people were more than happy to participate. However, seemingly in response to their discomfort with some readers' submissions, it appears that the editors suddenly changed the rules of the game, disqualifying some submissions. Bankers, bureaucrats, and cronies who dreamed of stealing themselves away into hermetic exile were recognized as following the proper rules of dreaming; radicals who insisted on food for all were disqualified for breaking the language-game's rules. The realist authors Ba Jin and Lao She treated the call for dreams with skepticism and flouted the rules in their submissions by protesting that the dire political conditions of the day made dreaming impossible, and thus they had no dreams to contribute. (Their contributions will be touched on in more detail in the next chapter).

Lu Xun stridently challenged the editors' notion that "authentic" dreams are irreducibly private in nature. For Lu Xun, Freud was not merely a psychologist of the personal: "Freud considers the repressed [*bei yayi*] to be the root of all dreams—but why are men repressed [*bei yayi*]? This is connected with the social system and customs. And yet dreaming is not considered something to be taken seriously, so to tell a dream, to ask about a dream, to analyze it, this suddenly becomes inappropriate."[27] Lu Xun intentionally borrows the Freudian term for "repression" (*yayi*) to also denote social repression. Lu Xun dismisses an exclusive stress on society's repression of the libido and instead points to another cause of psychic repression: hunger. But as he also points out, the bodily experience of hunger is inextricably linked with social and political realities. Hunger is as much a social reality as it is a private torment. The dreams of a hungry man cannot be separated from the collective, social forces that undergird hunger's manifestation. A dream that touches upon public concerns cannot be disqualified as lacking authenticity.

Moreover, Lu Xun expresses skepticism as to whether it is even possible to voice a dream that "speaks what is intently on the mind" when all printed materials undergo censorship. He redoubles Freud's theory of censorship as a psychological mechanism to repress inappropriate unconscious thoughts by alluding to Nationalist censors that emend and abridge all media, including the very magazine issue carrying dreams. Just as psychic repression finds its mirrored double in social repression, so Lu Xun demonstrates that what are considered merely psychological mechanisms, like censorship, also exist in the wider social realm. The internally contradictory structure of the individual's psyche parallels the structure of a social reality ridden with conflict; the mind is not a category shut off from the public and social but in fact illuminates and is illuminated by the society surrounding it. The editors' appeal to "authentic" dreams as having superiority over political dreams elevated private experience as unassailable. But this very act of installing the private as "authentic" effectively legislated which speech was permissible and what was irrelevant. By upholding an illusion of "authentic" dreams that can be communicated directly from one heart to another, they sought to veil how all utterances find themselves caught within societal, political, and discursive conventions, always subject to the changing rules of the game. The valorization of personal authenticity over contrived politicization was in itself an ideological act.

Lu Xun attempts to defuse the editors' charge that the vulgar agitators have subscribed to the pedantic *wen yi zai Dao*. Rather than "carrying forward the Way," he argues that intellectuals have merely been "carried by the Way": "But it is certainly not 'carrying forward the Way,' rather, [the intellectuals] have been carried about by 'the Way' for a bit, and if we want to be concise about it, we should say that [these dreams] are 'Way-carried.'"[28] A dreamer does not choose to speak out against social conditions; he is rather compelled, "carried" about by the needs of real circumstances. Lu Xun insists on the ineluctable social context that accounts for dreams' emergence and on their usefulness as an index to social conflict.

Lu Xun's pedantic explanation of the social overdetermination of dreams is lightened by his artful way of expressing a materialist theory of dreams. His ironic take on the Archaist slogan *wen yi zai Dao* as "to get carried about by the Way for a while" (*gei "Dao" zaile yixia*) demonstrates how he transforms a trite cliché about the utility of literature into a witty gem. By breaking apart the adage, switching the terms around, then cloaking the phrase in the garb of vernacular grammar, and then finally resting with the revised term "Way-carried" (*Dao zai*), Lu Xun demonstrates how by making a cliché strange he restores the sensuous materiality of shopworn language. His symbolic manipulation of the phrase seems to mimic the way dreams work in reorganizing lived experience into a mystified code. Lu Xun's affirmation for the social utility of literature (and dreams) also embraces language's playfulness.

While "Ting shuo meng" was written after *Wild Grass* and Lu Xun's left-wing transformation, this does not mean that its themes do not resonate with the moral and social concerns of *Wild Grass*. Sun Yushi argues that the dream pieces in *Wild Grass*, despite their strangeness, nevertheless "bear the deep, burning scar of real life."[29] However absurd and fantastic the content of the dreams, dreams nevertheless operate under the burning, lacerating sign of the real. Of course, writing in the People's Republic in the 1980s, Sun Yushi was making a case for the social referentiality of *Wild Grass*, one well in keeping with the PRC's insistence on the social utility of literature; on the other hand, this idea of "brand" or "scar" invites thinking about other ways in which society can be represented. A scar, or a brand, not only operates as a metaphor but also constitutes the very material trace of repression (an index). Lu Xun's writing thus invites us to notice how words can burn at the same they describe.

BODILY WAVES: "TREMORS OF DEGRADATION"

Lu Xun's prose poem "Tremors of Degradation" (Tuibaixian de chandong) is a complicated set piece that demonstrates how a dreamscape can force us to rethink the intellectual and moral basis of social conflict. As an aesthetic experiment, it makes strange the conventional narrative situation of realist fiction: the hierarchical relation between observer and observed. The tragedy of a woman degraded through prostitution, who raises a daughter in abject poverty, and then is callously driven out by her daughter years later offers a conventional image of social abjection that would have made a likely candidate for a May Fourth realist object of representation. However, were this a conventional realist narrative, it would indeed risk committing the kind of moral trespass of sanctimoniously depicting the plight of the poor. The woman's tragedy, while pitiable, is nevertheless at a distinct remove from a conventional narrator; she remains an object of curiosity, amusement, and even contempt for a narrator who is free to walk away. Recasting this conventional situation through a dream features a narrative twist that forces the narrator/dreamer to become unsettlingly intimate with the object of representation, one that precludes a convenient escape.

The narrator begins with the phrase "I dreamed I was dreaming" (*wo mengjian ziji zai zuomeng*). It might help to think of the second "I" (*ziji*) in the opening sentence as separate from the first "I" (*wo*), as an independent figure of dream representation. What the original narrator has dreamed up is a meta-vision about the process of representation itself. "He" is unsure of his surroundings, but similarly we are unsure as to who "he" is, the original dreamer or the secondary dreamer the former has produced? It is from this ambiguous and tenuous subject position that this shaky "I" is confronted with a strange sight: "The globe of the paraffin lamp on the wooden table had been newly polished, making the room very bright. In this light, on the rickety couch, under the hairy, muscular flesh of a stranger, a slight frail body trembled with hunger (*ji'e*), pain (*tongku*), shock (*jingyi*), humiliation (*xiuru*) and pleasure (*huanxin*)."[30] This unknown body, frail and trembling under the weight of a similarly unknown stranger, embodies something degraded, bereft of subjectivity or personality. The scene suggests an act of sexual congress. The narrator acts as voyeur, looking upon the primal coupling of two beings as nondescript as mating animals, two sensate beings lacking definite identity. To merely acknowledge the sexual nature of the representation would be one-sided; the "hunger" and "humiliation" suggest a socially tragic dimension to her experience that is equal to, if not overshadows, what "pleasure" may arise. The bodily sensations depicted are ones that will permeate the entire terrain throughout the sequence, thus inviting the dreamer and we readers to wander through a troubling atmosphere of feeling that envelops us at every turn.

The strange nature of bodies depicted, their barely palpable disambiguation into a "male" and a "female," invites us to view the polar positions of "male" aggressor and "female" victim as much more indistinct. Hunks of flesh lie before us, the gender of which can only be tentatively determined not by pronouns but by the contrasting descriptions of muscularity and frailness, of domination and submission. The diegetic "self" dreamed up by the primal narrator is free to identify with either one or the other being in this encounter. There is an overriding feeling of being smothered and pressed upon by another, even when it is unclear which body is whose. While pleasure may be one of the results of this bodily contact, so are the "hunger," "pain," and "humiliation."

The narrator continues by describing his surroundings: "The air was still pervaded, pulsating, with a wave of hunger, pain, shock, humiliation and pleasure."[31] The "interior" experience of the one being pressed upon is turned inside out, becoming palpable in the external atmosphere. The wave of "hunger, pain, shock, humiliation and pleasure" appears as a mantra-like refrain, suggesting a universal, undifferentiated bodily experience. The "frail body" proves stronger than it seems, for its affective experience threatens to overrun the limits of the text itself.

The dream suddenly skips a few temporal frames and the narrator now envisions a young girl of about two, hungry and pleading to her mother for food. Her mother, holding on to a last silver coin that she will use to buy food for her daughter, assures her that she will soon be fed and gently nudges her to sleep. The coin was presumably earned from her desperate profession, although this remains ambiguous. Suddenly the air is pervaded by another wave of affect that soon overtakes the narrator and causes him to "be unable to breathe," at which point the dream breaks and the first narrator awakes, "groaning."[32]

What affective stimulus represented in the dream proves so intense that it interrupts the dream and causes the narrator to wake up? The issue of hunger seems to be the overriding cause of emotional distress, one that even overtakes the power of sexual desire. This hunger, one that knows no bounds, drives the woman to prostitution in order to feed her daughter. In "Ting shuo meng," Lu Xun will insist on hunger being far more powerful than libido: "Surely, [Freud] will also tell us that because of the attraction between the sexes, daughters will love their fathers, and sons will love their mothers. However, not long after a child is born, no matter if it's a boy or girl, the child will purse together its lips, and move about this way and that. Is it not because the child wants to kiss someone of the opposite sex? No, we all know, the child simply wants to eat!"[33] Note the sympathetic likeness between the primal narrator's own body and that of the pressed-upon woman in the dream's beginning. Recall that the mother is trying to get her daughter to sleep in order to make her persistent feeling of hunger go away. Right when she coaxes her daughter into sleep, the emotional "wave" appears again. The narrator (either the original dreamer or the second) thus identifies with the daughter as much as the mother, because in an effort to escape hunger the speaker wishes to remain ever deeper within sleep. This sleep within sleep is a hoped-for escape from the bodily suffering caused by hunger, and on the part of the speaker, an ironic escape from dreaming itself. The dream proves even more frightening to face than reality. However, the sleep within sleep, the promised escape from bodily torment, is refused by the "wave" of hunger, pain, humiliation, and pleasure. Moreover, the mother lays her daughter on the very "rickety couch" upon which she herself sold her body; thus the daughter's sleep and escape from the pain of the body are shrouded in a deeply portentous and ironic gloom.

Rather than fall into an even deeper sleep that might perhaps escape the dream, the narrator is instead roused from sleep altogether:

> All of a sudden from the middle of the atmosphere arose yet another great wave, and it collided with the wave from before, spinning until it had become a great whirlpool, submerging everything, including me, and neither my mouth nor nose was able to breathe.
>
> I groaned and woke up, outside my window the air was filled with silver moonlight, and it seemed to be still very far from daylight.[34]

The sensation of drowning, and the panic that it inspires, epitomizes the effort of the body to resist death, the need to assert its own existence against forces bent on its destruction. In the beginning of the piece we are introduced to a secondary "self" who dreams of the sex scene. In what ways does that figure, that doubled self, act as a kind of buffer, a promise of distance between the narrator and his dream? On one hand, the creation of the secondary "self" stages a self-reflexive view of the process of dream representation and how an individual creates bodies through dreams. It reminds us of the formality and structure involved in all representation, either of "others" or "myself." On the other hand, such an ironic distance threatens to dull the visceral impact of the scene, and it seems as if the author feels compelled to restore this impact by taking away the narrator's sense of ironic self-awareness. Removing the buffer, taking away the "fourth wall" (after already having laid bare its existence), makes the sense of the narrator's suffering all the more stronger. The description of the narrator drowning and then waking up reveals to us the power of bodily experience described in the prose poem; it overrides even this provisional self and makes contact with the narrator. Both unmediated intimacy *and* ironic self-knowledge intertwine in contrapuntal rhythm in order to provide a dynamic view of the situation.

While being awake seems at first to save the narrator from his nightmare, he inevitably sinks again into another dream and realizes that his new dream is a continuation of the prior one. This time many years have passed, and the young mother is now an old and frail grandmother. Her daughter is now married with children, still living in poverty. The entire family rises in resentment against the old woman for having raised her daughter by means of prostitution. Her son-in-law accuses her of shaming the entire family and depriving the family of "face": "We have no face to show people, and it is precisely because of you."[35] It would have been better, he says, to allow her daughter to starve than to be condemned to a life of shame. The daughter also accuses her mother of causing shame, and her son-in-law accuses the mother of having now implicated him: "Hai yao dailei le wo." The daughter rejoins by claiming that her mother has implicated her own grandchildren to a doomed fate: "hai yao dailei tamen li!" Even the grandson points a reed at his grandmother, as if holding a sword, and simply yells, "Kill!"[36]

Dailei means to carry over a kind of harm or suffering to another person. It suggests harm's mobility, its ability to drag or weigh down the person unlucky to receive it. The son-in-law hardly conceals his resentment for having to carry a woman's shame, no less because he is not related to her by blood. The daughter is anguished over the fact that her mother's shame has now been transferred to her own children, and perhaps more cogently, carried over to the male heirs. This "carrying over" and "implication" are analogous to the wave of bodily sensation that overwhelms the narrator at the end of the first dream. The burning shame the family feels mirrors the bodily force that causes the narrator to gasp for air. Whereas in the first dream the young girl is pressed under the weight of male oppression (both figuratively and literally), in the second dream, the girl, now an old woman, is smothered by a relentless front of verbal abuse. The family has felt this "wave" and, resentful of having experienced it, throws it back against the mother. In disavowing their own kin, they exhibit a contempt that breaks the fundamental bonds of filial piety.

Having been driven out of the house, our dream heroine wanders aimlessly and listlessly: "While naked she stood like a stone statue in the middle of the wilderness. In an instant she saw everything from her past: hunger, pain, shock, humiliation, pleasure, and as a result she trembled; [she also saw] suffering, shame, implication [*dailei*], and as a result she convulsed; kill! . . . and she grew quiet."[37] Her body convulses in tremors, and these tremors, "radiating like sunbeams," break through the confines of her own body and overrun the universe, causing the narrator to feel the same tremors. The narrator suddenly wakes up: "It was a nightmare, yet I knew this was because I had pressed my hands on my chest. And in my dream I strained every nerve to remove these overpowering, heavy hands."[38] The piece thus concludes.

The dream sequence's brilliance lies in how it relates the conventional representation of abject sociality with the narrator's own bodily experience through the somatic logic of dreaming. The woman's representation is made surreal by the dream's fantastic elements, thus resisting a transparent realist mimesis. The dream, while eschewing such conventional representation, nevertheless betrays a token of realism's aim to depict and expose a social dilemma. The woman's tragedy appears to have a somatic effect upon the narrator. When he awakes he realizes that his hands are pressing against his chest, but while dreaming his hands had become a crushing weight that he could not remove. Thus the text reveals a formal parallel between the woman lying on the couch, pinned down by the man, and the narrator, pinned down by his own hands while lying on his bed. The rickety bed of shame upon which both mother and daughter lie in the dream is metonymically linked to the very bed on which the narrator sleeps, implying the exchangeability of the man and woman. The narrator and the object of his representation occupy the same position of being oppressed by a larger weight from above. The crushing weight becomes a sign for social oppression that the narrator himself senses by proxy. Through this parallel the narrator and the woman relate to each other not hierarchically but contiguously. The narrator is not separate from that woman, untouched by her suffering; he suffers with her in an analogous way. The text thus embodies the logic of contiguity, both literally (in the way the woman "touches" the narrator via his hands) and figuratively (in the use of symbolic metonymy).

"Tremors of Degradation," in its radical juxtaposition of the narrator with a sexually and socially exploited woman, allows its readers a pathway, through the dream, into a transgender cross-identification, thus opening up the simple reification of female suffering. The dream's potential in setting up a relationship between narrator, reader, and narrative object also extends to how the dream is itself a relentlessly queer form, a structure constantly twisting and distorting latent dream thoughts into manifest content. The most vociferous anger within the dream comes from the son-in-law, who is so incensed by having to carry a uniquely feminine shame. He embodies a misogynistic refusal to identify with his mother-in-law. In contrast it is the presumably male narrator who, through the logic of the dream, is made to feel this shame, precisely because the woman is a product of his own psyche, a separate figural entity, but simultaneously himself as well.

"Tremors of Degradation" constitutes an intriguing formal intervention into the problem of representing the social other and the oppressive relationship between author/narrator and hero. The charge may be leveled that the narrator is simply indulging in an egoistic, solipsistic fantasy, that the woman does not really "exist" but is simply a figment of his fancy. However, the piece is not concerned with the problem of "accurately" reflecting suffering women ontologically; the weight of concern, rather, is on the epistemic and moral quandary of how we can come to notice, view, and feel an Other in the first place. In this vein, "Tremors of Degradation" is a critique of realism as a form of naive ontological reflection that does not engage with the problems of how we come to know the "real" and how suffering bodies can be made intelligible and morally significant. The collision of the bodies of woman and narrator is undoubtedly uncomfortable, and yet the possibility of creating an equivalent of bodily consciousnesses between the two allegorically signals the possibility of Utopia, of the empathy and reconciliation between atomized individuals. The dream form thus effects a formal and functional solidarity between observed and observed, a formality that is itself allegorically symbolic of utopian desire. Consequently, this piece elaborates on a hidden desire within conventional realism itself: the desire to overcome individual subjectivity. Of course, realism can never completely overcome discrete subjectivities (whether of the omniscient narrator, the first-person narrator, or any of the characters) and indulge in a Utopian consciousness; to do so would be to utterly evacuate the possibility of knowledge itself, one predicated on a gap between self and other, and self and the world. While this piece cannot enact Utopia (for to do so would be to vitiate the necessary role of History), at the same time it seeks to go further than a conventional realism that simply represents but does not strive to truly "know" the Other.

The complex framing device in the beginning ("I dreamed that I was dreaming") attempts to de-center the role of the narrator as originating source of representation and meaning and defer the source of authorial presence into yet another dream representation. The self is just as textual as the woman being represented; both exist on the level of symbolic discourse itself. Even though this secondary self dissolves, the formality and structured quality of the dream reflect back onto the contrived nature of the solipsistic narrator himself. On one hand we are lured by the candid welcome of the sensitive, first-person narrator; it becomes easy to identify with him, to join him in his sleepy presence. On the other hand we become paradoxically aware that this narrative self is itself contingent, subject to the same overdetermination that rules over the dream. If the narrative "I" looms large in *Wild Grass*, it is one that is conscious to an obsessive degree to its rough edges, the tenuous boundaries of its own existence, the very liminality that threatens its existence but also provides the foundation for transcendence.

SOCIAL DIFFERENCE AND THE EDGE OF DREAMING: "THE BEGGARS" AND "THE DOG'S RETORT"

"The Beggars" (Qiuqizhe) touches upon the dimensions of social hierarchy. While not explicitly a dream poem, it has much in common with the pieces that deal directly with dreams. It was originally published in *Threads of Language* on the same day as "The Shadow's Leave-Taking" (September 24, 1924, nine days after the opening "Autumn Night" that ends with the narrator yawning), a piece that begins with this line: "When one has slumbered into a time which is unknown, that is when one's shadow will bid farewell."[39] Many critics have commented on the fracturing of subjectivity that occurs in the dialogue between speaker and his own shadow; moreover, this disintegration of unified subjectivity only happens in deep sleep, thus suggesting dreaming or some similar state. That "The Beggars" appears along with "The Shadow's Leave-Taking" suggests that the two can both be possibly read as oneiric visions, landscapes of illusion and reverie.

"The Beggars" deals with a perennial experience of urban life: the pedestrian's encounter with a panhandler. The contact between passerby and beggar encapsulates the quintessence of the experience of looking at a social Other. The conflicting feelings of pity, annoyance, contempt, and self-contempt are the contradictory emotions that accompany such an intense and unsettling social encounter. Moreover, beggars demonstrate one of the most notable forms of the Other's embodiment. A beggar calls attention to all its various poses of prostration; they kneel on the ground with hands outstretched, head kowtowing on the ground. Such bodies are meant to evoke pity or, more cynically, enough irritation that the passerby has to pay some fee in order to be free of harassment.

The piece opens with the narrator walking along a bare and decaying wall, stepping on ashen earth. He sees several children begging on the street; some are mute and gesticulating for alms, others are pleading and prostrating themselves for charity. The narrator's reaction is not sympathy but coldness and contempt: "For him I have only disgust, suspicion and hate."[40] Herein lies the paradox of the beggar's self-representation in society: to earn his living, he must present a form of embodied suffering that proves meaningful enough to a passerby that he will pay a price in exchange for the spectacle. And yet the challenge the beggar must overcome is the fact that most urbanites have already numbed themselves to the sight of suffering bodies; the pain and misery that are inscribed through their performance register nothing. The narrator is cynical of the beggars' sincerity; some of them seem to be even cheery and playful, and moreover, their thick winter jackets seem to downplay whatever misery they hope to project. One mute beggar is in fact play-acting, the narrator concludes, merely employing a "kind of begging device." The narrator thus seeks to conclude that this suffering is an inauthentic, contrived performance and thus unworthy of his charity. But the narrator does not examine how one is to gauge such "authenticity"; if one is to recognize suffering, must there not be some external sign that indicates such pain? But if these signs are external, that implies their ability to be replicated and mimicked. When the performance and reiteration of such signs are possible, how is one to tell between genuine suffering and its mere performance? The narrator has thus fallen into a hermeneutic trap; his insistence on being able to distinguish "inauthentic" and "authentic" forms of suffering covers up the fact that such a distinction is inherently unclear (much like the distinction between "authentic" and "inauthentic" dreams). As another scholar has pointed out, his insistence that these beggars are "false" only serves to justify his indifference and contempt.[41] Whether a beggar's street performance is "real" or "false" has no effect on his social status—he is still a beggar. The narrator's wish to believe that these beggars have chosen their lot belies a fanciful wish to believe that social status is a product of rational choice; moreover, it hides how his own seemingly secure existence as a passerby depends upon social forces, not his will. By the mere flip of a coin the passerby himself may be compelled to perform his own spectacle of suffering.

This appears to be what happens midway through the piece. The "I" is now walking along a similar crumbling wall, this time made of mud and full of cracks and crevices. He feels the sharp autumn chill penetrate his own winter coat; the beggars featured in the beginning were also wearing such a coat. The narrator wonders how he will beg: "I am thinking about what methods I will use to beg: if I make sounds, what tone will I use? If I play the mute, what gestures shall I employ?"[42] The "I" finally concludes that he will use the method of "non-action" and "silence" to beg, and thus earn the "irritation, suspicion and hate" of those who see themselves as being above charity. As disparate individuals continue to walk the streets, the piece dissolves into:

> dust, dust, ...
> . . . .
> dust. . . . . .

and thus ends.

The beggars' performance that the narrator witnesses and then attempts to enact constitutes a social script belonging to what sociologist Pun Ngai has labeled a "minor genre."[43] The narrator seeks to disenchant and lay bare this genre, to reveal its inauthenticity. But his attempt to "mimic" the beggars starts to blur into a real social embodiment, a performance that is ultimately ineluctable. The repetition of elements between the two halves—a crumbling wall, a breeze, and the pervasiveness of dust—seems to suggest, if not a kind of temporal rewind, then a sudden disorientation from the temporal progression that was initiated in the beginning of the piece. Moreover, the fact that this "I" notices the cold autumn air piercing *his* winter jacket (remember that the child beggars are themselves wearing similar coats) immediately creates a certain kind of suspicion as to the identity of this speaker. Is he the same "I" as before, or is he a beggar himself? How can we be sure that the speaker "fantasizing" about being an "ideal" beggar is not an "actual" beggar, one inured to the hatred of others and defiantly resisting humanity's indifference?

It is impossible to conclude whether the two "I's" are separate (a beggar and a passerby) or one and the same. The piece does nothing to resolve this ambiguity, and in fact, it is precisely this ambiguity that lends the piece its power. The sudden narrative recapitulation in the middle seems more like the repetition of a dream sequence but with a sudden uncanny reversal of embodiment; whereas in the first half one was merely a passerby, in the second, one now takes on the guise of the beggar. Rather than exposing the "falsity" of the beggar, this piece instead exposes the fragility and artificiality of the "I" that seeks to anchor his identity by disavowing such a beggar.

One might argue that this "beggar-I" of the second half is disingenuous, "stoic" and not "flesh and blood." But to argue that the speaker at this juncture has failed to conjure up an identity as a "flesh and blood" beggar reiterates the epistemological mistake made by the speaker at the beginning of the piece: the insistence between "authentic" suffering and "mere" performance. The "beggar-I," it should be noted, always uses the modal particle *jiang* along with each verb; *jiang* indicates the incipience of an action. It suggests a certain premeditation in regards to the action, a lack of spontaneity, and a hint of theatricality. One may argue that the presence of *jiang* shows that the beggar-I cannot be genuine, for every action is preceded by a theatrical intentionality. On the other hand, the presence of the modal particle stages the very problem of authenticity that is foregrounded in the beginning. All beggars must perform in one way or another; what this poem shows is that performance, for all its appearance of being a conscious act, willed by a rational individual, is in fact socially compelled.

That this piece was published alongside "The Shadow's Leave-Taking" in *Threads of Language* suggests that both works elaborate on a theme of duality and reversal. In "The Shadow's Leave-Taking," it is the nocturnal self that becomes split into a sleeping body and his shadow, one who bids farewell and sinks into darkness. In the other piece, however, the beggar appears as one's "social shadow," the reality of social suffering that follows us everywhere we go, asking for charity and compassion. Any and every attempt to disavow the reality of this embodied shadow only serves to disavow oneself. The crumbling, decaying wall along which the speaker walks suggests the fragility of separation not only between self and other but also between dream and waking reality; the "I" skirts along not only the "edge" of the reverie but on the borders of his own being. The persistent refrain of "dust" everywhere evokes the Buddhist and Daoist usage of the word to denote phenomenal reality as being but an illusion, a dream to be awakened out of, a façade of dust to be brushed away. Existence itself is an ephemeral performance whose curtain must be drawn and whose enchantment must end. It also, of course, evokes the Christian notion of the return to dust after death. The dusty ground underneath the speaker's feet is forever shaky, just as his own subjectivity threatens to dissolve and transmute at any moment. Consequently, the author is evoking a reality that goes even deeper than the rifts between social classes. Whether the reduction of all reality, of self and other, into "dust" invites a kind of socially disengaged quietism is left unresolved. "The Beggars," in its defamiliarization of the beggar's "minor genre," dismantles their script, supposedly revealing its theatricality. And yet the result is not an easing of conscience: if anything, the fact of beggary and social suffering clings all the more tenaciously upon our psyches. The attempt to reveal someone else's existence as an inauthentic performance only serves to reveal how our own assumption of sincerity can itself be unraveled as contrived; in any case, we remain in suffering's throes.

The prose poem "The Dog's Retort" (Gou de bojie) exploits the way in which dreams blur the dividing line between reality and unreality in order to similarly reveal the contingent arbitrariness that lies underneath social difference. Here the narrator dreams that he is a beggar dressed in rags, thus recapitulating the theme of mendicancy in "The Beggars." He runs into a dog that barks at him, and in response he insults the dog by declaring him *shili*, roughly meaning "snobbish." The dog retorts that he is "not up to man in that respect."[44] The dog continues to explain that he does not yet know how to distinguish between "copper and silver, between silk and cloth, between officials and common citizens, between masters and their slaves, between . . ." Before the dog can explain more, the narrator, suddenly terrified by the dog's lecture on social distinctions, flees. While the dog tries to persuade the man to come back and continue their rather one-sided discussion, the narrator will have none of it. "But I ran straight on as fast as I could," the narrator writes, "until I had run right out of my dream and back into my own bed."[45]

What scares the narrator in this dream is ambiguous. It could be his shock upon discovering a dog with the human capacity of speech and, moreover, speaking to the contradictions of humanly created distinctions. The dog points out a number of such distinctions, for example, the difference in value between "copper and silver." As he continues with his list, he mentions the differences created among humans, "between officials and common citizens, between masters and their slaves." Before he can go on with his list, the narrator takes flight. What seems to inspire the narrator's fear is the intractable reality of a hierarchical society founded on seemingly arbitrary distinctions among things and people. The narrator in his dream takes the guise of a beggar, a product of socially created difference. Despite his own status as a dispossessed subject, he nevertheless replicates the operation of social differentiation, telling the dog to "shut up" in an attempt to assert his human superiority over the animal. But the dream features a strange reversal whereby the dog is endowed with eloquence while the human is rendered a degraded and mostly speechless beggar, capable of saying only one complete sentence in the piece. Most of his speech seems to consist of barely articulate grunts and exclamations: he "thunders" (*chizha*), utters the onomatopoeic sound *dai!*, orders the dog to "shut up" (*zhukou*), and asks "What?" (*shenme*) in a fashion that parallels how an English speaker might quizzically exclaim *Huh*? This seems to be a reality that the narrator finds difficult to endure, and so he runs as far as the dream is wide until he finally breaks out of the dream and lands back in his own bed. The crisis is perhaps one of unbearable embodiment, trapped in the body and clothing of a beggar, bested by a loquacious dog, and unable to put up any possible spoken response (when the narrator runs away, the dog pleads with him to stay and "discuss it further," something of which the narrator is surely incapable). The crisis that tears the speaker apart is the fact that the social distinctions that were meant to safeguard his superiority have now come back to bite him from behind.

By waking up, the narrator has escaped his dream (and the dog) and seemingly attained some relief. However, while he has crossed out of the threshold of his dream (*tao chu mengjing*), he ends up within the confines of his bed, ready to dream yet again. Whether in dream or in waking reality, his "self" is always bracketed, subject to the pressures of what lies beyond the self. The narrator is trapped not only by the physical confines of his bed but also by the constant discursive repetitions that suggest the somatic rhythms of the body. *Wild Grass* is rife with such repetition; for example, in the dog's speech mentioned above, he uses the phrase "I still do not know how to differentiate" (*hai bu zhidao fenbie*) five times before the narrator decides that he cannot bear it any longer and runs away. The hypnotic, pulsating rhythms displayed in the narrator's somatic language maintain the sleepy atmosphere of the work and keep both narrator and reader under its dreamy spell.

The piece intriguingly conjures up the topography of the dream as a physical space. As significant as the topsy-turvy world depicted in the dream is the fact that the narrator can run through the borders of the dream and straight into his bed. On one hand this affirms the boundedness of the dream itself, its sense of self-containment; on the other, the ease with which the "I" physically moves from dream-space to waking-space suggests that awakened reality and dream are locked horizontally, neither more ontologically real than the other. The edge that seems to seal off the dream from reality in fact reveals itself to also be the same edge of the narrator's own bed. Wherever the narrator runs, there is no freedom from confronting the edges of his own existence. The portrait of reversal between the speechless beggar and the gabby dog would be rather tepid were it not for the fact that it is bound up with the dialectic between dream and waking reality.[46] The minimal difference that spawns antagonistic human relations revealed in the dream corresponds to the minimal difference between dream and wakefulness itself. In this vein, while these edges are a portent of entrapment, they are also an opportunity for insight. The narrative threshold between dream-narration and waking-narration stands in for the threshold between conventional existence and its other.

REALISM'S BEDTIME: "THE AWAKENING"

Having looked at two prose poems that are structured as dreams, the concluding piece, "The Awakening" (Yijue), invites us to ponder the boundary between sleeping and wakefulness. In this piece, the narrative register suddenly shifts to a more historic footing.[47] It opens with a description of planes conducting bombing missions of Beijing in the morning, a result of internecine fighting among warlord factions, causing fear and silent panic that make the narrator deeply aware of the fragile line between life and death; moreover, it brings to sharp awareness the contingency of his bodily existence, one that can easily disintegrate in a second. In the midst of warfare, the narrator goes through manuscripts sent in by young writers, excited by their energy, exuberance, and commitment but worried by their nascent cynicism.

In addition to representations of fear and violence, the piece is also overrun with inscriptions of discursive materiality that permeate the atmosphere. The morning bombings have a regularity that "seem[s] like attending lessons at school."[48] His bed is completely covered by a mess of newspapers (*sanluan man chuang de ribao*). Not only does the disarray of the newspapers reflect the chaos in the city, but the papers themselves serve to give the narrator a journalistic knowledge of what is happening around him. Moreover, the fact that these newspapers are on his bed suggests the interpenetration of language/text and the body of the narrator that is so prominent in the earlier pieces: the narrator's sleeping body and this pile of old newspapers are in fact metonymically related, one standing in for the other. The narrator's manifest corporeality, his bodily instantiation within a particular social space and time, is thus overdetermined by a discourse, both printed and verbal, that circulates throughout the land.

After having picked up the newspapers and tidied up his room, he sets upon his editing work. In the midst of warfare, the narrator goes through manuscripts sent in by young writers: "The spirits of the youth that refused to whitewash [reality] stood up in succession in front of my eyes."[49] These spirits correspond to the youths' manuscripts themselves, piled upon his desk. He wishes to "kiss upon the formless, colorless roughness dripping with fresh blood" (*wo yuanyi zai wuxing wuse de xianxue linli de cubaoshang jiewen*).[50] These youthful spirits pose a descriptive paradox; as spirits, they should be "formless," and yet they are pulsating with fresh, warm blood, rough rather than smooth and ethereal. What the narrator seems to be describing is the nature of language itself; at once "formless" and transparent, a clear mirror to reality, and yet on the other hand framed, textured, and intricate just as any other material. The fact that he wants to "kiss" these spirits/youths/manuscripts suggests a kind of bodily communion between the narrator and the youths with whom he wishes to connect. It should not be read as a belated desire to be "young" again; we are reminded of the narrator's desire to serve the youth with his writing in the "Preface" to *Call to Arms*. Reading their wistful tales, he finds that instead of having his spirit transported to faraway fictive landscapes, the texts remind him that he is "living in the world of men,"[51] a statement he repeats later in the piece. The narrator thus demonstrates his self-conscious awareness of his editing and mentoring responsibilities—his devotion to his young writers is not an attempt to quaff from the fountain of youth but to take part in a vital continuity between old and young, much in consonance with Lu Xun's own developmental thinking.[52] Through the narrator's mystic kiss, old and young are united into a greater, ever-progressing, dynamic body.

The text continues to forge symbolic linkages between text, youth, life, and corporeal/biological materiality. He recalls three years earlier being handed a youth literary magazine called "Shallow Grass" and being moved by the writing inside. He relates the story of how Lev Tolstoy was so affected by the struggle of a thistle to bloom that he writes his novella *Hadji Murat.* Writing is figured as a form of fragile, botanic life. The narrator continues to relate how plants and trees in the desert burrow their roots deep in the ground to find water and thus manage to flourish as well as provide shade and nourishment for thirsty travelers. Text is thus seen both as life and as a giver of life, something that makes bodily existence possible.

The narrator's editing work takes him well into the evening: "While I have been editing the sun has set, and I carry on by lamplight. All kinds of youth flash past before my eyes, though around me is nothing but dusk. Tired, I take a cigarette, quietly close my eyes in indeterminate thought, and have a long, long dream. I wake with a start."[53] This last paragraph of *Wild Grass* puts into doubt the idea that Lu Xun has stepped out of his bed, so to speak, and entered the properly social realm. The collection ends at the same time it started, the evening. The "youth," who have already transmuted into spectral images before his tired eyes, continue to stand in an indefinite but certain relation to his body in the dusk. The narrator has a "long, long dream" but does not, this time around, describe its contents. Is he dreaming about the youth whose manuscripts he is editing, the youth to whom the fledgling nation's hopes are entrusted? We do not know, and ultimately, we do not need to know what the dream is about. What is important is not the dream's content but its form. Like the youthful manuscripts he has been editing, the dream is also a text, a discursive transfiguration of the narrator's body. The narrator returns to the somatic space, the place where impressions that are repressed in the social order during the day manifest themselves upon the body of the sleeper at night.

The narrator suddenly wakes, finding himself in a space both mundane and enchanted: "Suddenly I woke, still wrapped around me was the yellow dusk; the seal-script cigarette smoke floated upwards within the still air, like several small, wispy summer clouds, softly conjuring images that are difficult to name."[54] The collection ends here, with a return to the sleepy body of the narrator, enveloped in a haze of twilight and tobacco smoke. The title, "Awakening," suggests in the original language a singular moment of awakening, a unique epiphany (*yijue*). However, there are at least two moments of awakening, not one. In addition to the narrator waking after his "long,

long dream," the prose poem itself, with its representation of contemporary Beijing undergoing warfare, is a kind of formal awakening from the dreamy sequences of images that followed beforehand. It is a belated nod to the demands of reality and socially engaged writing, an attempt to depict the waking world in historic and panoramic perspective. And yet the movement of this piece progresses inexorably toward the *telos* of twilight and evening, toward the somatic experience of sleep and dreams. The text constitutes a critique of a seemingly transparent realism that seeks to repress its nocturnal other, its dark inverse. When the narrator awakes from his dream, his corporeal, waking experience is still permeated with a sleepy, hypnotic haze, and upon closer inspection, there is also something dreamy about the beginning of the piece as well. The sensuous and strange ether of the dream leaks out of its boundaries and permeates awakened reality.

The haze, though, is not simply some kind of sublime, sensuous air. The narrator figures the cigarette smoke as a form of "seal-script" whose meaning is as yet unclear. Thus what constitutes the sensual, dreamy "haze" is, once again, the mystery of writing itself, characters in an arcane calligraphic form whose decipherment proves difficult. Again, it is the materiality of language that is emphasized here, not just what the characters mean but how they look, how they appear in their own discrete form. The difficulty in trying to "name" these quasi-discursive images is in consonance with the fullness of dream language, signifiers whose meaning is made difficult because of a sensuousness that defies semantic transparency. The end of *Wild Grass* stages a "return" to the body, but this body is thoroughly cloaked in the garb of discourse whose significance is always subject to displacement and deferment. We should take note that seal script (*zhuanshu*), like dreams themselves, has traditional associations with divination and access to hidden knowledge.

THE "PLENITUDE OF FORM" AND ITS ETHICAL POSSIBILITY

The generic form of *Wild Grass* has long been a topic for scholars. The work is usually classified as a form of "prose-poetry," or *sanwen shi*; as one critic has pointed out, the development of *sanwen shi* had its roots in the very beginnings of the May Fourth Movement. Well before Lu Xun began writing prose poetry many other May Fourth writers, including Guo Moruo, were publishing their own examples of the genre.[55] Moreover, the prose poems of Charles Baudelaire and Ivan Turgenev were translated and published in top literary journals. However, the form's novelty did evoke the opposition of some more conservative elements who refused to accept prose poetry as a kind of poetry by virtue of its lack of verse and meter.[56] Nicholas Kaldis notes the difficulty in defining the features of the prose poem itself, a hybrid form that seems to encourage "vagueness" in critics' attempts to define it, "occup[ying] hazy literary territory on the borders between prose and poetry."[57]

It has been argued that the prose poem not only foregrounds the conflict between the two generic forms of poetry and prose but simultaneously proposes a "dialectical" solution between them. Prose poetry becomes an opportune form for addressing conflict between social classes as well as envisioning a possible resolution of social contradictions. For this reason, the prose poem is an essentially "utopian" genre.[58] Traces of this utopian resolution certainly appear in Lu Xun's text; however, the use of dream as the dominant trope in the collection not only expands on the work's association with utopian thought but also suggests an entirely new level of mediation between self and other. The prose poem genre is itself the formal metaphor for both social contradiction and its resolution. In Lu Xun's handling of the genre, this formal "metaphor" is extended by yet another figure: the dream.[59]

As a consequence of its self-consciously hybrid nature, the prose poem calls attention to its own form precisely because its contours are as yet unclear and hazy. The prose poem acts as a kind of generic "monstrosity," whose corporeality is foregrounded because the genre is aberrant. In other less hybrid forms, like a poem or a short story, we tend to pay little conscious attention to form; form becomes naturalized in the very process of reading and seems transparent. Even with a form as notoriously hybridized as the novel, its piracy of other genres often slips below the radar as we are lured into the narrative movement. The prose poem, a genre still in the stages of emergence in the 1920s, obfuscates the transparency of form because it foregrounds the collision of different genres.

The dream itself is allegorical of *Wild Grass*'s hybrid, utopian genre. By its very nature, the dream is a queer form. In its confounding of the boundaries between the present, past, and future, in its manifestation of desired objects that are absent in real life, in its twists and contortions of language and signification into polysemic palimpsests, the dream is perhaps the epistemic and aesthetic form par excellence that expresses alterity. *Wild Grass* relates the strangeness of dreaming with the strangeness of its literary form: its genre is always relentlessly hybrid, inchoate, monstrous, unruly like wild grass. It also focuses on the strangeness of bodily forms: the narrator finds himself at level with a ravished, abject woman, disputes with a dog, contemplates his own disemboweled organs, and fixates on Christ's wounds.

The Russian Formalists, who were flourishing at the same time Lu Xun was writing his main fictional work, aimed to show that all art ultimately referred to its own artifice and construction. Boris Eikhenbaum, writing at the same time Lu Xun was working on *Wild Grass*, summarized his findings and those of his colleagues, and argued that reigniting an appreciation of form was essential to understanding the function of literature. For Eikhenbaum, aesthetic form was not a "mere shell" whose function was to contain ideological content but "a plenitude" that was "full of content in its own right."[60] Viktor Shklovsky, in his earlier and celebrated work "Art as Device" (1917), argued that the purpose of art was not to reflect reality but to in effect distort it, to make it strange and thus wrest it away from the deadening effects of "automatization" so that one may "regain the feeling of life."[61] As the Formalists argued, for many readers the form of a work often threatened to disappear from view; the literary critic's task was to discover how a work was "made," to extract and explicate its form. Along with "making strange" is the famous notion of "laying bare the device" (*obnazhenie priema*), by which a text points to its own artifice. This "laying bare" also metaphorically implies a kind of body that is suddenly exposed, brought to view, but one that cannot be equated with mere "content."

Summarizing well-known Formalist doctrines might seem banal to some readers long accustomed to these critical verities.[62] But the Formalists' ideas suggest a social and ethical dimension to the idea of "making strange." In *Wild Grass*, not only are bodies made strange, but literary form is as well. The "monstrous form" and the "monstrous body" share a structural homology, each enhancing the other's "strangeness." Coming back to Shklovsky's idea of "automatization," the point becomes clearer. It is important to make sociality and the literary forms that convey it strange because otherwise the body would disappear, "swallowed" by the automatization of quotidian perception and conventional form. Indeed this was the problem with conventional realism; reflecting human suffering only served to make it even less noticeable to a readership already habituated to everyday images of such suffering. It was not merely the fact that they were not noticed; they in effect disappeared.

What *Wild Grass* allows us to see is the body "made strange," distorted, reconfigured, made monstrous. What comes into view are the body's unruly edges, what captures our attention is not so much the body's "form" as a complete, stable image but the strangeness of its very formality. In the case of generic form, what results is not a new, stable poetic genre but the foregrounding of generic hybridity itself—the monstrous formality made possible by the collision of generic and modal registers. However, the aim is not to provide a corporeal freak show; the point is to rediscover the body, to be cognizant of its existence, and, moreover, one's ethical responsibility to the forms of sociality that anchor our existence. In *Wild Grass*'s primal mimetic ooze perhaps we can find an emergent formalism that might constitute the basis of a new life, one predicated on a reinvigorated sociality. By shaking the body from epistemic and affective complacency through grotesque literary form, perhaps the body can become once again a proper heuristic anchor for social knowledge. The body in *Wild Grass* is not merely a ground through which we can anchor feeling and knowledge; the body is itself, in every instance, an epistemic revelation. However, such a revelation cannot be made possible by relying on automated and manufactured corporeal common sense; it is only through radically redefining our bodies' edges that they, along with their mutual responsibility to one another, become intelligible. Against a narrative realism that relies on the conceit of the transparency of its descriptive discourse, *Wild Grass* suggests that language and bodies inaugurate a perpetual affective circuit: language and bodies reflect and amplify the visceral resonances between each other. It is improbable that *Wild Grass* can stand as a sustained model for a more effective literature of social address. Like its eponymous tender and fragile leaves, the work serves as an aesthetic flicker of an intervention, perhaps impossible to reproduce. But it serves as an allegorical hope, a wildly utopian one, of what literature should strive for.

The strong first-person orientation of the work is an invitation to personalize the moral act of representation. *Wild Grass* introduces a way of thinking about representation by explicitly inserting the observer's body into play—no more is he a disembodied eye, but also a figure who is as vulnerable to the power of his own work of representation as the object thereof. We sense representation as a uniquely ethical relation, not as mere observation but as an attempt at reconciliation between self and other. Thus we have a first-person narrator, presumably "Lu Xun," who is constantly aware of his own entrapment by the gates of his dreams and the edges of his bed, limits that bring to relief the contours of his bodily existence. And yet these "borders" also paradoxically serve as critical foils that allow him to rethink the intersubjective relationships between him and others, him and the world(s) around him. It is through a renegotiation of the borders of our bodies, and the relation between them, that reconstitutes the plenitude and value of the body.

Wild Grass, Lu Xun's engagement with modernist and Symbolist literary technique, maintains a muted dialogue with the promise and problems of realism. The tropes of awakening and alertness form the somatic parameters through which realist observation happens—in the daylight and through vision. Realism thus implies the presence of the always awake, always alert observer, who describes, narrates, and analyzes well through the night. Realism is a literary vigil to the social world, a tenacious and persistent accounting that never rests. *Wild Grass* questions whether realism can ever be a form of perpetual literary vigilance, and asks whether realism itself also needs its nighttime slumber and its own dreams, where the very desires, hopes, and energies that propel realism's social project in the first place can be nurtured and sustained. *Wild Grass*'s dream fantasies thus reveal realism's own psychosomatic ecology and shed light on realism's own unconscious spaces. It is in these hidden spaces that realism's radical hopes can be found: the reconciliation of self and other, oppressor and oppressed, discourse and the world, and history and utopia.

CHAPTER 3

Realism's Hysterical Bodies

Narrative and Oneiric Counternarrative in Mao Dun's Fiction

In 1935 Mao Dun (born Shen Dehong, 1896–1981), journalist, editor, revolutionary, and foremost realist novelist of the Republican period, published his own abridged version of *Dream of the Red Chamber* (Hong lou meng).[1] The 1930s were among the most prolific periods of his literary career; that he managed to find time in this busy period to lay his hands upon this classic of vernacular fiction is remarkable. In the foreword to his abridgment, Mao Dun noted Hu Shi's biographical reconstruction of the novel's purported author, Cao Xueqin.[2] Mao Dun thought that Hu Shi's research definitively demonstrated that *Dream* was in fact an autobiographical novel that drew from Cao Xueqin's own lived experience in a prominent Qing banner family that had fallen from grace. As such, *Dream* was revealed to feature "realism" (*xieshizhuyi*) in the Chinese literary tradition *avant la lettre.*[3] Mao Dun thus claimed that *Dream* signaled a "new stage" in the "development of Chinese fiction," an accomplishment that remained ignored by its first readers.[4] Mao Dun felt that Qing-era readers could not recognize the novel's realistic depictions of high society because of Cao Xueqin's skillful concealment of names and identities and his use of fanciful, metaphysical episodes that distracted readers from the real social content of the work. As a result, such readers were unable to recognize that the protagonist Jia Baoyu was no other than Cao Xueqin himself![5]

Mao Dun cited Chen Duxiu's opinion on *Dream* as pretext for his own abridgment: "I [Chen Duxiu] have always felt that only if a great author could take out all of the frivolous episodes from *Story of the Stone* and just leave behind the lovely parts that describe human affections, then the novel can finally be regarded as a representative work of Chinese modern vernacular literature."[6] Mao Dun took up Chen's call and reduced the number of chapters from 120 to 50. He excised three portions from the novel: (1) all of the metaphysical "fairy tales," including nearly all of the first chapter (which tells the fantastic story of the novel's creation from a magical stone), as well as Jia Baoyu's pivotal dream journey to the Realm of Illusion in chapter 5; (2) most of the lyrics and poems that weave through the entire novel that appeared outdated in terms of modern fictional prose; and (3) extraneous episodes and scenes that detract from the main plot. The reader was left with a compelling novel that detailed social mores and, moreover, addressed the pressing issue of arranged marriage. The abridgment reduced the novel's volume, according to Mao Dun's own estimate, by two-fifths. While Mao Dun felt the original novel was better left to literary scholars, he believed that his version had special pedagogical value for middle school students seeking to learn "something of literary technique."[7]

Though Mao Dun was not the only one to have produced an abridged version of *Dream* in the long history of the novel's reception, his presumption to possess the authority to cut out what he felt was "trivial" seems to post-Mao sensibilities to be retrograde, if not short of blasphemous to Chinese cultural patrimony. But this sort of cultural iconoclasm was not out of place in the May Fourth era. Mao Dun's zeal in trimming the fantastic fat from *Dream* in part stemmed from the prospect that, underneath the layers of mysticism, there lay an authentic, if embryonic, realist novel within the very bosom of Chinese vernacular tradition. Chinese writers thus did not have to strain much to adopt a foreign literary mode; their own vernacular tradition possessed native precursors of literary modernity.

Of course Mao Dun's excision of all the "fairy tale" elements in the novel still strikes one as somewhat egregious, for who now can even attempt to read the novel without its substantial metaphysical apparatus? *Dream* probes the edges of reality (rather than, in Mao Dun's eyes, merely narrating it); to cut out such a substantial bulk of the novel, one that affords much of its surreal pleasure, seems to go against the novel's spirit. Who, indeed, possessed the "authority" over the novel, Mao Dun or Cao Xueqin himself? Why did Mao Dun feel he could assume the right to censor Cao Xueqin's aesthetic dreamwork?

Of interest here is Mao Dun's sense of critical authority in legislating what could be considered realism proper and what had to be marginalized or excised completely. Mao Dun's abridgment of *Dream* highlights the great extent to which he approached realism as a practice of narrative management, one that implied the need to separate the real from the fantastic from within the text itself. However, Mao Dun's own fictional texts betray the danger of too fastidious a separation between reality and fantasy—the negation of a narrative desire that is necessary for the text's own flourishing. Such a balancing act between different modes of critique and fantasy results in psychic and narrative strain, as is evident in Mao Dun's texts. Mao Dun's realism is a hysteric literary mode, one vulnerable to instability as it searches for representational equilibrium. "Hysteria," it will be seen, is not a frivolous term; for Mao Dun, realism was a gendered enterprise, an attempt to wrest an essentially masculine critique from feminine fantasy. However, his attempt to draw the line between critique and illusion on gendered axes betrays the fundamental hysteria that afflicted his literary enterprise. Dreams act as symptomatic sites in Mao Dun's narratives where the lines between masculine critique and feminine fantasy, reality and hallucination, blur.

THE FUTILITY OF UTOPIA: MAO DUN'S RESPONSE TO THE 1933 CALL FOR DREAMS OF A NEW CHINA

As China in the early 1930s descended into increasing turbulence, Mao Dun became ever more realist in orientation, convinced of the power of realism's mission to convey critical knowledge about society and thus aid in its transformation. By the time he published *Midnight* (Ziye) in early 1933, his status as realist chronicler had become a part of his brand. A promotional advertisement in the first issue of *Eastern Miscellany* of that year gave prospective readers a summary of the scale and ambition of this work, soon to be published by Kaiming Shudian (Enlightenment Bookstore). The advertisement claimed that *Midnight* sought to answer this urgent question: "Exactly what kind of society is China?" After describing the novel's prodigious length (over thirty thousand Chinese words), its equally prodigious number of characters (over eighty), and its encyclopedic breadth of subject matter, the advertisement assured readers that the novel was not merely a literary example of "social science"; Mao Dun's "artistic hands" had reshaped this abundant social material such that there was not a single "dry or bland moment." *Midnight* was thus touted for both magisterially conjuring up a panoramic and empirical vision of Chinese society while also meeting aesthetic demands for pleasure and distraction.

But this same issue of *Eastern Miscellany* also suggested that realist narrative was not the only way to respond to history's tumult. The advertisement was located in a special New Year's supplement devoted to "Dreams of the New Year." Lu Xun's reaction to this supplement, his essay "Ting shuo meng," was discussed in Chapter 2. Some more words about this feature are in order.[8] The editors had put out a call a few months before to its readers to submit their answers to two questions. One asked readers to submit their dreams about a future China, and the other asked them to reveal a dream they held for their own personal life. One hundred forty-two participants mailed back answers, exceeding the editors' modest expectations.[9] In a summary article on the submissions, the editors noted that the majority of respondents were from Shanghai, with contributions also coming in from Nanjing, Beijing, Hangzhou, and Guangzhou. Only four respondents were women. Thirty-eight respondents were university professors, thirty-nine were writers and editors, and twelve were government officials. The editors lamented that 90 percent of the respondents were "middle class" and for the most part belonged to the "cultural aristocracy." "Although these 244 'dreams,'" the editors wrote, "cannot represent the 50,000,000 'dreams' [in China], they at the very least can represent the dreams of a large part of the intellectuals."[10]

In this same article the editors made a distinction between "orthodox/authentic" dreams (those that express a genuine, personal wish of the dreamer) and "heterodox" dreams (those that are programmatic calls for social change), evincing great preference for the former. But the careful analysis of these dreams, replete with chart graphs divided by class, profession, geographic origin, and gender, seemed to betray the editors' own treatment of these submissions as an object for quantitative social analysis. While the editors insisted that dreams were the unmitigated expression of personal desires, the very methods of analysis implied the inextricably social and material basis of these dreams. Dreams were on one hand the voicing of a wish unsullied by reality; on the other, they were a very function of that reality.

This inconsistency between dreams as authentic expressions of private desires and dreams as indices to social circumstances touched upon a certain complexity of the dream form that befuddled the editors. Indeed, dreams involve the presence and desire of the dreamer in a way unique among forms of representation and narration; it can be a personal, intimate genre. But dreams also draw from a collective pool of symbols that belong to the culture as a whole and address longings and desires not just of the dreamer but of the broader society as well. The dream form uniquely intertwines both collective and personal desire, making what is personal and intimate also speak to the yearnings of the nation. The editors' decision to split their call for submission into two parts, one public and one personal, betrayed how dreams invite a slippage between the social and the intimate.

However, the push to promote dreaming in the face of crisis caused other contributors to express deep reservations about the usefulness of dreaming, with some realist writers questioning aloud whether in such bleak times dreaming was even possible. Author Ba Jin was one of these skeptics: "In the present atmosphere, I cannot even dream up a good dream. Moreover, I cannot rely on a dream in order to deceive myself. In this long winter night I only feel cold, I only sense hunger. I only hear the cries of people all around, and all of this only makes me have nightmares."[11] Lao She equally had reservations: "My hope for China's future is not great, nor do I see in my dreams a rose-colored world. Even if I do end up dreaming, and especially if it is an auspicious one, I still am not bewitched by it. So that leaves daydreaming. I can fantasize that the heavenly kingdom is near, but if [this dream] does not solve my own hunger, then it is of even less use to your average Li or Zhang."[12]

Mao Dun's own contribution to this collection is worth noting. Though he is known for his long, sprawling narratives, Mao Dun's answers to the call were surprisingly curt:

> In regard to China's future, I never dream; I only seek with great effort to know reality. Dreams are dangerous. In these times there are various dreamers here and there. If they haven't now sobered up to the point of lifelessness, then they might as well be on the brink of suicide.[13]
>
> In my personal life I have two dreams, and based on reason I should very well be able to realize them, but till now I have been unable to do so; these two are (1) I hope that my nervous ailment will not get worse, and (2) I hope to get a half hour of exercise every day.[14]

Dreams were invidious to knowing "reality." One should strive, as Mao Dun himself wrote, to "know reality with great effort." Dreaming's dangers were dire, ending in both spiritual and physical demise. Mao Dun saw the consequences of dreaming in somatic terms; indulgence in dreams seemed to suck the very life out of dreamers. Dreams were a dangerous distraction from the more urgent task of figuring out reality.

By the mid-1920s Mao Dun had already transcended a strictly empirical naturalism in favor of a more fluid, nuanced type of critical realism.[15] Yet his patent unwillingness to afford any room for dreams in his thought betrayed a lingering pedantic stodginess. He seemed at pains to repeatedly reject and dismiss any last vestiges of his own youthful romanticism, seeking to firmly project the authorial persona of an observer and critic unafraid to face reality in all its ugliness.

The appearance of the advertisement for *Midnight* at the end of a collection of dreams ironically demonstrates how a sense of historical crisis can engender two different forms of response. Mao Dun's narrative sought to illustrate, reflect, and diagnose, to walk the reader step by step through the unfolding of reality. The readers' dreams, however, encouraged a form of categorical transcendence, emphasizing the possibility of transformation of reality over its careful narrativization and diagnosis. Despite Mao Dun's insistence on how he preferred the strain of sifting through reality in order to pull out its essential narrative thread to the easy lures of dreaming, there is something fantastic in his belief that narrative can actually encapsulate such a reality. A theorist of narrative has remarked how narrative features ideal structural continuities in space and time. As such, narrative functions like "a daydream, a wish-fulfilling fantasy that . . . is grounded in the real conditions of the dreamer's life but goes beyond these to the imagining of how, in spite of these conditions, things might be otherwise."[16] Mao Dun's strident disavowal of dreams sounds more like the guilty conscience of someone who has the sense that he is indulging in daydreaming but is trying to keep it under the rug. Another critic makes similar claims for the utopian potentials of writing in general in his analysis of Mao Dun: for the author, "writing in itself projects a utopian wish, mediating human conflicts at different levels and letting truth speak on its own terms."[17]

Narrative also bears an important relation to the thematics of the body. In Mao Dun's "dream" about his personal life, he speaks in explicit terms about his body, hoping to recover from his nervous breakdown and find physical recuperation. As with his first dream, he begins with a disavowal, saying that his personal dreams are not really dreams, as he should "very well be able to realize them." Realizable or not, his "dreams" involve a transfiguration of the body, namely, his own. Whereas "dreaming" of China's future can only lead to the body's annihilation, his own "personal" dream is about the rehabilitation of a body that already seems broken. Mao Dun's body is one that has been tortured by a reality and history that he is straining to comprehend.[18] The body exists wedged tightly between the proverbial rock and hard place of dreams and reality. If narrative is an attempt to create utopian "structural continuities" in forms that do not otherwise exist in reality,[19] then in what ways does it also promise the rehabilitation of the body's fullness, as well as its reconciliation within the body politic? Mao Dun's attempt to create narrative can be read as a reconstitution of the body in both physical and social forms.[20]

Mao Dun's realist narratives are thus as much attempts in envisioning political utopia in formal terms as they are analyses of the historic crises he and his readers faced in content. Ironically enough, dreams, which he so dismissed in his real life, appear frequently in his fictional work. Ostensibly, Mao Dun featured his characters' dreams in order to demonstrate how they are mired in subjective illusion. However, the presence of these dreams occasionally looms so large they threaten to overwhelm the realist text's ability to contain them as mere subjective fancy. Read another way, these diegetic dreams are symptomatic of the realist text's own continual struggle to maintain its own sense of reality; they offer a glimpse on how the text seeks to manage or otherwise divert libidinal and utopian desires. They address not just the subjective states of the characters but the formal issues of realist writing as well. One can read these dreams as hysterical symptoms of the realist mode and observe not only how these dreams reveal realism's internal contradictions but also how the text responds in an effort to maintain narrative coherence.

A DREAM OF HYSTERIA

Despite Mao Dun's opprobrium against dreams, in 1928 he did publish one of his own, a short essay titled "Dreaming During a Hard Frost" (Yan shuang xia de meng). In his memoirs, written fifty years later, Mao Dun insisted that the impetus for writing the piece was to express his "confusion, incomprehension and disapproval" of what he called "blind action-ism," or what he felt to be reckless revolution-mongering by all too earnest rebels unchastened by the failures of left-wing revolutions of the 1920s.[21] Mao Dun, in his recollection, argued that he used "symbolist techniques" to express his opprobrium for unthinking political action, thus implying that the dream was merely an artful fabrication meant to express a political opinion.[22] Whether he actually had the dream he describes in the essay, or merely made it up, remains unclear.

Mao Dun begins by noting that dreams belong to the carefree province of childhood, while adults, occupied by the requirements of livelihood, have little time to indulge in fantasy. Only children are capable of crossing "the rainbow bridge" into the dream world.[23] Real, waking adult life is ceaseless toil, suffering, and disenchantment, while dreams are the infantile remnants of a past that serve to ironically highlight life's very drudgery. Mao Dun steadfastly refuses to give in to dreams: "With my razor-sharp rationality, I never allow myself to fall into that realm of the mystery upon mysteries, and allow the caresses of such fantasies to comfort the scars of reality."[24] Dreams are a hallucinogenic palliative to the "scars" of real life, a puerile intoxication that can only serve to make reality's pathology all the more serious.

Nevertheless, the author goes on to describe one of his dreams. It involves a carnivalesque, joyful gathering of young revolutionaries. The imagery quickly becomes ever more bizarre, as the dreamer and his fellow revolutionaries find themselves regurgitating their hearts, which in turn float about in the air and coalesce into a blood-red banner featuring barely legible revolutionary slogans. The dream precipitously descends into a cascade of blood-soaked images, and the final sequence features the dreamer gazing rapturously at a "valkyrie" singing the melody of the "Sirens." The dreamer wonders if a wedding or a funeral is about to happen. He is suddenly overcome by the smell of putrefying flesh and hears a "girl's cry of hysteria."[25] Wolves surround the girl and set about devouring her.

The dreamer wakes up in a terror and realizes that it was all a nightmare: "Ah, it was also a dream! A malicious, mocking dream! The cold light tenaciously broke through the vent underneath the window, and like a mocking laugh landed on my face; the frost must have been even thicker, but when would the daylight finally come? When will Aurora's gentle fingers brush away the dominion of this cruel nightmare?"[26] Part of the nightmare's terror stems from a dispiriting truth about the confusion, chaos, and failure of revolution. The beautiful "Valkyrie," the ostensible bride of an allegorical wedding, ends up torn apart by wolves. While "Dreaming During a Hard Frost" is a form of symbolic personal fantasy rather than realist narrative, it nevertheless resonates with themes of dreams, the body, and hysteria that will appear in his realist texts. Realism, it would seem, is the arrival of Aurora, illuminating epistemic darkness. The psychic intensities, existential urgencies, and libidinal forces that give rise to Mao Dun's phantasmagoria also express themselves, in altered form, in his realist texts. What changes, however, is the way Mao Dun's realist mode manages these volatile intensities in order to sustain a representational equilibrium in the midst of ongoing mimetic crisis.

BURSTING THE BUBBLE: *DISILLUSIONMENT* (1930)

Mao Dun's 1930 trilogy *Eclipse* (Shi) offers a glimpse on how narrative seeks to manage the forces of volatile affect, libidinal tumult, and mimetic crisis. It was written shortly after Mao Dun participated in the 1926–28 revolution, or Northern Expedition, during which the Nationalists fought warlord factions and brought the nation closer to unification. In 1927, the Nationalists, led by Chiang Kai-shek, turned against their own members who were suspected of being Communists, culminating in the April 12 Shanghai massacre, when thousands of Communists were purged from the Nationalist Party, rounded up, and executed. Mao Dun wrote his trilogy as a reaction to both the euphoria and succeeding disappointment felt by radical youth involved in these events. The first novella, *Disillusionment* (Huanmie), centers on the tumultuous emotional life of its main heroine, Jing (which means "tranquility"), a young student. Despite her aspiration to serenity and her outward appearance of quiet (thus earning her the nickname of "stone maiden"), Jing's psychic life is anything but tranquil.[27] Along with her childhood friend Hui, Jing must wade through a series of fantasies, deceptions, and disappointments as they pursue happiness, romance, and a sense of meaning.

Disillusionment aspires to a feminine bildungsroman, and one critic has argued that Mao Dun sought to productively use the Marxist-Hegelian notion of the dialectic in order to convey a narrative trajectory in which contradictions are transcended.[28] *Disillusionment* suggests progress and maturation fueled by the power of negation and disavowal. As this critic has noted, one of the key functions of realism is "demystification" of "conventional pretensions, desires, or ideals."[29] Moreover, the form this progress takes is appropriately sentimental; as Jing's name suggests, she is an affective barometer of the worlds she inhabits, both romantic and political. Changes in her worlds are registered as impacts upon her sensorium, and we readers vicariously experience her corporeal oscillations.

Fantasies, dreams, daydreams, rumors, and wishes abound in this novella, waiting to be deflated one after another. Dreams are featured throughout the work in a variety of ways, sometimes as a concrete motif but mostly as a descriptive metaphor. In the beginning Jing is "a girl who was a little behind in conjuring fantasies" in comparison to other women, one who "had never dreamed of the filth and dangers of humanity."[30] By the end of the novella, she concludes that her seemingly idyllic romance with soldier of fortune Qiang Weili is "one great dream."[31] Dreams and fantasies provide a useful foil in order to illustrate the edifying process of disillusionment and realization. The more daydreams and fantasies a hero falls for, the more opportunity for insight. Within this realist text dreams function as formal devices that provide the impetus for the narrative's motivations. Ideally, the narrative would conclude with a heroine finally free from all illusion and fantasy, ready to forge her place in society.

Even though they feature only in order to be disavowed, dreams and fantasies become structurally necessary for the text's revelation of reality; they thus act as reality's necessary "support." As Slavoj Žižek has suggested, it is not enough to simply dismiss fantasy and accept reality: "The only way to break the power of our ideological dream is to confront the Real of our desire which announces itself in this dream."[32] Only by "traversing the fantasy" of these dreams may we come to a better understanding of reality. If "unreality" structurally inheres in the very narration of reality, then reality proves to be a far more complex object, one that contains multiple layers of ontological texture. The realist narrative's reliance on illusion's immanent unraveling entails a great faith in the power of the dialectic as a mechanism of disillusionment; should it fail, not only has enlightenment been dashed, but a sad trail of deflated dreams remains.

Focusing on narrative's uninterrupted progression risks ignoring the felt materiality of the narrative as a totality. Mao Dun attempts to instill a cognitive dialectic movement in his readers through which, by following the travails of the protagonist, they transition through dream to reality. We are to read these narratives diachronically, allow ourselves to be pulled by the movement of diegetic time, realize our illusive mistake, and then forget. But a synchronic, spatial view of Mao Dun's narrative reveals that these dreams do not easily disappear from the text; they remain, not as chance episodes but, in the case of *Disillusionment*, as large, fundamental building blocks of the text. It becomes difficult to differentiate what exactly is dream and what is reality, within the same narrative. The text often attempts a clear separation between the two by proclaiming self-referentially what is "real" and what is merely "dream," as if the rhetorical power of naming will keep the spheres separate. Moreover, the very presence of these dreams risks blurring the edges of reality. By announcing the finite, contrived parameters of the dream, the text invites attention to the finitude of the entire text, if only because the parameters of the dream constitute part of the text's edges as well. The dichotomy is not so much one between a fictitious dream and a triumphant reality as it is between a deflated dream and a reality that will be revealed to have been a dream as well.

In this vein, the dreams and fantasies that act as the negative examples of the realist narrative of disillusionment are not merely straw men to be scrutinized and then cast off; they also reveal a more complex view of narration. Narrative disavowal constitutes the necessary framing device that legitimizes dreams' presence in Mao Dun's fiction. But ignore the disavowal for a brief moment, and one discovers that dreams are not merely empty fantasies but also that they represent other narrative possibilities. As fiction, realist narrative aims to describe faithfully an objective reality that exists, both in its historical and psychological substance. Yet realist narrative is not merely a straight retelling of History's movement; key to the story's flourishing is the sustaining of a narrative desire that may transcend external ideological demands and constraints. It might help us to think of the "narrative line"[33] not as a complete, teleologically oriented thread, with a clear beginning and end, that structures the text. Rather, what obtains is a sequence of diegetic moves within the background of many other possible moves. Mao Dun's fiction does not feature a single monolithic narrative but rather a tentative narrative thread that is shadowed by the traces of other narrative possibilities and desires. These moves left untaken may be in the same register as the dominant narrative or may fly off toward more fantastic worlds. In a realist text these impermissible storylines are often legitimized, as well as neutered, by encapsulating them within the dream form. These alternative narratives then are seen as merely fantastic, merely impermanent, evaporating under the aurora of realist narrative. But these dreamscapes are narratives in their own right, traces of alternative plotlines that hint at hidden desires (narrative, libidinal, and political) from which the narrative proper must demur. What results is a complex narrative structure holding both conscious and unconscious modalities. The presence of dreams is symptomatic of a far more complicated, and interesting, narrative fuzziness.

In *Disillusionment*, dreaming is primarily associated with the heroine, Jing. The schizoid nature of the narrative is evoked through its focalization of the often turbulent flux of Jing's emotions and physical state. The sprawling nature of the plot, including its geographic excursions through Shanghai, Hankou, and Jiujiang, is suggestively analogous with Jing's own varied emotional and psychosomatic terrain. The first half of the novella narrates her and Hui's romantic entanglements with Baosu, an attractive rake who is later revealed to be a spy for the Nationalists reporting on radical students. When Baosu succeeds in deflowering Jing, she is overwhelmed and loses consciousness. The next day, while assessing the loss of her virginity, she tells herself that the events of the previous night were "just like a good dream." In her post-coital languor, images of her rural hometown "appeared floating in front of her tired eyes." A beautiful pastoral scene unfolds in front of her, including cows and lush, green rice paddies. The splish-splash of the waterwheel turning in the wind and the intermittent notes of a folk song being sung far away can be heard. Soon after, "a fantasy unfolds," whereupon Jing feels herself physically transported both back to her hometown and back in time. She is at home, reading a "newly published magazine" outside her front door. Her mother and Baosu soon come out of the door. The mother wears a light smile of contentment, and Jing responds in kind. But before the dream is allowed to continue, "reality immediately pulled apart the brocade curtain of fantasy, and once again snatched away its sacrificial victim."[34] As the narrator instructively informs us, "fantasy and all sorts of stimulants are one and same. It gives you a momentary anaesthesia, but when it passes you must compensate for it many times over."[35] Immediately after, Jing discovers Baosu's true identity as a spy and realizes how much of a pipe dream her recent fantasy has been.

Jing's status as the "sacrificial victim" of her fantasy also points to a structural narrative logic that reflects the formal economy of gender in Mao Dun's fiction. It is often the women who are mired in dreaming and illusion; their repeated suffering in the throes of unrestrained desire takes on a ritualistic significance for the narrative. It often seems as if the sacrifice of a woman's desires or even sanity is a necessary condition for the narrative's continued flourishing. This logic is repeated in Mao Dun's other texts.

Jing's reverie that occurs before "reality" self-consciously cuts in is a nostalgic pastoral scene; utopian desire moves backward, rather than forward, forming a phantasmatic image of the past where woman and nature exist in harmony, untouched by the chaos of modern time. Here, for once, things seem truly quiet, at peace, to the point that it actually irritates Jing: "She furthermore was annoyed by the backwardness of her hometown and its stasis."[36] As she enters more deeply into this reverie she reads the "current" magazine of the day. The timeless, somewhat backward countryside, beautiful yet cut off from the world, is juxtaposed with her magazine, hot off the press. It is a wishful admixture; a sensuous and timeless landscape surrounding a modern girl pursuing knowledge. The scene involves both a physical escape from the frenzy of the city and yet an exaltation of intellectual activity. Pastoral and modern time seem to find, if not a synthesis, then a cozy cohabitation. The contradictions between countryside and the city, feeling and knowledge, and traditional mother and modern daughter are seemingly reconciled. The appearance of Baosu suggests an element of erotic fulfillment. Jing's carnal experience, along with its lingering resonance upon her body, generates this fantasy scene. But Baosu does not merely represent carnal sexuality. As a replacement for a long-missing male presence (Jing's father died long ago), his integration into the family suggests a form of reunion.

The way both narrator and plot collude to destroy Jing's dream smacks of narrative overkill. Not only does the narrator caution the reader about the intoxicating nature of dreams, but by fortuitous coincidence, Jing quickly discovers that Baosu has been snitching on fellow students to the government as well as maintaining an affair with yet another student. Jing finds her romantic rival's picture in a book that Baosu has left by mistake in her room. Included is a letter in which the girl professes her absolute love for Baosu. She imagines how much like herself this other girl is: "Right at that time this pitiful girl was busying herself with beautiful, satisfying, honeysweet dreams!"[37] She realizes that her own dream is not unique but shared with other girls duped by Baosu, each in her turn a "sacrificial victim." This "revelation" seems sudden, so quick on the heels of Jing's own deflowering. The narrative seems in a hurry to disavow its own indulgence in fantasy.[38] Jing is made to compensate heavily for her mistake; she falls gravely ill with scarlet fever and rushes herself to a hospital, where she stays in convalescence for a number of weeks. Jing the "dreamer" must ultimately pay the price and act as sacrificial victim for the narrative's own indulgence in desire; her penance is the deferred punishment the realist narrative spares itself.

In a span of less than twenty-four hours, Jing veers from sexual climax, post-coital satisfaction, and reverie to disillusionment and complete physical breakdown. If she proves to be the antithesis of what her name suggests, then the narrative responds in kind with its own manic leaps. The speed with which the realist narrative charges against its own fantasies leads to diegetic paralysis, and the story finds itself marooned in hospital. Reality principle and utopian wish violently clash, leading to physical and narrative incapacitation. As if by another strange and rather unbelievable coincidence, two of Jing's female classmates find themselves in the exact same hospital for reasons that remain unknown, suggesting that all the women characters are breaking down one way or another. They coalesce in the hospital, and it is here that the main characters among them decide to join the Second Northern Expedition. The narrative, having undergone its own kind of recuperation and now regaining a sense of direction, transports the reader forthwith to Hankou.

The second major "dream" scene is at the end of the novella, when Jing, after a number of failed attempts at finding meaningful work in Hankou, becomes a nurse in the military hospital. There she meets the swashbuckling Qiang Meng, also known by his courtesy name, Qiang Weili. As others have noted, his names bear august martial connotations: "[Qiang Meng's] name means something like 'strength and ferocity' and [his] style, Weili, means 'by force alone.'"[39] His various appellations also carry a hint of a primal, phallic virtuosity, one that complements both Jing's intellectual gifts and her own sexual desire. As Jing nurses him back to health, a romance ensues. Their passion reaches its peak (both figuratively and geographically) with yet another geographic displacement and, appropriately, another shift in Jing's state of mind, as they saunter off to Guling and Jiujiang for an "ecstatic week" of frolicking in a wondrous natural setting.[40] As the two lovers hike their way up the mountains, "Miss Jing for the first time tasted a life as sweet as a dream." Jing ascends both physically and emotionally, her legs taking her to high peaks, her mind seemingly floating up into a dream world. She sighs to herself (via the narrator's free indirect discourse), "now, the dream life, it has finally arrived." At one point, shielding themselves from a rainstorm, the two find shelter underneath a rock. As she lays her wet body against Weili's likewise wet chest, she repeatedly sighs, "Weili! Oh, Weili!"[41] Given the literal meaning of his courtesy name ("By force alone! Oh, by force alone!"), her cries seem like orgasmic paroxysms.

The "dream" ends when Weili is called back to service, and Jing must fight her bitter disappointment. Jing goes through another cascade of emotions but in the end is able to accept the separation and learns to cherish her romantic interlude: "She loved him too much, and deep down in her heart she thanked him for giving her an unforgettable time; although it was almost over, Jing still treasured this final scene of happiness, and was unwilling to completely tear apart her own fantasy. But she was also unwilling to cause Qiang Meng to have lingering regrets."[42] When Weili finally does leave, she falls into her bed and sighs to her friend Wang Shitao:

> "Sister Shi! Now that we've separated, I've simply been having a dream! A great, big, happy dream! Now I've awoken from this dream, and just like before, it's just you and me. It's just that I don't know where Hui is these days!"
>
> "With someone like Hui, she surely won't be disappointed."
>
> That was Miss Wang's answer.[43]

The story ends by announcing itself as a dream. As one critic notes, Jing subjectively transforms both of her romantic liaisons into mere fleeting dreams.[44] However, the question of dreaming is not merely an issue of what Jing does with her imagination. Her imagination is ultimately our narrative experience, and the romantic interlude is no mere fantasy. For the text to label two whole chapters of diegetic activity as a dream risks more than invalidating Jing's own experiences and, perhaps, naive wishes but also undercuts the text's own narrative effectiveness. The novella, by puncturing holes in Jing's dream, hints at its own unraveling.

It is easy to wax cynical about Jing and Weili's romantic and sentimental idyll, filled with caresses and coos amid the rumbling of a river. In fact, by constantly reminding us that this interlude is a dream, the narrative is registering its own embarrassment that it felt compelled to go there in the first place. While it is Jing who calls out in pleasure, the force of her cry threatens to collapse both woman and narrator: the woman who experiences orgasm and the narrator who indulges in voyeuristic delight seem to partake in the same ecstasy. No wonder, then, that this episode must be reduced to a mere "dream" in Jing's imagination; her hysteric transformation of narrative experience into dream memory functions to displace the reader's attention from the sentimental contortions of both text and narrator. Wang Shitao's final word, a sort of streetwise crack, aims to kick us back into "reality"—it attempts to shift the narrative terrain from exalted romantic reverie to something more down to earth in register, but it does not succeed in writing off the realist text's guilty pleasure. Even so, whatever the affective excesses of this "dream," Weili is still no Baosu, and the love the two feel for each other is genuine if foolhardy. It is not a dream because Weili is duplicitous. It is a dream because their love has been created by war and, in the end, is undone by it. Even their idyll, Jiujiang, is not wholly separated from worldly strife; it had only recently been wrested from warlords a year earlier. Their shared dream, both its joys and its heartbreak, is in effect a function of history's own violent disjunctures. It is not because of naiveté on Jing's part, or a lack of trustworthiness from Weili, that their affair is a fantasy; it is the problem of historic time itself that has rendered their love a reified experience that Jing can only fetishize in the end. The way in which pastoral time and modernity seemed to hang together, if tenuously, in Jing's first nostalgic fantasy in the end fails here, rendering the recent past as a "dream" and the present as "reality." In this sense, the oscillation and confusion between dreamtime and historic time within the novella are, in their own way, mimetic of the epistemological pressures involved in trying to apprehend historic upheaval and change.

If the transition from "dream" to "awakening" fails to work in *Disillusionment*, then perhaps we can talk about the relationship between the narratives of dream and reality as a kind of architectonics, a collision of surfaces upon which it is the fault lines between reality and dream that are most significant. Rather than conceiving of their relationship as one of transcendence, where one narrative (the dream) is merely sublimated into the other (reality), perhaps we should see both competing narratives as imbued with comparable symbolic weight. At the same time, then, that the narrative of *Disillusionment* aims to create an objective mimesis of historic reality, it also more subtly stages the epistemological drama of trying to "recognize" reality. It betrays that reality is as much an ontological substance out there waiting to be analyzed as it is also a shifting stream of consciousness itself. The manic shifts of consciousness that heroine, text, and reader undergo are perhaps the best index to the power exerted by the historic Real itself on our attempts to formulate, articulate, and ultimately experience reality.

Mao Dun's intense focalization of the narrative through Jing's psyche and body, often aided by free indirect discourse, cannot merely be attributed to authorial voyeurism. One critic notably argues that Mao Dun was successful in trying to capture the "contradictory" nature of a "capricious" reality by featuring what she claims are Western-influenced descriptions of his heroines' thought processes.[45] However, Mao Dun falls into his own trap; while emphasizing women's inner psychic life, he also indulges in detailed and perhaps lurid descriptions of women's bodies, a kind of sexual objectification that threatens to delimit the power of these women's inner mental lives.[46] Another critic has argued that Mao Dun's use of women characters "accentuated male delectation of both the female body and female emotions" and that he "proved to be a connoisseur of female emotions as well as the female body."[47] Women characters, while ostensibly signifiers of modernity and progress, nevertheless become frozen within Mao Dun's leering gaze.

That Mao Dun was unable to overcome a measure of chauvinism in his fictional work is undeniable. But what if we were to read his repeatedly clichéd, even banal, depictions of women as symptomatic of a deeper conflict of narrative management within Mao Dun's writing itself? Mao Dun privileges the female body with a heightened emotional and corporeal sensitivity; it is they who dream, lose consciousness, cry, suddenly contract scarlet fever, and so forth. Their hysterical bodies function analogously to the chaotic tumult of the historical moment. Mao Dun's female hysterics are allegorical of his own narrative: seductive, passionate, and volatile. Moreover, the problem is not one of whether Mao Dun was authentically sincere in his fictive empathy with women or a "misogynist" in feminist drag. Indeed, Mao Dun's championing of women's plight suits him well insofar as it promotes him as a progressive champion of women, and insofar as women constitute the major trope for national modernity and sovereignty. However, what ultimately risks being revealed is the hysterical nature of the narrative itself; staging the hysterical breakdown of the heroines appears to be a strategy to somehow exorcise this volatility from the text and to project it upon the female characters. Feminine hysteria, as we saw before in Mao Dun's dream, is ultimately a fantastic displacement designed to cover up male hysteria and preserve the integrity of author and text.[48] As Mao Dun promoted himself as faithful to a robustly empiric and masculine form of realism, affectations for such things as romance and daydreaming must be rigorously disavowed. Semicolonial subjugation is conceived of in gendered terms, the victim nation seen as a woman ravaged by unscrupulous male colonizers. Resistance to such subjugation is often troped as a reclamation of political masculinity. That Mao Dun's narrative seems to police itself betrays an anxiety of succumbing to hysterical dreams; the narrative's careful delineation of what is dream and reality, what is hysteria and rational observation, allows us to observe the narrative's attempts to manage its own story.

The second novella of the trilogy, *Vacillation* (Dongyao), famously ends with a hysterical hallucination on the part of the hero's wife, Mrs. Fang.[49] She hides in an abandoned temple with her husband, Fang Luolan, a liberal Nationalist officer, and his mistress, Sun Wuyang. Meanwhile an angry peasant mob, egged on by conservative members of the Nationalist Party, viciously cuts its way through the village, targeting the womenfolk who have attempted to modernize by cutting short their hair. Mrs. Fang imagines herself to be a spider she sees hanging by its thread as she envisions the entire temple collapsing spectacularly around her. The story ends with Mrs. Fang letting out a scream and falling to the ground.[50] Her hysterical breakdown not only is a description of psychological collapse but, both as allegory and as actual reading experience, stages the collapse of realist representation itself, as it loses its mimetic bearings and suddenly veers into figurative nonsense. Mrs. Fang observes the spider tenuously climbing up and down its thread; the spider and the fragile line it relies on for support are suggestive not only of the fragility of the body but of the perpetual mimetic crisis of narrative itself. Mrs. Fang's hysterical collapse is on one hand evocative of the narrative hysteria that the author is loath to admit; on the other hand, her sacrifice allows the narrative to continue on without her.

In this vein, the experience of history as filtered through feminine sensuality may be mimetic in its own way of a certain historical experience. This sentimental appeal to the body, however, is at odds with the equally realist convention of the dispassionate observer. The frenzied woman corresponds, if uncomfortably, with the sprawling, mercurial texture of the narrative itself. At a remove is the realist authorial position that seeks to claim the mantle of objective observer. However, as Mao Dun's own statements about himself reveal, he was by no means a stable observer. His frequent illness and nervous ailments are tantalizingly symptomatic of his own hysteria, even if he refused to diagnose himself as such. Mao Dun thus holds two different ideals of the "real" in tension: corporeal experience and critical apprehension. At points this feminine sensuality and imagination escape the author's control and must be reined in and disciplined through the strong assertion of male narrative authority; Jing must physically and mentally break down and recuperate in the hospital as a kind of narrative penance in place of the author. However, her mental flights, her "dreams," are themselves fantasies of physical apotheosis, a bodily redemption through romance. In her dreams Jing finds the healing and calm that seemed to plague her creator all too persistently. In the end, Mao Dun offers up a narrative corporeal poetics that is as volatile and contradictory as both the women he narrates as well as their author. What gets represented is not so much reality but the very "effort," the strain the author must undergo to reach that elusive goal. This strain is apparent when the narrative falls into discursive excess, when the abundance of language seems to block mimesis rather than facilitate it, when even the word "reality" is marshaled as a superfluous and self-conscious trope. Perhaps, then, the most revealing aspect of Mao Dun's attempt to write "reality" is not so much his historical narrative but the very moments when realist mimesis and discursive excess collide and produce a mass of figurative meaninglessness, a hysterical shriek that encapsulates the author's impossible desire to reconcile himself with an incomprehensible world.

WU'S WEB: NARRATIVE STRATEGY, NARRATIVE ESCAPE, AND THE LOOPHOLE OF DREAMS IN *MIDNIGHT* (1933)

The discussion on *Eclipse* focused on the fraught resonances between volatile sexual desire and an equally mercurial revolutionary politics. Mao Dun's *Midnight* takes aim at speculative desire and the incessant pulsations of capital.[51] *Midnight* portrays the heady economic frenzy in which Shanghai was engulfed during the early 1930s; national industry struggles against cheaper foreign imports and speculators duel for control of the stock market through underhanded trading while workers resist declining wages, oppressive working conditions, and the violence meted out by their exploiters. Amid the dozens of characters that appear on stage, the text centers on Wu Sunfu, an unscrupulous and irascible owner of a silk factory trying to keep his company solvent by battling against his industrial competitors as well as playing a risky game with government bonds. Mao Dun, in memoirs he wrote late in life, detailed the many maladies that accompanied the preparation and writing of his masterwork. He suffered from an eye infection, stomach ailments, and a general nervous breakdown (also alluded to in his submission to *Eastern Miscellany*). Despite these ailments, he proceeded to work on a panoramic literary trilogy about contemporary Chinese society and economy. His three linked novellas would deal, respectively, with cotton manufacture, financial speculation, and a match factory. However, in November 1930, his vision, already damaged by trachoma, began to deteriorate, and he sought treatment from a Japanese-trained doctor. Treatment entailed having injections in his right cornea to cure an abscess that had formed inside. He was largely prevented from engaging in reading or writing for three months, monitored by his wife's strict supervision. While effectively blind during this convalescence, his "thinking, nevertheless, was very active,"[52] and he mentally revised his outline for his project. Still, the irony is not lost that for the foremost Chinese practitioner of realism, a mode that privileges empirical observation over inspired creation, Mao Dun was at risk of losing the very faculty most identified with observation.

During these three months of intense brainstorming, Mao Dun decided to combine his three planned novellas into one long novel. Moreover, he switched the light industry emphasized in the first novella from cotton manufacture to silk production; the protagonist of the third novella, an owner of a match factory, was transformed into *Midnight*'s main character, Wu Sunfu, a silk filature proprietor. Mao Dun wrote that he turned to silk because it was the main industrial Chinese export and was thus a major industry within China; however, the domestic industry was suffering because of intense competition outside, in particular the popularity of cheaper Japanese imports. In addition to these material considerations, the centrality of silk production in *Midnight* also functions as a handy metaphor for the novel's own structure as a tangle of various narrative threads trying to form an overall coherence and pattern. In an insightful reading of the novel's structure, one critic argues that *Midnight* consists of five interlocking narrative threads: Wu Sunfu's ownership and management of his factory; the duel between Wu Sunfu and his financier rival Zhao Botao on the stock exchange; Wu Sunfu's struggles with the workers; Wu Sunfu's problems with his properties in the countryside; and Wu Sunfu's struggles to maintain control within his own family.

Within this extended metaphor of a narrative web of interlocking threads, it is Wu Sunfu who pulls the strings.[53] The centrality of silk has symbolic connotations: an invention that is often thought of as a quintessentially Chinese export, the industrialized manufacture of silk was in no small way allegorical of China's attempt to maintain its national sovereignty while modernizing itself. The novel itself is an attempt to "weave" a uniquely Chinese, but also modern, tapestry.

Mao Dun's decision to concentrate on economics was no doubt inspired by his commitment to a conception of realism as an empirical method of observation, a demonstration of "knowing reality with great effort." Rather than focusing on intellectuals, revolutionaries, or students, Mao Dun wanted to focus on someone he thought was most emblematic of the historical and economic zeitgeist: a capitalist. Marxist critic Qu Qiubai thus praised the result as being "the first successful realist novel in China. It clearly bears the influence of Zola (Zola's *L'argent*)."[54] Mao Dun, while appreciating Qu Qiubai's approval, admitted that he had never read Zola's novel about financial speculation in nineteenth-century France. But his focus on money betrays an advocacy of literature more as sociological investigation than belles lettres. In his memoirs he defended himself against the charge that, as a writer, he had no background in financial speculation. He himself witnessed a flurry of speculation in his hometown in Zhejiang province over the price of mulberry leaves that happened every year and that coincided with the spring hatching of silkworms.[55] His 1932 story *Spring Silkworms* addressed silk cocoon harvesting and catastrophically bad commodity speculation in a rural town. Wu Sunfu, Mao Dun noted, was inspired by his own personal acquaintanceship with a number of industrialists: "I simply synthesize and analyze the personalities of real people you are most familiar with, and then come up with the most approximate typical personality. By this principle it is natural to be able to create the typical personality of an industrialist. Wu Sunfu's personality was created just like this."[56] Wu Sunfu not only reflects a realist and materialist novelistic approach but is also himself a product of type, a composite specimen meant to be a representative sample of an important segment in Chinese society. But he is not the most pleasant or compelling figure; he is greedy, arrogant, and conniving, given to fits of rage and poutiness. However, he has greater aspirations, professing that the resuscitation of national industry is key to China's future. In his industrial ambitions he seeks to embody a national narrative, one where the key players are businessmen and entrepreneurs, not scholars and intellectuals.

Mao Dun's decision to narrate the story of a businessman is emblematic of his wish to provide a material basis for his narrative; concentrating on economics rather than belles lettres, poetry, or even politics conveys the author's attempt to bring a more thoroughly objective framework to his storytelling. But an economy that runs on credit and money is essentially a symbolic economy, predicated on tokens, promises, and faith. One critic, writing about the nineteenth-century European realist novel, argues that the story of money is essentially a form of dream making: "In the nineteenth-century novel, money bolsters and fuels the romantic dreams of heroes and heroines from all classes of society at the same time as it discredits those dreams—that is, establishes the limit of their realization."[57] Mao Dun's reliance on economic discourse attempts to materially ground his narrative that nevertheless unravels itself as a fantasy. The author in a sense wants it all, both the material backing that economy provides the novel and the radical epiphany of collapse and awakening. The rhetorical move is not unlike that attempted in *Disillusionment*; the creation of a house of cards that, in the critical last instance, founders. The novel sets in motion a struggle between two sets of values, one economic, the other poetic. But the poetic does not easily triumph over the economic; only through the catastrophic unraveling of the economic itself do the utopian, poetic values seem redeemable. Hence Mao Dun has nothing but scorn for those who naively wax lyrical without attending to the necessity of critiquing the economic; on the other hand, we see throughout the text a hidden lament that poetry must be forsaken in the present term.

The conflict between entrepreneurs and poets is demonstrated in a scene where Wu Sunfu is dismayed to find his younger brother, Axuan, reading a book of poetry by a family acquaintance, Fan Bowen, a would-be romantic and ostentatious aesthete. Both poet and industrialist gather around Axuan, debating the merits of poetry and business. The elder brother is visibly vexed by Fan Bowen's intrusion in Axuan's life, and even more irritated by the poem that catches his eye: romantic doggerel bemoaning the loss of the natural beauty of West Lake as it chokes in the exhaust fumes from cars owned by the vulgar "bourgeoisie."[58] Poetry duels against the market, and the conflicts between culture and commerce find their incarnation in Axuan, would-be inheritor of Wu Sunfu's enterprise but enraptured by Fan Bowen's verse. Fan Bowen embodies a parodic nostalgia for the literati past, one in which power and prestige were conferred upon those harboring literary skills (his name can be read as "a model of broad knowledge"), an era now disenchanted by industry. The text makes it clear that Fan Bowen is an irrelevant and incompetent vestige of the past, and in a scene soon after we find Fan Bowen brooding near a lake and thinking about emulating the great poet Qu Yuan by throwing himself in the water.[59] Qu Yuan's realist incarnation, Fan Bowen, is a fanciful parody of his premodern icon. While he intones against the cultural vulgarity of bourgeois life, he is dependent on his capitalist connections to stay alive. Fan Bowen is a laughable figure that hardly anyone takes seriously; however, his presence nevertheless brings up the question of what happens to lyrical values in a disenchanted age. While the text points to the inadequacy of traditional literature to speak to the present, it hesitates from completely severing ties with the "lyric" past.[60]

Midnight also signals a contrast in its mobilization of gender. The story is geared prominently toward male protagonists engaged in the masculine occupations of finance and industry. While women do appear in the novel, often recapitulating the same motifs of dreaming and disillusionment, their general marginalization within the narrative makes them far easier to contain. By focusing on men and economics, it would appear that we stand on more solid narrative ground; however, by the end of the novel the world of business proves no less fickle, no less hysterical, than that of women's inner lives.

Axuan is not the only member of the Wu family to feel the conflict between a lyric past and a disenchanted, mechanical present. Wu Sunfu's wife, Lin Peiyao, longs for her days as a carefree student, frolicking in the literary landscapes provided by such texts as Shakespeare's *The Tempest* and enraptured by grand gestures of chivalry inspired by works like Walter Scott's *Ivanhoe*: "She never would have thought that this cup full of the fine wine of youth would one day be emptied."[61] The narrator, through free indirect discourse, conveys how Mrs. Wu's own thinking waxes lyrical with the cloying metaphor of a "cup full of the fine wine of youth." Are these solely Mrs. Wu's thoughts, or are they the narrator's as well? Following Shakespeare, the text refers to this period of her life as a "midsummer night's dream," one soon to be dispersed: "The deaths of her father and mother by illness in quick succession forced the true taste of 'reality' into 'Miss Lin Peiyao's' virginal heart."[62] Reality here entails the social obligation to find a husband with the means to support her and her siblings. For Lin Peiyao, this means entering into a union with a "stern, purple and pimply faced husband who just happened to be the knight and 'prince' of the mechanical and industrial era of the twentieth century."[63] Poetry has been replaced by industry, nature by mechanics, and handsome knights have been switched for ugly and cruel businessmen. What Mao Dun not so subtly suggests is the sexual revulsion that Wu Sunfu evokes; Lin Peiyao is forced into a loveless marriage with a revolting protagonist arranged by a literary mode that must be faithful to economic "reality." She herself is a "sacrificial victim" of material necessity. Dashing knights and romantic literature as objects of desire must be disavowed. However, the narrator's use of free indirect discourse to convey Mrs. Wu's disappointment suggests that it is also narrator and text itself forced into a shotgun marriage with realism.

The former Miss Lin's train of thought is disrupted by the unexpected appearance of her former suitor, Colonel Lei, a knight of a more chivalrous stripe from the Nationalist Army. She is thrown into a state of bewilderment: "Mrs. Wu was startled into a panic. 'Reality' and 'dream' within an instant flowed into each other, and she almost could not believe her eyes."[64] Again, free indirect discourse blurs the line of who is trying to decide what is dream and reality, the narrator or heroine. But what seems to be a hoped-for realization of a long-held romantic dream becomes yet another disappointment, as he announces that he is leaving for battle the next day. He pulls out an old copy of Goethe's *The Sorrows of Young Werther*, and clasped between its pages is a dried rose. Mrs. Wu had given this volume to Colonel Lei years earlier when he was a poor student and unsuccessful suitor for her hand in marriage. After years of near-fatal battle, Colonel Lei returns the book to Mrs. Wu for safekeeping, informing her that he likely will not return alive. They share a final kiss:

> "Dear brother!" suddenly chirped the parrot that was in the cage.[65]
> The embracing couple was startled. Mrs. Wu awoke as if from a dream and forcefully pushed away Colonel Lei, and holding onto her *Sorrows of Young Werther* ran out of the drawing room, up the stairs and into her own room. She fell on her bed, and a stream of hot tears shortly soaked her flower embroidered, white pillow.[66]

Colonel Lei and Mrs. Wu enact the romantic plot of their shared Sturm und Drang favorite, Lei playing the young Werther tortured by his beloved's marriage to another. Colonel Lei sees no way out of his romantic predicament other than to die in battle, while Goethe's hero commits suicide. However, their star-crossed love also mirrors that of Jing and Qiang Weili in *Disillusionment*. Both characters express a yearning for a romantic era by enacting an eighteenth-century epistolary novel. They also both express nostalgia for the act of reading. Whatever dreams of romance the former Miss Lin Peiyao holds onto, each one is closely related to an act of reading as an affective exercise of libidinal imagination. It is not just romance that has been threatened by a mechanical age but the very act of reading as well. The parrot's voice rudely interrupts this dreamy vignette, suggesting that the love shared by the two has already lost its aura of authenticity, a portent borne out by the fact that Colonel Lei does not die but eventually finds his way back to Shanghai and into the arms of a harlot.[67] Even a noble death is rendered out of reach.

The novel thus makes a case for its own status as a "realist" text by thoroughly debunking the "dreams" of romantic literature, and it does so in a self-conscious manner that invites the charge of defensiveness. Even as this scene is meant to be a parody of the "Mandarin Duck and Butterfly" leisure literature that was far more widely read in the 1930s, such scenes are often more compellingly written than many of the scenes concerning Wu Sunfu's struggles with his economic rivals. "Narrative desire" is not just a way of conceptualizing the reader's libidinal investment in a text; it also invites us to think about how the text itself struggles with its own mimetic self-identification. In what sense is the text trying to mask its own guilty desire to break into full-fledged sentimentality by framing such emotions in terms of dreams? Despite all of the realist disclaimers, the text nevertheless betrays a fascination with the values of romanticism, a desire that need not be rigidly muffled by an overcompensating realism. Mao Dun's realism is a literature of strain, exhibiting both doctrinal fastidiousness and sentimental excess, both a defense of its purposefulness and a lingering regret of what must be forsaken. Mrs. Wu's trade-off between a romantic knight and an ugly, rich industrialist mirrors the literary trade-off the text makes. Realism, in Mao Dun's hands, dreams of literature as pure pleasure, now seemingly lost under the imperative to represent and analyze. The epistemological binary of dream and reality becomes writ large in an unexpected fashion as the opposition between literature and realism.

Intertextual nostalgia makes its appearance in yet another dream scene in the novel involving another female character, Wu Sunfu's sister, Huifang. Wu Sunfu's family is rooted in the landowning class in the countryside; however, because of threats of revolt from "Communist bandits," Wu Sunfu decides to move the rest of his family, his brother, Axuan, sister, and father to the relative safety of Shanghai. Wu Sunfu's father dies immediately upon arrival to Shanghai, pushed over his cardiac limit by the sensory overload of the city. Huifang, who was especially close to her more feudal father, finds her new urban life deeply alienating. As a result of her closeness with her father, she has inherited his moral values, including his devotion to a Daoist text, the *Treatise of the Most High on Action and Retribution* (Taishang ganying pian).[68] Popular among pious masses, the text is formed of laundry lists of good and bad deeds and their corresponding reward and retribution. Wu Sunfu's father rejects the dynamics of capitalist exchange in favor of the moral exchange outlined by the scripture. Huifang clings to this scripture as she longs to return to the countryside. Her loneliness in the city is only compounded by her brother's ironclad control over her life, and she quickly descends into fits of desperation and paranoia. Haunted by a number of unsettling dreams, one in particular holds special power over her:

> Suddenly last night's dream came back to her. It was an old dream that she had had repeatedly, although now Huifang was simply convinced that it was not merely a dream, but reality [*zhenshi*]; she seemed to think that the dream referred to an event that had occurred three weeks ago during the evening—it was a thunderous and rainy night, and it was after she and Fan Bowen had finished chatting near the fish pond by the flower garden facing the hexagonal pavilion that was on the artificial hill when she lost her precious maidenhead under cover of night; she was truly convinced that among her strange dreams this particular dream that tormented her repeatedly and with little variation was surely not a dream, but was real [*zhenshi*]; and this real dream precisely took place at that hexagonal pavilion, in that thunderous and rainy evening, that moment when the heavy rain first roared, as she lazily lay back on the reclining chair in that pavilion with Fan Bowen sitting opposite her, and with her eyes closed she could feel him walking to her side, and she felt her whole body suddenly become weak and paralyzed, as if intoxicated.[69]

The narrator again employs free indirect discourse by means of one long, meandering sentence in order to convey a sense of Huifang's tumultuous mind; we see a more sensual and racy recapitulation of Mrs. Wu's "dream" sequence. The frequency with which the words "dream," "real," and their related cognates appear reveals a dizzying dialectic that far outstrips what occurred in the earlier sequence. In earlier instances, the narrator does not hesitate to delineate what is reality and what is merely fantasy; here the narrator finds itself ventriloquizing Huifang's voice, telling us that her dream is indeed reality. Moreover, the text leaves unresolved whether Huifang is completely imagining her rendezvous with Fan Bowen or whether there was indeed an actual assignation at some earlier part of the narrative that the text never hinted at. However, the passage's focus on the precise location, time, and setting when Huifang was suddenly ravished cements a sense of the concrete palpability of the event, its unmistakable "realness," even if it is a fabricated memory. The text, usually so eager to separate reality from fantasy and romance, seems to have suddenly collapsed.

We might ask how Huifang's dream reveals a naked desire that complicates Mao Dun's search for "reality," a desire so strong that at certain points it threatens to warp the integrity of that narrative reality into something beyond recognition, carrying the text to the edge of hallucination or complete breakdown. Huifang's supposed affair with Fan Bowen may be utter fantasy, a willful and violent creation of reality from an unfulfilled desire. The text wavers between two possible scenarios and seems unsure of its own reality: Huifang's coupling with Fan Bowen as hallucination or "actual" event.

Just as Mrs. Wu's dream sequence was inspired by Goethe's *Werther*, so does this scene suggest an intertextual connection to the past, this one more native: the pivotal dream-scene in Tang Xianzu's sixteenth-century *Peony Pavilion* (Mudan ting). The heroine, Du Liniang, not only discovers her future lover and husband in a dream but consummates her love with him. After the dream, she pines over her spectral beau, Liu Mengmei, and dies. Du Liniang eventually reunites in the phenomenal world with Liu Mengmei after first being his ghost lover, and then dug out of her grave and resuscitated. Their love for and devotion to each other are recognized by Du Liniang's erstwhile doubtful family and sanctioned by imperial fiat, thus making what was a love that existed only in a dream into a socially recognized reality. In Tang Xianzu's well-known preface to the work, we find rhetoric that is similar in spirit to the passage from *Midnight* above: "Love is of source unknown, yet it grows ever deeper. The living may die of it, by its power the dead live again. Love is not love at its fullest if one who lives is unwilling to die for it, or if it cannot restore to life one who has so died. And must the love that comes in a dream necessarily be unreal?"[70]

Love, or *qing* (a term that also denotes desire and affection, encompassing both civic *agape* and passionate *eros*), is so powerful and so compelling as to transcend life and death and to establish itself as the ultimate reality. Mindful that the literati of sixteenth-century China were not as engaged with questions of empiricism in the May Fourth sense, we should note that the word used to denote "real" is simply *zhen*, a more flexible term that emphasizes truthfulness and authenticity, and that not need necessarily include the sense of empirical reality.

Whether Mao Dun actively sought to use *Peony Pavilion* is at best a speculation. But placing the two dream scenes side by side illuminates realism's complicated relationship with depicting desire. *Peony Pavilion* demonstrates the power of *qing* to create multiple narrative worlds to accommodate its trajectory. In the end, *qing* constitutes an ultimate reality that proves more lasting than the existence bounded by life and death, man and ghost, and the paternalistic strictures of Neo-Confucian morality. Whatever the doubts of the other characters as to the reality of Du Liniang's love, the spectator remains functionally convinced of its reality through the very act of watching the performance. The actors inside and outside the dream are the same; there is no "set change" to demarcate that we have entered "dream space." Whatever our private doubts about the dream's reality, the dream is real "functionally," for the play *itself* believes for us. This "externalized belief" that the play creates structurally heightens the sense of love's reality.[71]

For a split second this also seems to happen when we read Huifang's dream. The onslaught of the meandering prose collapses dream and reality, objective narration and interior monologue; it is not difficult to believe that something utterly magical is taking place. But as a realist novel, only one sort of reality exercises hegemonic control over the text. Du Liniang exists in a textual realm where multiple worlds are possible; moreover, her ability to traverse these worlds makes her a heroine. Huifang, however, does not exist in such a pliable world; her insistence on her "reality" threatens to condemn her as psychotic, not heroic. What are merely parallel universes in Tang Xianzu's play are the teetering footsteps lurching toward insanity in Mao Dun's novel. And yet even this psychosis has a silver lining; her insistence on the reality of her dream and desire inspires her to a stunning rebellion against her brother: "her entire body was a flame of revolt."[72] She makes a bold declaration of independence by moving out of her brother's house, leaving Wu Sunfu livid.

The text leaves ambiguous what will happen to Huifang. On one hand she wishes to pursue an education. On the other she is enthralled by a group of new decadent friends, and at one points muses that frolicking in the Rio Rita Gardens is far more pleasurable than reciting her Daoist treatise.[73] They frolic in gardens, near lakes, in pavilions, and on artificial mountains, poor imitations of a wished-for Eden or a pavilion filled with peonies. But even they are aware of their precarious existence. Fan Bowen, the poetic clown, has a prescient sense that things will quickly change as he remarks on a White Russian émigré waiter serving drinks: "'You see that White Russian over there? He probably was a count or marquis at some point, probably lived half his life having other people pour wine for him. But now it's his turn to wait on other people; he's a quick study, though. He can pick up six soda bottles in one hand!'"[74]

Even the aesthetes are not unaware that their continued life of pleasure will most likely come to an end; it remains to be seen where Huifang's life will lead. Nevertheless, Huifang succeeds in being one of the few characters that successfully escapes Wu Sunfu's "web," and as such, drops out of the novel. Mrs. Wu, unable to escape the unhappiness of her loveless marriage to a capitalist, finds herself secretly "sympathizing" with Huifang's plight and her escape, even as she is unsuccessful in retrieving her sister-in-law from the YWCA where she is staying.[75] Whereas *Peony Pavilion* allows us to follow Du Liniang to whatever spectral realms she may wander, *Midnight* can only abandon Huifang, leaving her fate to our imagination.

Huifang's dream, along with Mrs. Wu's dreamlike fantasy, both involve the lingering intertextual traces of older, more romantic literature. Following the logic of negation, the text is proclaiming what it is not: it is not a tragic romance in the style of *Werther*, nor is it a romantic drama with a happy end as in *Peony Pavilion*. However, the invocation of both of these works in the dream form also installs them as a powerful form of intertextual nostalgia, whereby the realist text discreetly reveals what it cannot allow itself to be. Mao Dun's critical realist novel, then, evinces two forms of desire: one for the kind of social transformation that the work implies is yet to happen (and perhaps is imminent), and the other for a nostalgic fantasy of literature as a form of beautiful romance, something that is also, by necessity, lacking in the novel. In both cases the barrier to desire is History itself, as that which seeks to be transformed, and whose necessary transformation prevents the author from writing in a more aesthetically inclined mode. On the other hand, these two forms of desire, for utopia and for literature, are also the end goals that the reader will ostensibly feel emboldened to pursue through the means of social struggle. In as much as these desires are deferred because of History, they are also the inspirations that spur its transformations as well. Thus to characterize the text's relationship to its intertextual predecessors as merely lament would be one-sided, for while the text bemoans the loss of literature, it also evinces a hope of its reclamation.

In addition to Mrs. Wu and Huifang, our protagonist also starts dreaming toward the end of the novel as his financial schemes go awry while, in his own home, he starts to lose control over his family. His wife is described as "groaning and whimpering in [her] dream,"[76] suggesting that perhaps she is thinking of Colonel Lei. Her husband, on the other hand, is torn by nervous fits, feeling as if "his body was completely surrounded by landmines," feeling a "kind of terror that repeatedly battered his swollen and feverish brain." In Wu Sunfu's dream he finds Huifang with her hair shorn going off to a nunnery while the other siblings raise a ruckus over dividing the elder brother's property. Suddenly the dream takes a happier turn and finds Wu Sunfu in a hotel, cradling Liu Yuying, the mistress of his archrival Zhao Botao whom he secretly covets.[77] Wu Sunfu's dream is both a nightmare and a reverie. He witnesses the complete dissolution of his power over his family; his property is parceled away among family members, his sister rejects all familial duty and runs to a nunnery, while his brother finds a new home in the theater, as if his family has decided to reject the twentieth century and return to a premodern existence where monasteries and village dramas play an important role. Wu Sunfu's accumulation of capital is also a project of familial modernization, an effort to bring his rural family into the urban fold; the dream undoes that trajectory. The only bright spot in his dream is in the end, when he can finally be at ease with the object of desire; the only place where his body can find a measure of respite is in the arms of an unattainable woman. The novel seeks to finally undo Wu Sunfu's power over both his surroundings and the text by undermining him from within and dispatching a Trojan horse into his unconscious. The last chapter begins with Wu Sunfu flailing in the "black waters" of a dream.[78] As his bedroom clock strikes nine in the morning, the ring transforms into the sound of the bell at the stock exchange, the site of his final, desperate rally, as well as the solemn knell of his financial doom. In the end Wu Sunfu causes his own undoing along with his financial rivals and the global economic system that strangles China's industrial development.

The rise of the clock in Shanghai was a function of a dramatic change in the sense and use of time in an industrial and commercial society. To that end, "time had to be experienced as standardized measurements that synchronized and structured the rhythm of life."[79] The novel's title, *Midnight*, indicates a moment in time that can only be accurately pinpointed by a mechanism like a modern clock; on the other hand it also marks the point of transition between one day and the next, but in an allegorical fashion, between capitalist time (night) and revolution (day). Moreover, the nostalgic dreams the text indulges in occasionally are not merely passages backward into time but yearnings for different forms of time, whether it be romantic Europe, late Ming China, or, as in *Disillusionment*, the pastoral, where time is felt by the rhythmic turning of the waterwheel instead of the ticking of a clock.

In the end, however, it is the tale of economic development, the story of national industry that forms the backbone of the novel, that itself becomes a "dream." Zhou Zhongwei, the owner of a match company, finds himself unable to secure a loan to keep his factory afloat. Faced with such a dire end, he reminisces about headier days with his fellow businessmen:

> "Hey, do you remember? The day of old Mr. Wu's funeral! Miss Xu Manli was there too! Remember? She was dancing on the tables! Miss Xu then lost one of her brocade high heels! Haha! It was real fun, a dream!" . . .
>
> Colonel Lei and Xu Manli both laughed, but Wang Hefu furrowed his brow while his face changed color. That time from Old Mr. Wu's funeral up till now really was all a dream! Their dream of developing industry! Was it soon time to wake up from the dream?[80]

In the end, Zhou Zhongwei has no choice but to accept a predatory loan from Japanese lenders, thus selling out a national enterprise to a colonial rival. As he announces the reopening of the factory to his workers, he disingenuously tells them that his work is motivated by a deep sense of nationalism:

> "Even though our factory was in the red, I still decided to keep going; why? First, if we closed the factory, you'd all be starving. You're all Chinese, and your boss here is also Chinese, and Chinese bosses need to help Chinese workers! Second, our markets are saturated with

> foreign matches, and the cash of the Chinese are going to the pockets of foreigners, who knows how many millions per year! . . . Chinese workers also need to help Chinese bosses! If the operating costs are too heavy, then we can't sell our goods; if you guys help me out, that is, accept a wage cut of a few dollars, then once the factory starts earning money, we can all live happily! . . . Alright then, long live national industry!"[81]

In his short speech Zhou Zhongwei mentions the word "China/Chinese" twelve times, varnishing his words with a gloss of vulgar nationalism that only heightens the irony of how the factory is now de facto a Japanese venture, leaving Zhou the proprietor in name only. The workers are more dumbfounded than inspired and glumly return to work. As the machines begin to hum, Zhou Zhongwei reflects on his life: "First he was a compradore, then he was his own boss, and then he was yet again a compradore,—but a different sort of compradore, from now on a proprietor in name only! It had been a dream, it had come full circle!" In the end, Zhou Zhongwei has lost his business and his pride, and is only left with his ability to laugh at his predicament.[82]

Wu Sunfu, as a "typical" specimen of the industrialist, stands in for the greater tragic hero of Chinese capitalism itself. With hopes of creating wealth and power for a new, modern China, national industry falls victim to its own economic hubris, becoming merely a "dream" and rendering the nation little more than a crude slogan. It has been argued that the novel's obsessive attention to details prevents the text from suggesting, in Lukácsian fashion, the imminence of historical movement; it thus fails to show how history gradually unfolds toward a revolutionary end.[83] Mao Dun's singular focus on Shanghai, one that does not take into account the great historic forces of the peasantry and colonialism, thus inhibits him from conveying a diachronic sense of historic progression.[84] However, the deployment of the dream trope to encapsulate the failure of economic development returns us to a different sense of dialectic. This one is well represented by *Dream of the Red Chamber*, a novel that delights in material sumptuousness, description, and detail, only to suddenly and tragically reveal the vacuity of it all. The logic of movement in *Midnight* is not one of progression, as we would expect in a realist novel, but one of sudden enlightenment, an instant transcendence of the phenomenal world. However, such a transcendence can only occur alongside a great historic trauma.

Moreover, if the nationalistic development of China's industry is compromised by the forces of imperialism outside and uneven development inside, how much more can we expect a realist mode, a "novel about China," to exist comfortably on Chinese soil, a terrain that is constantly shifting? Colonialism and globalization thus compromise the very reality that Mao Dun seeks to reflect, for underneath any seemingly solid image of "Chinese society" lurks the far more powerful web of global connections and power relations that not only overdetermine national identity but undermine it as well. The problem lies in mistaking the temporality of historic reality as narrated in *Midnight* as a form of unfolding immanence, a developmentalism that will steadily hint the way forward to emancipation. As opposed to a gradual evolutionary lurch toward communism, *Midnight*'s realism suggests a temporality that might be more readily described as living through a slow burning crisis that does not yet recognize itself as such. There is no comfortable stasis, no stable "picture" of Chinese reality on which to hold, for reality exists within the modality of perpetual crisis. The realist mode itself exists, and exuberantly so, within crisis, constantly managing the manifold shifts of narrative tone, shuffling between competing discursive desires. The relative fragility of Mao Dun's realism, its "hysterical" shifts into a dream world, do not only point to the relative novelty of the mode but also suggest that any claim to a realism that depicts a society in stasis has only depicted a society whose immanent crises have been temporally and spatially deferred onto other spaces.[85] In those lands on whose backs the safety of the first world's stable and cozy lived existence is assured, the naked desire for revolutionary Utopia can gleam all the more brightly, as a fledgling epistemology of static "realism" can only try in vain to obscure it.

A case can be made for an analogy between dreaming and the economy as described in *Midnight*: just as a dream seems ethereal and impermanent, so does the capitalist economy essentially run on an engine of emptiness, of fictive speculations and hypothetical prices, values flitting and transforming in a speck of time. On the other hand, a dream can nevertheless feel very "real," and in the way that the phenomenon is somatically involved, so does capitalism have very real, and often traumatic, effects on bodies: wage labor is exploited while the reserve army of labor endures hunger, workers' protests are met with violence. That the text renders the national economy as "merely" a dream not only exposes the "emptiness" of the whole enterprise but also implies the hysteric political violence that renders an entire economy oneiric pageantry. The dream is not simply a nostalgic figure for the hopes of the past but a trembling index to the horrors both presently occurring and yet to come. In the end Mao Dun was perhaps wiser in his fear of dreams than he himself knew; their danger lay not so much in their indulgence in utopian allegory but in suggesting a more horrifying mirror to reality than mimesis itself.

CHAPTER 4

Sleepless Nights in Fast Socialism

Dream Rhetoric and Fiction in the Mao Era

For the Communists and their supporters, the establishment of the People's Republic of China in 1949 marked the new nation's confident proclamation of being in synchronicity with the rest of the world. No more a backward, colonized, and feudal nation, China could now claim to stand on par with the rest of the world as a sovereign power. Literary critic Hu Feng celebrated Mao Zedong's ascendancy atop the balustrade of Tiananmen Square by publishing the first part of an epic poem on November 20, 1949, titled "Time Has Now Begun!" (Shijian kaishi le!).[1] In his lyrical epic, the poet reveals how his "dreaming eyes" and "dreaming heart" have been awakened in the sublime moment of liberation and redemption. In this moment of transfiguration, the whole cosmos recognizes China's ascendancy:

> Fatherland, my fatherland
> Today
> In this sacred time of your rebirth
> The entire globe pays respects to you
> The entire universe extends its congratulations to you[2]

For many citizens, October 1, 1949, marked a moment of triumphant celebration, a majestic "now" that a newly confident and victorious citizenry could proudly proclaim. However, it did not take long for the sense of a glorious present tense to fade, as the country now embarked on the arduous path of modernization and politico-economic transition. The glory of a present "now" had to be deferred to the future, as the nation struggled to meet the challenges of creating a new society in the aftermath of decades of war and revolutionary turmoil. If Hu Feng's poem spoke to a sense that a fully transfigured and redeemed present had finally arrived, later discourse would grapple with the paradox that while the revolution had indeed happened, the country was still far, far away from socialism. In the span between the moment of Liberation and that future moment of true communism lay a period of unruly and difficult transition, a period marked profoundly by a sense of temporal disjuncture, of being betwixt and between but not at all settled.

SOCIALISM OUT OF JOINT: THREE FORMS OF TEMPORAL DISJUNCTURE

The theme of temporal disjuncture in the Mao era played out in three forms, reconfiguring the relations between dream and reality, night and day, and sleeping and awakening. The first is the rhetoric of transition not long following the celebratory moment of Liberation. How were the Chinese now to embark on the task of modernization and transformation after the revolutionary mandate had been conferred, and how was the populace to be convinced of the surety of the path to be taken? The links between early Chinese socialist rhetoric and nineteenth-century Russian aesthetic criticism illuminated how Russian aesthetic notions about dream and reality informed Chinese political notions of socialist transition. However, as tensions emerged between the PRC and the Soviet Union following the death of Stalin, the Chinese started to ponder ways of accomplishing an accelerated modernity independent of Soviet Union control and aid. Whereas the Soviet Union had played an important role in shepherding China toward socialist modernity, the Chinese sought to persevere alone through a process of accelerated transition, culminating in the Great Leap Forward of 1958. Here, sleeplessness figures as a cultural logic of accelerated socialist accumulation, one that had severe consequences not just on artistic production but on the bodies of the populace themselves. The third form of temporal disjuncture takes the form of revolutionary nostalgia: Yang Mo's 1958 novel *The Song of Youth* is read as a symptom of an obsessive attachment to the "dark" pre-revolutionary era, one that betrays a certain uneasiness with the present, post-revolutionary moment. The novel indulges in historical and stylistic nostalgia ostensibly to overcome it and thus demonstrates how both historical and unconscious darkness are cleared through socialist illumination; however, this putative attempt to "cure" the wounds of the past betrays a persistent desire for the symptom itself.

Weaving through the investigations of these three forms of temporal disjuncture is an exploration of the rhetoric of dreaming during the early years of the People's Republic. In a period when official discourse celebrated the majesty and grandeur of a new reality, the rhetoric of dreaming, once prominent in pre-1949 intellectual discourse, faded away. The socialist imperative for a transparency and legibility of all social meaning rendered dreaming, in its symbolic density and in the privacy of its operations, ill-suited to offer any insights. This comprehensive management over knowledge and desire resulted in an ideological and cultural landscape in which the sunlight of communism shined so brightly that not only did dreams barely figure, but even sleep itself was hard to come by.

A REALITY GREATER THAN ANY DREAM: NIKOLAI CHERNYSHEVSKY, ZHOU YANG, WANG RUOSHUI, AND THE ARTICULATION OF TRANSITION

The publication of the 1933 special New Year's edition of *Eastern Miscellany*, with its collection of readers' submissions about their "dreams" for a future China, acted as a historical benchmark and index to the depth of crisis into which the nation had plunged on economic, political, geopolitical, and spiritual fronts. At once a plea and cry for much-needed change, it was also, conversely, an expression of hope that such change was indeed possible. The new regime's ideologists were not ignorant of the evocative historic power that this publication carried, and the *People's Daily* (Renmin ribao), the national news organ of the party, weighed in with its own assessment. In 1953 Wang Ruoshui (1926–2002), then a young editor in the theoretical department of the *People's Daily*, made the 1933 *Eastern Miscellany* issue the subject of his own commentary. According to Wang, the dreams written down in 1933 were expressions of a much darker time; the crevasse between the readers' dreams and the grim reality that surrounded them constituted a "sharp contradiction" that they struggled, yet failed, to resolve. Their dreams were a direct index pointing to the nation's misery, a pathological symptom pointing to substantial social ills.

However, the passage of time and the unfolding of history have produced a radically different present:

> Twenty years have passed that have spun around our heavens and upturned our earth.
>
> Those beautiful dreams of twenty years ago, brushing aside the merely absurd ones, have for the most part already become reality, and there are still some that are gradually becoming reality; moreover, the reality has in some places even surpassed those dreams. The reality of today is far more abundant than that volume of vivid dreams written twenty years ago. Not only do we see a number of things of which we once dreamed, we also see things of which we never even dreamed.[3]

The "beautiful dreams" of the past have been validated by their historic realization. It was not enough, however, to merely celebrate the realization of these "dreams"; the point was to demonstrate how the reality of socialism was so resplendent as to outstrip and outshine even the prettiest of dreams. Dreams and reality dramatically switched places after 1949, the dark and grim existence of colonialism, war, and poverty turned into fleeting nightmares, while those dreams of a transfigured nation suddenly materialized in front of our very eyes. Just as the "heavens" and "earth" changed their positions, so have dreams and reality reversed. As Wang Ruoshui wrote: "In the past we used dreams to beautify our reality; now we use reality to beautify [reality's] dreams."[4]

While the 1933 issue of *Eastern Miscellany* forms a structural and temporal benchmark against which Wang Ruoshui constructed his polemic, there was another horizon, from another country, that also informs the content and logic of his argument. The piece begins with a single quote from radical Russian writer Nikolai Chernyshevsky (1828–89): "Reality is grander than dreams."[5] Chernyshevsky wrote *What Is to Be Done?* (Chto delat'? 1863), the utopian novel that inspired the Russian radicals of the 1860s and later Vladimir Lenin. As one of Chernyshevsky's most authoritative critics has argued, the novel "had the greatest impact on human lives in the history of Russian literature."[6] The novel's heroine, Vera Pavlovna, realizes her aspiration of creating a utopian community; in her journey toward utopia she has a series of pivotal dreams. In her last dream she envisions a palace made of glass and metal, the triumphant meeting place where the liberated masses congregate, dine, and revel after a hard day's work, the famous "Crystal Palace" that became emblematic of socialist utopia. This dream of collective revelry acts as an allegory for the last scene in the novel, which shows the protagonists reunited in joyful song.

The epigraph, however, does not derive from Chernyshevsky's main claim to literary fame. It instead comes from his 1853 master's dissertation, "The Aesthetic Relation of Art to Reality." Zhou Yang (1908–89), who would become the most prominent literary theorist of the Mao era, produced a Chinese version based on an English translation in 1948. The epigraph that Wang Ruoshui cites is drawn verbatim from Zhou Yang's translation. While Wang Ruoshui, in his editorial, does not discuss Chernyshevsky's dissertation in depth, it is clear that his argument and rhetoric draw heavily from the content of that polemic.

Chernyshevsky was the spokesman of the new, more radical breed of Russian intelligentsia who were impatient with the slow pace of reforms, even under the relatively liberal reign of Alexander II, who emancipated the serfs in 1861.[7] While they inherited the long influence of Hegel and German philosophy that had so nurtured the intellectuals of the 1840s, they rejected the previous generation's dalliance with Romantic philosophy, aesthetics, and idealism. The radical intelligentsia of the 1860s were staunch materialists and were also attracted to advances in the natural sciences and in physiological explanations for human phenomena.

Chernyshevsky sought to remold a concept of aesthetics that would bring it in line with the materialist vogue of the times. His dissertation was an attempt to articulate the place of aesthetic appreciation and creation within a materialist conception of the world. If reality and matter were primary, then what possible justification could there be for a work of art or, for that matter, any illusory fantasy? Chernyshevsky sought not only to realign the relationship between art and reality but to assign a new function to art that would be compatible with the radical intelligentsia's philosophical and political program.

Chernyshevsky asserted the primacy of reality over the aesthetic; he identified beauty with reality itself—in his immortal dictum, "beauty is life."[8] The conjecture that beauty can be equated with life posed a paradox: how could one account for works of art that portray sublime, otherworldly things and places that had little mirror in reality and that would exhaust any politico-economic system that attempted to realize such fantasies? Chernyshevsky's answer was both ingenious and audacious. Man's desire for a fantastic form of "perfection" was ultimately a perverted, aberrant desire, one formed by a mind and body lacking in robust health and confronted with a "stinting" reality.[9] He likens the situation to dreams, which he argued often compensated for real deficiencies: "Lying on bare boards, a man is sometimes given to dreaming of a luxurious bed, a bed made of some unheard-of precious wood, of an eiderdown quilt, of pillows bordered with Brabant lace, of a canopy made of wonderful Lyons silk; but will such dreams occur to a healthy-minded man who sleeps not on a luxurious, but on a sufficiently soft and comfortable bed? 'When you have sufficient you don't seek more.'"[10] Dreams were indices to a "stinting" reality that, by depriving the body of its sufficient needs, will give rise to such irrational fantasies. Chernyshevsky's ideas about dreaming anticipate both Freudian psychoanalysis (dreams as contorted expression of repressed desire) and Pavlovian psychology (the role of somatic conditions affecting nervous phenomena). "Dreaming whips up desire to fever heat only when wholesome, even though fairly simple, food is lacking," argues Chernyshevsky. "It is beyond doubt that the human organism does not need and cannot stand titanic desires and satisfactions."[11]

Dreaming thus operated as an important conceptual figure to explain how art, and in particular its fantastic representations of beauty, in fact pointed to a compromised reality. Implicit in Chernyshevsky's argument was the presumption of a "normal" standard of sufficient life, a healthy, robust mode of existence that would mitigate against the sickly and pallid psychosomatic conditions that gave rise to fantasy. Chernyshevsky juxtaposed the beauty of high society, a thin, idle, and lax girl bred from generations of inactivity, with the energetic, hale beauty of a peasant girl, one who bore "a very fresh complexion and rosy cheeks" borne out of a healthy amount of daily work coupled with hearty food.[12] Chernyshevsky's philosophical discussion of the aesthetic carried within its rhetoric an implicit and unmistakable place for the role of biopolitics; it becomes impossible to divorce discussion of a work of art (or a dream, for that matter) from considerations of the relative health and sanity of the mind/body that creates it. Questions about whether people have the basic necessities of life, including food, clothing, proper sleep, and so forth, inevitably touch upon political issues of social justice and material reproduction. While Chernyshevsky focuses upon the aesthetic, the dialectics of his argument necessarily involve political concerns.

Wang Ruoshui's figural rhetoric about the primacy of reality over dreams seemed to parallel Chernyshevsky's view that art was irrational, oneiric fantasy and that "life" itself was the source of all beauty. For Wang, reality did not simply stand above dreams; it outpaced them, frustrating any possibility that dreams could ever surpass reality. No longer was reality merely that which a realist like Mao Dun strived "with great effort to know." It did not sit passively, waiting to be probed, analyzed, and transformed by someone else. Rather, reality emerged as a powerful force in its own right, acting on its own behalf, uncovering and producing its own truth: "Reality corrects those dreams of desperation: in the past it was possible to use dreams to criticize reality, but now we should use reality to critique dreams. Reality has smashed those dreams that sought escape from the world: most of those dreamers have since woken up; otherwise, if they continue to abandon reality, they will find themselves forsaken in turn by reality."[13] "Reality" emerges as a terrifying angel of vengeance; Wang Ruoshui writes that whereas prior to Liberation dreaming was a way of escaping or sugarcoating reality, after Liberation, reality has returned to actively dispense with those dreams. However, according to Wang Ruoshui, this did not mean that dreaming was completely abandoned in socialism. Instead, the way one dreams has been radically altered by the new reality:

> Reality has taught us how we should dream. From now on we will never again have those blurry dreams, those empty dreams, those fearful dreams; we now will have rational dreams, Five Year Plan dreams, socialist and Communist dreams. Beautiful reality will not bring an end to rational dreams; instead, it will give those dreams' potential for realization a wide pathway. . . . An unbridgeable chasm between dream and reality already does not exist anymore. Our eyes have seen the great Soviet Union; their reality is precisely our dream. This fills our hearts with conviction: dreams can be transformed into reality.[14]

Reality did not kill dreaming per se but tethered it to "rationality" and meticulously laid-out schemes of economic development. Moreover, these post-Liberation dreams were "rational" and "realizable" because they had concrete backing: the "reality" of the Soviet Union. Dreams and reality were bridgeable because there was fundamentally no chasm between them except for that of time and a mere geographic border. The "dream" world was, after all, just next door. If, in the time of *Eastern Miscellany*'s special 1933 New Year's issue, dreams were a plea of desperation and hope in response to a reality that seemed on the verge of collapsing, then in 1953 dreaming takes on a decidedly different tenor, one of a challenge or dare, probing reality's ability to respond. As Wang concluded:

> As we are in the very beginning of building our economy on a grand scale, these [aspirations] are still dreams, or half are dreams and half are reality. Our readers perhaps will have even more beautiful dreams than these.
>
> Those dreams will be surpassed by reality.
>
> We have great dreams, but we have an even greater reality.[15]

Wang Ruoshui's last lines resemble Chernyshevsky's epigraph. His use of Chernyshevsky via Zhou Yang's translation provides an interesting window to the intermingling of political and aesthetic philosophy. Rather than the commonplace about how art becomes rendered utilitarian under socialism, Wang Ruoshui's commentary suggests the reverse: his political discourse is one that is indelibly shaped by aesthetic thinking. There is a good reason for the transitive nature between politics and aesthetics. For both Chernyshevsky and Wang Ruoshui the common denominator is "reality," against which dreams, both aesthetic and personal, act as a sort of feedback loop informing us that reality needs to be made better. Political and aesthetic dreaming are thus indicators that reality has still yet to reach its potential "beauty." While Wang celebrated the invincibility of reality over all dreams, he still recognized the need for "rational" dreams to help spur the nation toward a more ideal reality. The relationship between dreams and reality was not one of mutual disavowal or negation but one of temporal transition. After all, the Soviet Union that was a "dream" to the Chinese was already a reality for the Soviets themselves.

In realizing the dreams of the past and bringing about a new reality, the Communists seemed to diminish the enchantment dreams once held over their subjects. Their space over the cultural imaginary was diminished as reality was imbued with revolutionary vitality.[16] Wang Ruoshui's commentary was as much a paean to the triumph of socialism as it was a farewell to dreaming. The rhetoric after liberation was one of profound ambivalence. While the dream had become reality, it was not quite there yet either. Socialism was paradoxically both present and deferred. Utopian desire was exploited in order to fuel the revolutionary momentum, but at the same time this desire had to be carefully managed so it did not turn into a counterrevolutionary deviation. Dreams posed the possibility of constituting a critique of the present: if people continued to imagine worlds other than the one they were presently in, were they not implying that the current reality was still "stinting"? While the contents of such dreams may be benign and merely beautiful, their form constituted an implied critique of repression, injustice, and want, a dark knowledge that was an unwelcome competitor to the slogans and affirmations of liberation.

If we move away from dream as a utopian rhetoric and turn our attention to the fate of dream as a psychological object of study, we will see a similar hesitance to deal with the subject. In the 1950s psychoanalysis, while having thrived in intellectual and aesthetic discourse during the Republican period, virtually disappeared in the socialist period. Psychoanalysis and virtually every other Western school, including Gestalt, behaviorism, and pragmatism, were lumped into the category of "idealist" psychology, regarded as patently inferior in light of the materialist orientation of Marxism-Leninism and Maoist philosophy. Psychology followed the Soviet model, deriving much inspiration from the theorist of conditional reflexes, Ivan Pavlov.[17] Psychological research was to be experimental and materialist in nature, not speculative and analytic, and it had to "serve the Chinese socialist construction."[18] Physiology and social psychology took precedence over speculative investigations of the unconscious. Freud, Jung, and other Western figures were denounced as "idealist," "subjective," and "bourgeois."[19] Moreover, following the Soviets' cue, Freudian psychoanalysis was viewed as the tool of American imperialists, for whom the concept of the unconscious was a way to keep the masses mired in mysticism and superstition.[20]

Aside from the scientific disdain for psychoanalytic theories, the popular press also tried to dispel superstition associated with dream phenomena. In a *People's Daily* article printed shortly before 1949, the origin of dreams was explained as a psychological response to a physiological stimulus. The article was signed, notably, by the "North Chinese People's Government Hygiene Bureau."[21] Both mental and bodily illness could induce dreams, and dreams in general were harmful to health. The authors instructed readers to avoid dreams altogether and gave practical tips on how to achieve such a state (e.g., not eating too much and using light blankets).

Ten years later, Fu Lianzhang, a vice-minister for public health, declared in the *People's Daily* that dreams, while common to all sleepers, were "essentially void and absurd, and have no real meaning."[22] He took aim at Freud as well as at traditional beliefs regarding dreams, in particular the practice of dream divination (*yuanmeng*). As dream divination often took place within the context of political governance, the criteria for such interpretation were therefore arbitrary, dependent upon the unequal hierarchy between lord and seer.

While Fu Lianzhang affirmed the materialist view of dreams as inherently devoid of significance, he did admit that "dreams perhaps reveal a person's true feelings. An individualist will dream about the realization of his own extravagant wishes [*shewang*], whereas a person who enthusiastically loves to work will dream of a sudden increase in production." Fu Lianzhang marked a contrast between the "individualist" whose dreams were merely fanciful, and the lover of labor whose dreams were purely within the realm of rational production. One dreamer was selfish, the other dreamed of the greater socialist good.

It is most likely not accidental that the rhetoric of the "dream fulfilled" as heralded by the socialist revolution, and the rise of a materialist, Soviet-inspired explanation of dream phenomena, coincided. Both approaches ultimately tried to lay dream discourse to rest. Socialist psychology was foremost concerned about how to foster a new kind of subjectivity appropriate to the socialist state, how to mold the nation's citizens into responsible and enthusiastic subjects. Psychologists were primarily focused on educational psychology and emphasized the importance of researching the psychic and social development of children. The role of materialist psychology was to make its subjects conscious of their existence not as private individuals but as actors within history, contributing to the collective construction of the new socialist society.

The relegation of dream discourse to "superstition" or, more damningly, "absurdity" (*huangmiu*) reveals not only the empirical thrust of socialist scientism but also the dominance of official discourses over forms of signification at odds with collectivized semiotic authority. Of course, this did not come out of the blue; May Fourth scholars of psychology were also engaged in filtering out superstitious beliefs from new insights into the psyche. But socialist ideology inaugurated a regime of semiotic normativity, whereby speculative hermeneutics of alterity, such as dream interpretation, whether traditional or modernist, were deemed as being utterly devoid of meaning, "absurd." The Freudian method was rejected because of its clear connections to American imperialist false consciousness. But on a more fundamental level, the Communists simply followed a very different model of the relationship between individual and collective. They rejected the notion of a private unconscious that expressed its latent thoughts and desires in oneiric code. Instead, they subscribed to a much more porous paradigm that saw the individual as being in constant relation with the social world around him; this model promoted a notion of "spirit" (*jingshen*) over the unconscious as the preferred trope for describing the mind.[23] Fu Lianzhang's demarcation between the narcissistic and altruistic dreamers essentially demonstrated the divide between a person ruled by his unconscious and one who was attuned to revolutionary spirit.

The semiotic itself was recast as a form of collective production, along with agriculture and industry. Not only was cultural meaning to be collectively produced and distributed, so was the appropriate mass hermeneutic that could make proper sense of it. Dreams, as described by Republican-era writers and psychoanalysts, indulged in complex forms of meaning inaccessible to the great mass of barely literate readers. They upheld a model of mind that had to be rejected. Moreover, such opaque forms of signification threatened to conceal counterrevolutionary content.

SLEEPLESSNESS: THE CULTURAL LOGIC OF FAST SOCIALISM

By the end of the 1950s, the rhetoric of socialist transition proved too tame and gradualist for Chinese leaders (and, in particular, Mao) who sought to torpedo their way into first-world modernity through a contracted process of massive and superhuman transformation. Moreover, as tensions with the Soviet Union simmered throughout the 1950s, culminating toward a de facto Sino-Soviet split by 1960, China relied all the more on a voluntaristic rhetoric of the masses' self-sufficiency, unobstructed by a Thaw-era USSR. The cultural and literary forms that coalesce around this period aesthetically express what may be dubbed "fast socialism."[24]

Fast socialism rejected a temporal model of gradual transition into socialism; rather, it affirmed the need for a compressed period of productive accumulation to bring about the conditions for true socialism to flourish. Fast socialism acknowledged that this radical effort would be exhausting, but necessary so that normal life in socialism could emerge. Everyday life was thus mortgaged into the future, to be underwritten by extreme measures. The relative ease of the quotidian had to be replaced with an epic heroism that would bring about such necessary and radical change.

Literary texts of this period featured a chronotope that sought to realize the promises of fast socialism. Literary theorist Mikhail Bakhtin, who developed the concept of chronotope, argued that literary texts represent a universe that is governed by its own rules regarding space and time. Fictional characters exist and behave according to the conventions of the chronotope they inhabit, which may or may not bear resemblance to historic actuality.[25] The chronotope of fast socialism bore three features that are closely connected: temporal compression, pervasive illumination, and sleeplessness. The need for high productivity required the extraction of value in the most efficient way possible. Time could no longer be divided into a productive day spent in the workplace and a leisurely evening spent at home. Instead, time was compressed such that every hour provided maximum opportunity for production. During the Great Leap Forward the time that would have been spent at home virtually disappeared as People's Communes and mass canteens effectively erased the boundaries between public and private. Night was marshaled as equally productive terrain, and the night shift (*yeban*) capitalized on the opportunity to extract value from what would have been a time of rest.

Accompanying this temporal compression whereby night was reclaimed by the day is the pervasive presence of light, in both its literal and figural meanings. Night shifts could not be feasible without appropriate illumination. The rural electrification movement typified this ideal of bringing light into darkness. Physical illumination had obvious symbolic meanings as well; as the populace colonized the night through the help of technology, they also dispelled forms of epistemic darkness and superstition that held them back. The Chinese thus reached toward the light, whereas the imperialist world was held back by its own capitalist darkness.

Temporal compression and constant illumination could not help but have their effect on the body. Humans subjected to unrelenting production and unremitting light often had no choice but to forego sleep or else radically reorganize it in order to meet politico-economic imperatives. Literature of this time either depicted heroic figures who persevere against sleep or refrained from describing sleep at all, leaving it as an unspoken lacuna in the narrative. As such, literature of the period rarely touched upon the topic of dreams.[26]

The question of how time and space were experienced by the Chinese masses and represented in aesthetic production in the late 1950s and early 1960s tells us a lot about the intensity of the state's extraction of value in its attempt to rapidly construct a socialist infrastructure. Whether, how, and when people sleep during this period was symptomatic of how time was reorganized to meet the politico-economic imperatives of the moment. The radical changes the Communists introduced, and their catastrophic results, seem to us now in the present to be absurd and inhumane. However, one must bear in mind how many saw the initiatives of the Great Leap not as voluntaristic hallucination but as absolutely necessary in order to bring about a socialist modernity that was independent of both the USSR and the United States. Nevertheless, for a regime that prized dialectical materialism as a guiding epistemology, it is troubling that many could not see the worth of night as an important check upon the day. While they endorsed the dialectics of permanent revolution, they shut themselves off from the important insights that the dialectics of night, dreams, and personal life could provide. Although bathed in the proper ideological illumination, the Communists nevertheless seemed blind to the question of whether the Chinese masses themselves could weather such a relentless drive for maximum productivity in their quest to build socialism out of virtually nothing.

Literature in the socialist period had an explicit social purpose; it was supposed to aid the political transformation, to educate and enlighten the populace, a "cog and screw," to borrow Lenin's oft-abused phrase, in the socialist machinery.[27] Literature, as the most exemplary form of collective semiotic production, was a uniquely social public works project, following Mao's famous dictum that "revolutionary literature and art should create a variety of characters out of real life and help the masses to propel history forward."[28] The Chinese were inspired by the model of Soviet socialist realism in literature and the arts, producing their own works celebrating the heroic travails of model workers, peasants, and revolutionary warriors.

While socialist realism is often lampooned for its patently unrealistic depictions of enthusiastic masses, it was certainly no disavowal of earlier, critical realism. Rather, socialist realists saw themselves as the inheritors of the realist tradition who bore even deeper insight into the nature of reality and, more fundamentally, its potential transformation. As a leading scholar of Soviet literature noted, socialist realism exhibits a "modal schizophrenia," the oscillation between the worlds of "what is" and "what ought to be."[29] Critical realism had only addressed reality in a static fashion, stuck in its baneful reflection of social injustice. Socialist realism revealed the progressive ferment underneath seemingly still appearances and could show how utopian aspirations were thus imminent within present reality. The mode of "Revolutionary Realism plus Revolutionary Romanticism" (geming xianshizhuyi yu geming langmanzhuyi), which rose to prominence during the Great Leap period, sought to extend socialist realism even further. It arose as a response to debates among Communist intellectuals about the extent to which it was possible or necessary to address the darker aspects of life and society through socialist realism and whether such exposés compromised the ideological purpose of literature.[30] It responded to politico-economic imperatives to bring about socialist transformation even faster and was called upon to model an even more dynamic reality on the imminent threshold of socialist apotheosis.

Much has been written about the propagandistic nature of socialist-era writing, and most of this scholarship has concluded that such literature, whether of the socialist realist variety or Revolutionary Realism plus Revolutionary Romanticism, constituted nothing more than utopian fantasia. While this literature was produced under certain political imperatives, many writers and critics who engaged in the formation of socialist literature believed that they were producing a literature that could both reflect and model a new reality of rapid transformation and infinite possibility. As author Wang Wenshi noted, literature of this style needed to depict the "nonstop transformations [*buduan tuibian*] in the struggle for life."[31] As conventional, formulaic, and even simplistic as the chronotope of fast socialism seemed to appear, there was a genuine wish that a world of unrelenting effort and heroic self-sacrifice would both reflect and model historic actuality. The formal transformations of this literature, however dubious they may seem, corresponded to a political aspiration that reality be far more dynamic and mobile than previously thought. A critical realism that sought to relegate utopian desires into their legitimate form as dreams or reveries was now supplanted by a new, dynamic realism that could illuminate the links between present and future. If dreams within critical realism preserve the separation of history from utopia, socialist-era realism sought to show how history would directly unfold into such utopia. Socialist literature thus promoted a form of realism where the bar between dream and reality had been removed, and where dream became life. As such, the presence of dreams as an autonomous entity becomes redundant, and their own borders dissolve within the narrative.

While "Revolutionary Realism plus Revolutionary Romanticism" obscured the catastrophes of the Great Leap period, it sought to capture a zeitgeist of radical transformation. As such, it featured a chronotope that was quite appropriate to its historic context: a world where the productive day continued at all times, where every space seemed illuminated, and where people took on a superhuman effort to transform themselves and their nation. Even "Revolutionary Realism plus Revolutionary Romanticism," socialist realism's wayward offspring, was not so much a "mask" over reality as it sought to capture a novel, if ultimately tragic, understanding of reality and its radical possibilities. The mode bespoke a hope that reality itself could be fashioned with the integrated perfection and wholeness that one would demand from a literary text. Enthusiastic illumination and mournful blindness featured in comparable measure.

In relation to the ideology of the patently visible against the murky phantasms of shadows, it is worthwhile to note the dominance of the motif of light, lamps, and electricity in the 1950s and early 1960s, one that surely helped precipitate the full-blown cult of Mao as the "bright red sun" during the Cultural Revolution.[32] But what is left unmentioned is the opportunity cost of ever-increasing light: night. When everything is illuminated, nothing is hidden. A poem from 1957 extols the image of children reveling in the street while holding festive lamps. The author equates the light with their happiness:

> But as for the children,
> In their hands there are lamps,
> On the crown of their heads there are lamps,
> In their hearts there are lamps,
> Even in the land of sleep,
> The sunlight of Communism nurtures their dreams.[33]

It is hard to imagine how these children can even fall asleep when they have been figuratively transformed into human torches.[34]

In contrast to this celebration of light, political discourse in the Chinese 1950s and 1960s often used dream discourse to pejoratively denigrate foreign and internal rivals, including the Dalai Lama, John F. Kennedy, and Liu Shaoqi. An instructive example is that of John Foster Dulles, secretary of state to President Eisenhower. In response to Dulles's anti-communist policy of diplomatic isolation in regards to the PRC, the *People's Daily* called Dulles's fantasy of politically containing China a "dream" and "daydream."[35] This was fitting for a country that Chinese psychologists considered the "second homeland" of Freud and his ilk.[36] Two years later, a poem appeared in the March 1959 issue of *People's Literature* titled "Dulles' Dream Ravings" (Dulesi de mengyi). During this time Dulles was terminally ill with cancer and died only two months after the poem's publication. The poem opens uncharitably with an image of Dulles in his sickbed:

> The dim light
> Emanating from the dark green edge of the lampshade,
> Shines upon Dulles' sickbed.
> . . . .
> Only Dulles' groans can be heard,
> In this exquisite desolation and loneliness.
> The night is deep,
> And the capitalist world is stuck in deep winter.
> Dulles has fallen sick.
> . . . .
> His troubles, like a viper,
> Grab hold of his heart,
> Often had he thought of swallowing the world in one gulp.
> But it was of course only a dream![37]

While Dulles bitterly approaches his demise, China is luxuriating in a verdant spring, the "sun as usual rising in the East." The difference between socialism and capitalism was as clear as the difference between day and night, between glorious sunlight and dark, sickly hallucination. Furthermore, this rhetoric heralded the triumph of socialist knowledge against bourgeois fantasy and speculation, the victory of one hermeneutic, one way of reading the world, over another. Socialists relied on the incontrovertible truth of dialectical materialism; imperialists, however, used dreams to dupe not only the working class but themselves as well.

It is clear that light functioned as a central trope that lay at the heart of an ideological fantasy central to the Mao era. Fantasy is often seen as the opposite of knowledge; however, thinkers such as Sigmund Freud, Octave Mannoni, and Slavoj Žižek have noted that fantasy is structured along the logic of the fetish. It involves the simultaneous holding of knowledge ("I know very well [that this is not true]") and non-knowledge ("but all the same [I will act as if I do not know]") in suspension.[38] Mannoni and Žižek elaborate on the structure of the fetish to describe how fantasy involves not a rejection of knowledge in favor of illusion but actively involves the delicate interplay between knowledge and its opposite. Fantasy is not pure illusion;

what accounts for its effectiveness, for its active structuring of our relation to reality, is precisely how it affirms our rational discrimination *at the same time* it extends our phantasmatic desire indefinitely.

The Maoist desire for correct knowledge in itself took the form of an ideological fantasy. Whereas Žižek and Mannoni point out how ideological fantasy engages both knowledge and non-knowledge in suspension, a certain Maoist "epistemic fantasy" installed knowledge itself as the very phantasmatic object. This special knowledge, in the very act of demystifying bourgeois ideology and feudal superstition, inaugurated its own fantasy of what such knowledge could conjure within socialist society. The process by which Maoist knowledge simultaneously demystified false consciousness while installing its own ideological fantasy finds its symbolic manifestation in the trope of light: light is that which illuminates and renders visible the truth, but it is also that which sweeps away and overpowers competing dark forms of knowledge. This fantasy of the "light of knowledge" bespoke the capability of humans to radically transfigure their world and the hope that knowledge could transform, via its proper application, into an illuminated, new reality. Light as trope thus united both theory and practice; on one hand it constituted the insight of correct theory, and on the other it illuminated a transfigured reality made possible only through the correct application of said theory. However, the enthusiasm with which Maoist discourse negated false forms of non-knowledge (dreams, fantasies, hallucinations, and such) seemed to veil over the possibility that Maoist knowledge could itself be negated. The lingering realization that must be continually disavowed is that knowledge, however correct, may not be able to guarantee its effectiveness in transfiguring the world. The tropological transformation of Maoist knowledge into the visual metaphor of light made it an attractive ideological object; on the other hand, this symbolization rendered knowledge from a dialectical process to a reified, binary fantasy of illumination versus darkness. Octave Mannoni's formulation can perhaps be revised to better fit the Mao era: "I know I do not know, but all the same I will act as if I do."

Fan Yanqiao (1894–1967) devotes an essay to the topic of artificial light in a 1962 issue of *People's Literature* (Renmin wenxue), telling the story of rural electrification by way of discussing an old village woman made ecstatic by the new arrival of light bulbs.[39] "Our village now has electric lights," he reports the old woman as saying. "I've lived over seventy years now, but even in my dreams I could not have dreamed of such a happy occasion."[40] In a remarkably meticulous manner Fan Yanqiao goes on to trace the evolution of artificial light throughout history, remarking how Mao was able to craft powerful essays even in substandard lamplight:

> Just like the never-ending evolution of human tools from pottery to bronze, and then to magnets and tin, the form of artificial light has also gone through many changes. The use of vegetable oil, soybean oil, peanut oil, cottonseed oil and hempseed oil [for lamps] over thousands of years have seemed like a single day. Kerosene lamps, gaslight and electric lights followed monopoly capitalism's entry into China. With the new always outstripping the old, not even the lamp can avoid this law, and those things that fall behind will be weeded out. However in that sacred land of revolution—Yan'an—our great revolutionary leader, under the light of a hempseed lamp, wrote majestic essays. Even though the light was dim, his words shone brightly for thousands of yards, illuminating the great land. . . . Today, under even brighter electric lights, what kind of things can we now write? This is worth deep reflection.[41]

Fan Yanqiao applies the materialist laws of history to the evolution of lamps and light bulbs throughout the ages, each new form of lighting replacing the previous one, and identifies electric light with the arrival of capitalist modernity. However, he indulges in a form of catachresis when discussing how Mao's revolutionary writings shine even brighter than his hempseed oil lamp. On one hand, he is endorsing the common evolutionary discourse of modernity, the obsolete making way for the new. However, Mao's use of a hempseed oil lamp signals a revolutionary leap over the usual laws of development; although the revolutionary leader is in a country backwater far, far away from the city, with not even a proper lamp at his disposal, it is precisely here that he produces his transcendent knowledge, one that pushes the peasantry into the forefront of revolution and brings him to the capital. In this sense the ideological and figural importance of enlightenment always outstrips light as physical phenomenon. Rural electrification had double implications; on a literal level it allowed people to produce and work uninhibited by nightfall (something that would be of great importance during the Great Leap Forward), but on an ideological level it drove away the darkness of ignorance, superstition, and false consciousness. The progress in the technology of artificial light promises, as the author suggests, an even greater advance in ideological insight. Moreover, electric light has won a significant battle against the wavering unreliability of nature:

"In helping us read and write, the lamp and the sun serve the same function, but the sun's power is occasionally weak while the lamp is affected by neither darkness, wind or rain, and even in darkness can shine brightly . . . the lamp will always be our greatest companion [*zhiji*]."[42] Light has contributed to collective happiness, and Fan Yanqiao ends his essay by describing a joyous New Year's banquet in the capital: "There was a banquet inside the Great Hall of the People, and the festive lanterns, numerous as a canopy of stars, bright as moons, illuminated the old and young as they toasted each other. As I told this old lady from the village, this is truly what cannot be dreamed of. Light, in the new China, is happiness; people under the light of today are far happier."[43] Again, the author easily equates the evolution of artificial light with themes of spiritual and social illumination, of how material modernity is always already its own figure. The most important advance is neither light nor electricity but Maoist knowledge. The essay itself, by beginning in the countryside and then ending in Beijing's Great Hall of the People, formally demonstrates the dynamism of the Maoist ideological ether, galvanizing the country and triumphantly zooming into the center of power. Under the guise of celebrating the forward march of lighting, Fan is in fact writing a joyous panegyric to the liberating power of socialist ideology over forms of epistemic darkness.

The loaded combination of temporal compression and pervasive illumination manifested themselves as a de facto "sunshine policy" in Chinese texts of this period. Characters are so engaged in building socialism that they often fail to sleep, and when they do sleep, only rarely do they dream. Sleeplessness, insomnia, and "all-nighters" at the cooperative constitute a common motif in this literature. The goal was to represent a world in the midst of transfiguration, a country suddenly illuminated to reveal its hidden reserves of energy and abundance. The light of knowledge finds its practical application in the wholesale transformation of the material world. Theory and ontology were inseparable; the material transfiguration of reality is only made possible when guided by the light of theory. A brief examination of three stories from this period—Wang Wenshi's (1921–99) "Night of the Snowstorm" (Fengxue zhi ye, 1956), his "Summer Night" (Xia ye, 1960), and Li Zhun's (1928–2000) "The Story of Li Shuangshuang" (Li Shuangshuang xiaozhuan, 1959)—will illustrate how literature of the late 1950s and early 1960s demonstrated this peculiar chronotope of total, constant, exhausting production.

In "Night of the Snowstorm," a group of village party leaders, guided by the township and district Communist Party secretaries, spend all night hammering out production quotas for the coming year on New Year's Eve.[44] The hero of the story, the district secretary Yan Keqin, is an indefatigable political leader traveling from village to village in order to promote higher productivity. His inexhaustible drive to work both intimidates and inspires the local villagers, who are prone to a more leisurely existence. But the seemingly inexhaustible gap between him and the more prosaic locals is bridged by Keqin's protégé, Yang Mingyuan, the township secretary. Through an intense period of personal tutelage by Keqin, Mingyuan has raised himself to comparable heroism.

The narrator, a colleague of Mingyuan and Keqin, notes how neither has slept much. In fact, they have the locals rouse the village leaders from their beds during a snowy night so they can hold this important meeting. Mingyuan and the villagers observe that Keqin has not visited his wife, a worker in the county hospital, for over two weeks, and what ensues are jokes about how long men can last without engaging in conjugal relations. Keqin ribs his protégé Mingyuan:

> "I am certainly not like you, a person who would fall ill if he goes half a month without visiting home [and seeing one's wife]!"
>
> Mingyuan guffawed, and retorted, "Now that's just slander! Old Wang [the narrator, a local official], say a word in my defense!"
>
> I said to the district secretary, "Perhaps you dropped by the clinic beforehand to 'sign in' [*guahao*]."
>
> The district secretary laughed, "No. I applied for a leave of absence from my leave of absence [*qingle ge jiaqi de jia*]!"
>
> We all laughed. The district secretary feigned seriousness: "Don't laugh! This is a matter of family discipline!"[45]

The joke about whether it is possible to persist in work without indulging in domestic pleasures reaches its height when Keqin argues that he has, in essence, taken a vacation not from work but from spending time with his wife. The narrator euphemistically refers to sex as "signing in," thus suggesting that sex is in fact "work." "Work" and "play" are thus ingeniously reversed, and desire is turned inside out, having effectively been kicked out of the bedroom and into the workplace. In addition to foregoing sex, Keqin suggests that the villagers engage in night shifts to keep productivity high.[46] Such sacrifices are necessary because, in Keqin's words, "socialism is arriving so fast [*shehuizhuyi lai de zheme kuai*] that our actions and attitudes must also speed up and become more alert—if we miss just a small step, we'll be left behind."[47] The temporal compression of socialism's imminent arrival necessitates deferring the joys of home life to another time.

The central task of the meeting is to determine the production quota for the next year. The village has ordinarily produced an average of 290 catties of wheat per *mu* (roughly one-sixth of an acre). The villagers agree, after much back and forth, to try to push the quota to 360 catties, but Keqin finally suggests that they push it even further up to 420. The villagers are aghast and incredulous at the proposal, but Keqin, who already has a ready knowledge of the specific conditions of the village's farm conditions, walks them through a series of calculations, taking account of each possible efficiency saving. The villagers finally arrive at a calculation of 410 as an average yield in the most optimal conditions. Disappointed that they seem to be missing 10 catties from Keqin's proposed estimate, they run through the calculations one more time and come up with the same result. However, at this point, Wang Zhenjia, a local village leader who had once been skeptical of Keqin's ambitious proposals, is so persuaded by Keqin's mathematical acumen that he seems like someone "who had just awoke from a dream."[48] He is confident that 420 will indeed be possible: "It is not a problem. For what kind of folks are we? We're folks who are 'walking the road of socialism.' As long as we push ourselves a little further, we'll figure out ways here and there to find more. Just ten catties of wheat is no big deal!"[49]

The crux of this story is, essentially, a math problem. How does a village move from 290 catties of wheat per *mu* to 420? After every rational calculation, they can only come up with 410. The remaining 10 are left up to the villagers' collective faith in socialism, and it constitutes an expression of their voluntaristic zeal. The 10 catties thus suggest the moment when rational knowledge slips into fantasy. But knowledge is not negated; after all, it was only through meticulous calculation that they raised their quota to 410. But the extra 10 symbolize the power of political faith to supplement ratiocination.

Even so, it is clear that these 10 catties must somehow be reckoned for. The story already suggests that this is possible ultimately through the sheer reinvention of everyday life: night will collapse into day, sleep into wakefulness, and home into work. Only through the complete inversion of everyday life can these 10 catties be extracted. Yan Keqin, the district secretary, is a revolutionary type (*dianxing*); he is meant to model optimal behavior and comportment, to be a flesh-and-blood incarnation of an ideological ideal. And yet the story suggests that the collapse of everyday life necessitated by fast socialism is precipitating a collapse in Keqin's own body. After the meeting has concluded, the villagers insist that Keqin take a nap: "His eyes had become bloodshot, surrounded by black rings, and his eyelids were heavy. They urged him to take a rest."[50] However, he only lets his eyes close for a moment before he bolts out of bed, his shoes still on, and trudges through a snowy morning to make his way to another meeting in another town.

While this story appeared two years before the beginning of the Great Leap Forward, it is uncanny how this story already anticipated the monumental, and ultimately cataclysmic, changes that would occur in the Great Leap's wake. It presages the collapse of the diurnal cycle in order to welcome the arrival of fast socialism. The story also epitomizes how knowledge and fantasy comingle in order to promote faith in socialism's promises. Moreover, when read against the grain, the story seems to reveal its own ambivalence about the toll such sacrifice will take and seemingly presages the heavy cost the masses would come to bear.

Li Zhun's "The Story of Li Shuangshuang" narrates the positive effect of the Great Leap Forward on a modestly educated but underappreciated peasant wife.[51] Sun village is mobilizing its citizens for a great collective project, the creation of a water channel leading from an uphill reservoir to the village.[52] Shuangshuang, itching to lend her efforts to the task, is dissuaded by her boorish husband. After a long evening of arguing with him, Shuangshuang finds herself awake and alone in her house. Outside the window she discovers the bright flicker of lamps wielded by jovial workers on their way to the night shift. "Outside the Great Leap has turned the night-sky red," she thinks to herself. "How can I let these household duties entrap me forever?"[53] She converses with a female neighbor, both of them professing their inability to sleep amid all the excitement, as the work is progressing nearer toward their neck of the woods. Concerned that there is not yet a communal mess hall to feed the workers, Shuangshuang and her friend forthwith head to the village secretary to propose an idea to build such a hall. Encouraged by the village secretary's wife to put up large announcements (*dazibao*) proposing the idea, Shuangshuang returns home to find her husband fast asleep and then spends the rest of the evening, until "the east was bright," writing her announcements. Toward the end of the story, just as night becomes day, her domestic household is turned inside out and traditional roles are reversed, as she manages construction and operation of the new mess hall, and her husband is employed as the noodle maker.

The radical reversal of gender roles in "The Story of Li Shuangshuang" runs alongside the other reversals we see in the story: the illumination of night, the abolition of private kitchens, and the dismantling of kinship ties that obstruct maximum collective productivity. While the story has been noted for its positive portrayal of women, it is clear that its ostensible advocacy for the status of women is directly tied to the wholesale transformation of Chinese society. The gender iconoclasm embodied in the character of Shuangshuang is perhaps more of an index to the political and economic extremism of the period than a promotion of feminist ideals.

Nevertheless, even if the rosy depiction of a woman's emancipation seems a little far-fetched, the story makes an implicit connection between ideological illumination and the visibility of women's domestic sphere and plight. By bringing the Great Leap's light into the home, private and domestic space (*nei*) is illuminated and made available to public view. Rather than remaining obscured and oppressed in the shadows of home life, Shuangshuang breaks out into the public sphere, visible to all. As the story notes, even her own proper name, and not her usual moniker as "Xiwang's wife," "leaps out" into view as a result of her heroic activities.[54] By aligning herself with the Great Leap's figurative illumination, Shuangshuang almost singlehandedly brings womanhood out of the obscurity and darkness of *yin* and into the realm of *yang*. As a result, the domestic sphere is itself turned inside out and forever transformed.

Another story detailing the collapse of day and night during the Great Leap Forward is Wang Wenshi's "Summer Night." While published right after the Great Leap, its focus on nighttime mechanized agricultural production suggests that it was composed in concert with other Great Leap texts that glorified accelerated production. Again, as with the other stories, the diurnal cycle, along with gender roles, is reversed. The main character is a skilled female tractor driver, Yunyun, assigned to the neighboring village to work the late-night shift (*yeban*), sleeping during the morning so she can plow under moonlight and lamps. Harassed by a playful laborer, Shuhong, who joy rides her tractor, she complains to the widow of a house in which she takes her morning sleep. She does not realize that the widow is Shuhong's mother, and she also fails to realize that both her father and his father worked together in the Communist underground before Liberation and that she and Shuhong were once childhood playmates. The first time she takes her sleep at the house, she enters a dream that is not quite a dream:

> It seemed like a dream, yet was not really a dream either. Yunyun hazily heard someone's footsteps treading lightly in her room, quietly closing the window slats and shutting off the sun's rays shining westwards, softly placing something besides her pillow, and quietly stepping out and bringing the doors to a close, after which from the courtyard could be heard some halting words: ". . . Mother . . . you should . . ." In reply she heard Auntie say "Don't worry and go ahead now." Several hours later, Yunyun awoke, and the few rays that seeped through into her room had dimmed. She opened a window and saw the setting sun immediately flood the room. Looking about the room, she discovered that by her pillow had been placed a large cattail leaf fan, and on the little stool was a washbasin to clean her face.[55]

In addition to the fan and washbasin, she discovers slices of cucumber to quench her thirst, as well as a note informing her that the gifts were from the village youth Communist league and meant as a token of appreciation for their "comrade engaged in mechanizing agricultural labor." Just as night has been artificially transformed into day through the magic of electric lamps, so must day be artificially turned into night by blocking out the sun's rays so that Yunyun can fall asleep. However, Yunyun does not really dream at all but merely perceives her surroundings through her flagging consciousness. When she does sleep, nothing happens, an absence marked by the narrative's ellipsis ("Several hours later, Yunyun awoke"); her mind shuts off, and both brain and body get the necessary rest needed so that she can be refreshed to work the next shift. Her fellow tractor-driving sister-in-arms tells her, "You must sleep your fill, otherwise you'll have no energy for the night shift."[56] This skilled laborer, bringing the wonders of mechanization to the village, is herself an automaton that needs sufficient periods of downtime.

The ambiguous use of oneiric rhetoric here, the dream which is not a dream, seems to evoke a sort of subtle sexual desire in the form of Shuhong, who spirits himself into the bedroom like a specter, quietly and softly placing his gifts in the room, even suggestively stepping right near her pillow, and then leaving. The language of dreams thus acts as a romantic foreshadow, hinting at the eventual union of the two lovers, a fate predestined by their fathers' close comradeship a generation earlier. However, all libidinal energies are eventually diverted toward the collective labor, not romance. When Yunyun and Shuhong in the end coalesce and initiate a proper courtship during an evening party, the two slip away from the festivities to work the night shift together, Yunyun acting as tractor instructor to Shuhong.

At the very end of "Summer Night," we see Yunyun and Shuhong head to their tractor together, bathed in the moonlight that illuminates the fields and riverbank along which they will be working. In this last scene we see the symbolic consummation of the aesthetic transformations the Great Leap Forward wrought. Night is associated with light rather than darkness, with work and awakening rather than sleep and rest. Work is associated here with a skilled woman who will tutor her male protégé in the skill of tractor driving. Yunyun and Shuhong will become lovers, and thus the boundaries between work and intimate life are dissolved. As the moonlight paints the scenery in a luminescent, picturesque glow, work is linked not only to intimate life but to aesthetic beauty as well. Yunyun and Shuhong are born of revolutionary comrades who died in their struggle for Liberation; hence their union, along with all the diurnal and gender transformations it entails, will act as an apotheosis to the struggle of the dead generations.

The story's quaint end does seem saccharine. But there is a genuine beauty and simplicity to the story, even with all the talk about tractors and night shifts. The story's charm lies, in many ways, in its exalted banality—an ordinary couple that finds love in the midst of work. However, the alluring "ordinariness" of the story's ending cannot hide the fact that while the beauty it expresses is banal, the social transformations to which the story gives witness were dramatic, radical, and destructive. Beneath a "simple" love story is another more complicated and violent narrative of a drastic transformation of time, space, and home. Night was eradicated, homes were turned into communes, and the country more or less transformed into one massive factory that operated incessantly, at all hours of day *and* night. The Communists sought to rationalize and control time and, after having brought it under their dominion, to extract as much value from it as possible. This transformation had visceral effects upon the bodies of those working in China, whether they were farmers, industrial workers, or writers. In this frenzy of accumulation, personal time was set aside for the greater collective project, and while some (like Yunyun) managed to rearrange their sleep schedules to meet the new demands of the night shift, others (like Yan Keqin) seemed to have done away with sleep altogether. Alas, the darkness that night brings, along with its space for dreams and personal reflection, had itself been swept away through electrification. Life had become a dream, and dream had become life.

As is self-evident, the negation of darkness and, in certain instances, of night itself was not for the sole purpose of extending working hours. A field illuminated by lamps was also saturated by ideology. Light drove away forms of epistemic darkness so as to preserve correct forms of knowledge. However, by banishing these forms of dark knowledge, Maoist rhetoric immunized itself from potential critique about the viability of its epistemic fantasies. In Freud's account of fetishism, the "fact" of women's castration is both disavowed and acknowledged through the installation of the fetish object.[57] Later theorists have moved away from the emphasis on the missing phallus and have instead emphasized how the fetish structure covers over (but does not replace) a constitutive "lack" that must be overcome in order for one to assert a discrete subjectivity. One wonders whether the treatment of knowledge in the Maoist era followed a similar dynamic. In strongly denouncing the vacuity of false delusions, bourgeois ideologies, and feudal superstition, did Maoist knowledge in some way cover over the risk of its own opacity, its own impotence to transfigure reality? In its celebration of complete illumination, did Maoist knowledge obscure murky doubts lingering in its own dark corners? The power of light to overwhelm, and thus disavow, any traces of darkness seems to cover over a constitutive lack within the structure of knowledge itself; no matter how correct, there is always a risk that knowledge may not translate into effective practice. The catastrophic results of the Great Leap Forward and other Mao-era projects seem to stand as confirmation of this skepticism.

TOUCHED BY A BOLSHEVIK: THE NOSTALGIC ADDRESS OF THE REVOLUTIONARY PAST

Yang Mo's (1914–95) novel *The Song of Youth* (Qingchun zhi ge, 1958), about a young woman's transformation from naive, earnest schoolteacher to emboldened and heroic Communist activist in the early 1930s, provides both a counterpoint and foreshadow to more contemporary tales of socialist construction.[58] Because the novel deals with a period prior to the revolution, it can and does display a certain stylistic nostalgia, and features more introspection and personal reflection than a contemporary panegyric to the countryside.[59] Unlike contemporary stories about the glories of collective agriculture, this tale instead indulges in the dark world of wicked Nationalist agents, feudal landlords, and the decadent bourgeoisie. The novel is a form of feminine bildungsroman that bears strong resemblances to women's literature of the Republican era, one that stresses the political evolution and development of its heroine, Lin Daojing.[60] Moreover, Daojing's tale is also a narrative of working through trauma and finding psychic recuperation through the agency of the underground Communist Party. The model of "traumatized consciousness" is itself a retrospective throwback to a Republican-era, Freudian-inspired account of mind. As Daojing's revolutionary consciousness strengthens and matures, we also witness the replacement of a Republican-era model of mind with a socialist one.

There is only one major dream scene in this novel of over six hundred pages, but it is a significant one. Trapped in an unhappy union with Yu Yongze, a Peking University literature student and petty-bourgeois dandy, Daojing is charmed and inspired by Lu Jiachuan, a masculine and robust Communist who begins to teach her the tenets of the Communist creed and encourages her to tackle a vast list of books on dialectical materialism. Laying besides an aesthete for whom she has long stopped feeling affection, she dreams of the true object of her desire: "That night she had a strange dream. Under a dark, murky sky she paddled a small boat, floating about on a sea buffeted by foamy waves reaching up to the sky. The wind, rain and black clouds were all pressing against this small boat, pushing it down. She was afraid, very afraid. She was all alone in this frightful sea, all alone!"[61] As she battles against the torrential elements, a man suddenly appears in the boat bearing an uncanny resemblance to someone she has met before. He softly smiles at her, eliciting her annoyance and frustration. In anger and desperation she flings herself at his throat, only to discover up close the identity of the familiar stranger: "She let him go. The sky seemed to clear, and the waters turned azure. He sat silently opposite her, and the two fixed stares upon each other. Was he not Lu Jiachuan? Taken by surprise, she dropped her oar into the water, and Lu Jiachuan immediately plopped right into the water to fetch it. But then the black waters swallowed him whole, and the skies in an instant turned black. Crying, she let out a yell and cast herself into the water."[62] The description of the water and Daojing's tumultuous emotions are thickly saturated with desire, one that finally culminates in the materialization of her beloved Communist mentor. Their naked attraction for each other is evidenced by their fixed, mutual stare, and when Lu Jiachuan disappears into the ocean, Daojing immediately follows her beloved.

While the dream certainly expresses a conventional trope in both premodern and modern Chinese literature, the erotic encounter with a beloved, a significant ambiguity abides in their union. They both fall into the sea, a motif that looms large throughout the novel. The novel opens with Daojing looking upon the sea after leaving the train in northeastern Beidaihe, where she has arrived after escaping the clutches of an abusive stepmother and an arranged marriage back in Beijing. Not long before her escape, she learns the fate of her birth mother and grandfather, poor farmers in Jehol.[63] Her mother was raped and kidnaped by their landlord; her grief-stricken grandfather shortly drowned himself in a nearby river. Shortly after her birth, Daojing was seized by the landlord's wife and her mother driven out. Her mother also eventually flung herself into the river. While both her mother and grandfather drowned themselves, the sea is abundantly associated with the maternal figure. While in Manchuria, Daojing finds employment as a schoolteacher. She goes to the sea every morning and discovers a visceral maternal attraction to it: "She would always spend the whole day sitting on a giant rock that reached deep into the water. She was drawn to the sea as she was drawn to her beloved mother. Her melancholy eyes stared firmly into the waters, and from time to time she would hang her head and cry 'Mama!'"[64] As one critic points out, this moment is only one instantiation of "a subtheme of searching for the mother" in the novel.[65] This is not the only time that the sea is directly associated with a mother figure. At one point Daojing meets a beggar woman near the water who is so starved that she is unable to breastfeed her infant. Only a few days later she discovers that this woman, in hunger and desperation, has flung herself into the water, child in tow. Not long after Daojing is herself on the verge of the very same fate, having learned that her erstwhile trusted schoolmaster is trying to pawn her off to a rich man. Pleading to her long-dead mother for help, she dashes into an angry sea, saved in the nick of time by the man who would be her first love, the Peking University student Yu Yongze.[66] The heroine likens the entire tumultuous episode as a kind of "bad dream."

Freud brings up the "oceanic feeling" to describe the sensation of "something limitless, unbounded—as it were, 'oceanic'" that constitutes the "true source of religious sentiments."[67] Freud, however, insisted that he felt nowhere inside of him any inkling of this "oceanic feeling," although he accepted that others felt this sensation.[68] He insisted that such a need sprang from a childhood psychological source, the child's desire for "a father's protection."[69] While Freud locates the desire that underlies the "oceanic feeling," and religion in general, as essentially a desire for fatherly protection, he also mentions the undivided consciousness of the infant prior to ego-formation, and the union of mother and child.[70] Freud seeks to explain religious drives as fundamentally psychological in nature, deriving from childhood experiences. In analogous fashion, the sea in *The Song of Youth* also has a very powerful association with childhood and, quite particularly, the maternal, characterized as a natural force that draws the heroine ever closer, even to her own oblivion.

The trauma of an absent mother haunts Daojing, most significantly in her dream. Motivating her deep desire to become an activist on behalf of the Party is her overriding feeling of being an orphan. Daojing's nocturnal vision of the sea is not the only instance where mothers and dreams are drawn together. In the last half of the novel, Daojing returns to Beijing after another stint teaching school in the countryside in order to evade the authorities. Having spent all night shortly after arrival unsuccessfully trying to find lodging, she sleeps outside a Peking University dormitory where she had hoped to find a friend and a bed:

> Suddenly a weak sound, like falling rain, softly resounded in her ear:
>
> "Mom! Mommy . . ."
>
> She woke with a start, thinking she was dreaming. Rubbing her eyes, that weak sound continued to reverberate:
>
> "Mommy! Mommy! I want mommy! . . ." She then heard someone sniffling.
>
> Fully awake she realized what was happening: it was not a dream, but the faint sound came from nearby. She stood and went looking for its source. She finally discovered it: across the girls' dormitory, under the eaves of a store there lay two children leaning against each other, sleeping on the icy stone steps. Under the faint light of dawn, Daojing leaned forward and could make out who they were: two boys, the older about nine years old, the younger about six, their faces filthy, bodies frail, not a single rag on their naked bodies. The two seemed to be sleeping soundly, but the younger one's mouth was left hanging, catching his tears, and he continued to cry out for his mommy.[71]

What is remarkable about this scene is how the author describes the heroine's inability to ascertain where the cry is coming from, either from her unconscious or from some external source. The cry of "mommy" is at first a disembodied voice, belonging to no one and everyone at the same time; it is only after Daojing fully awakens that she recognizes its true source. What she had mistook as her own dream turns out in fact to be that of the poor child, hungry and cold. And yet for a moment the text indulges in the fantastic, and in some ways this is the most truthful and poignant point; the dream of "mommy" is a collective cry. Yang Mo's constant evocations of the mother figure "paradoxically express the author's deeply personal desire for an emotionally nurturing mother and a functional maternal model."[72] However strong the autobiographical coding may or may not be in the actual novel, what is undeniable is the strong maternal pull that seems to overwhelm consciousness itself. It seems, also, that the maternal is strongly associated with a certain collective unconscious, a psychic "spontaneity" that must be illuminated and resolved through narrative development. The constant cries of "mother" throughout the novel resemble a nervous tic that imposes itself upon the narrative and thereby obstructs its flow, an unconscious symptom whose etiology must be traced in order for it to be resolved.

A similar instance where mothers and dreams are linked occurs later when Daojing is arrested by Nationalist agents and subjected to vicious torture. Thrown into a dungeon with two other women, an older, more seasoned revolutionary and a young girl of sixteen rounded up as a suspected sympathizer, they lean on each other for moral support and spiritual survival. The torture is so brutal that Daojing is left in a "dreamlike" state, an effect of the violence against her body but also a psychic defense against the trauma inflicted on her. The younger girl, also subjected to torture, is traumatized to the point of speechlessness: "She was held by terror, and didn't speak a single world. All day she would lie on her wooden board and cry. At night, Daojing could hear her cry out fearfully in her dreams: 'Mommy! Mommy! I'm afraid, so afraid!'"[73] In order to survive, the three women act as a surrogate family, Daojing acting as a mother to the younger girl and the older revolutionary as mother to both.

The encounters with mother-surrogates are so frequent in this novel as to be obvious.[74] Where mothers are absent, the revolutionaries step in to fill the gap. Daojing, in a letter she writes to her revolutionary love, Lu Jiachuan (one that is never delivered because, unbeknownst to her, he has already died after a fantastically gory trial of torture), refers to the Party as "our great Mother."[75] However, what is also significant is how the theme of the lost mother informs the psychological trauma that afflicts not only Daojing but, collectively, nearly all of the revolutionaries and, allegorically, the nation as a whole. While this trauma spurs Daojing to action, it also causes her psychological pain and thus is something that must be eventually overcome. What Daojing needs is therapy, socialist-style. Daojing's transformation from vulnerable, naive intellectual to brave, heroic activist is as much a process of political development as it is a kind of therapy, one that helps her heal her broken psyche. This therapeutic aspect of socialism is common to socialist realist literature; such novels stage the hero's ritual transition from "spontaneity" (*stikhiinost'*), the visceral and unthinking reactive behavior of the oppressed protagonist, to "consciousness" (*soznatel'nost'*), the hero's deliberate and disciplined exercise of knowledge gained only through a proper understanding of political theory.[76] In Daojing's case it is not merely a matter of acquiring new knowledge and replacing the old; it is a drawn-out, retroactive process of illuminating and displacing the psychic non-knowledge that lurks deep in her unconscious (one, as we have seen, associated with the maternal). Ultimately she needs to rewrite her own psychic history into a new, conscious political script in order to succeed as a cured socialist subject.

The discourse of motherhood in *The Song of Youth* is thus not confined solely to the issue of absent mothers and grieving daughters. The obsession with motherhood, and in particular absent mothers, is also figurative of a discourse about consciousness and its origins. The trauma of the absent mother incites us to inquire as to the source of traumatized consciousness itself, in particular when the psychic wound lies deep in the primordial unconscious, and thus as yet is unknowable to consciousness except in the form of symptoms. While revolutionary consciousness is supposed to travel from spontaneity to purposive awareness, that elemental spontaneity does not exist in an ahistorical vacuum; it bears in its very structure the traces of a traumatized history. The move from spontaneity to consciousness requires a therapeutic examination into the historic causes of psychic pain itself. In other words, the linear progression from spontaneity to consciousness is only possible by retrospectively inquiring as to the origins of one's own scarred, inchoate psyche; it compels one to explore the collective history that engenders one's very existence. If Wendy Larson is correct in stating that two competing models of mind were current in twentieth-century China, one built upon the idea of the unconscious and the other constituting "revolutionary spirit," then Yang Mo's novel seems to enact the very process by which revolutionary spirit synthesizes and then finally supersedes the "petty-bourgeois" model of unconscious mind.

At one point Daojing comes to an understanding of her mother's wretched life through studying socialist theory and reading exemplary literature like Maxim Gorky's *Mother*. Daojing's suicidal yearning for her lost mother is de-pathologized through the lens of class struggle; her family melodrama is not merely a private tragedy but emblematic of larger social forces. Through the aid of the Party and its representatives Daojing is able to translate her personal angst into social insight, a transformation that allows her to not only free herself from her mental shackles but take an active part in collective liberation as well. The Party thus acts as both a surrogate for her lost mother and, in an analogous way to psychotherapy, the object of psychological transference.

The novel ends with Daojing organizing a student strike against Japanese imperialism. Even in the face of artillery fire, Daojing loses herself in solidarity with her fellow protesters:

> The crowd, like an upturned mountain and a roiling sea [*paishan daohai de renqun*], the far-off sound of rifle shots, the free-flow of fresh blood, the surging tenor of a majestic song. . . . it all appeared before her eyes, rushing like a great sea wave. Because her body was weak and, moreover, exhausted from excitement and fatigue, she suddenly felt faint, and almost collapsed. But a girl student standing beside her held onto her, and although they did not know each other, they held tightly to one another.
>
> The closed city gates could not hold against the fearless, heroic young demonstrators, and they were bold warriors, marching in lines and in groups, one after another [*yi hanghang, yi duidui*], in the howling wind, as if drummed up in a frenzy and beginning to boldly attack their enemies. The city wall was finally broken by the wave of people—the enemy had no choice but to open the gates in front of the fierce and angry crowd. The ranks, vast and surging [*haohao dangdang*], continued to advance ever forward.
>
> "Defeat Japanese imperialism!"
>
> "Masses! Organize yourselves! Arm yourselves! Rise up, fellow Chinese, and save China!"
>
> The endless waves of people, the bright and arresting banners, the cries of solemn slogans, continued to swell up in the streets and atmosphere of this ancient capital, and the heroic march continued to move without cease ever forward—without cease ever forward.[77]

The novel ends in a lyric rhapsody organized, both in symbol and in syntax, by the sea trope. The protestors are likened to "waves," they "swell up" and are "vast and surging." The staccato syntactic repetition, as well as the use of ellipses, suggests a surging, roiling quality to the prose.

This scene also recapitulates Daojing's dream, where both she and Lu Jiachuan flung themselves into the ocean. The novel thus restages the dream in daylight and narrative real-time through a process of transcoding whereby the sea, which had previously been closely associated with Daojing's lost mother, transforms into the protesting masses, led by the Party. Like the city walls that eventually give way to the sea of protestors, so do the confines of her own mind also crumble. Daojing loses herself and her subjectivity to the crowd; in the last few paragraphs the heroine of our revolutionary bildungsroman completely disappears, a nameless, faceless wave in a multitude of waves that surge together as one. Individual subjectivity gives way to utopian consciousness, and a revolutionary "oceanic feeling" pervades the novel's conclusion. Daojing's personal dream becomes decoded through a socialist hermeneutic, transforming it into a collective experience. Through the interpretive agency of Party ideology, dream and reality have become fused as one. In contrast to Freud's treatment of the oceanic feeling, in which religious sentiments are translated into an individual pathology stemming from childhood, the reverse trajectory takes place in *The Song of Youth*. Daojing overcomes the traumatic symptoms arising from childhood in order to give herself to a quasi-religious ecstasy of solidarity.[78] Daojing's trajectory also mirrors the novel's formal shift from its nostalgic imitation of a 1930s intellectual novel, a literature in which dreams and reality are separate, into a full-fledged socialist realism, whereby the two are joined as a unity.

One of the reasons for the novel's popularity and renown may be found in its reliance on "feeling," whether oceanic, maternal, or both. One scholar has noted the role of visuality in creating an aesthetic sublime and points to a number of painterly tableaus throughout the novel that engage the ocular faculty. The experience of the visual sublime, embodied by the vast sea, ignites Daojing's revolutionary transformation.[79] The sea trope encapsulates the heroine's dialectical journey from an appreciation of the sublimely beautiful that transcends reality to an adoption of a revolutionary praxis that requires a reentry into reality. However, as a supplement to the role of visuality, there is an equally significant place for the haptic as allegorized by the maternal embrace and the oceanic feeling. The poetics of touch create a compelling and unique case for framing the Party in affective terms in contradistinction and as complement to the paternal and totemic discourse of Party and Maoist heroism. The sea is not merely a picturesque manifestation of the sublime. It is also a figure for an all-encompassing, total embrace, the dissolution of the self as it reunites with the multitude. Various scholars have rightly argued that fantasies of embodied collective unity threaten to shut off any space for dissenting voices, for aberrant waves that go against the current. There is a troubling analogy between Daojing losing her consciousness during torture and her doing the same in the protest that closes the novel, inviting a comparison between the two that was certainly unintended.[80]

It is easy, especially in hindsight and with the nightmares of the Cultural Revolution still so fresh in mind, to see something authoritarian and sinister in any expression of solidarity. But Yang Mo was not merely ventriloquizing an authoritarian discourse; what is so prominent, perhaps even overly sentimental, is the emotional sense of loss and trauma, figured by the absent mother and crying orphan. If we read sympathetically, then the sea stands not so much for the power of authority to smother all individuality and dissent but as a curing embrace meant to heal a sense of loss, both personal and national. The way the mother figure seems to haunt the dreams of a number of characters in the novel suggests how a sense of parental loss burrows deeply in the collective unconscious of these characters and causes them grief and misery. The psyche itself bears the imprint of an embrace that has long been lost, something it tries to re-create in oneiric form. To cry for one's mother, essentially, is to lament physical separation from her and demand reunion.[81] The text employs the potency of this affect to make a case for the Party not merely as a mother surrogate but as the mother figure par excellence, holding the peasantry and proletariat in its universal embrace. One of the ways the Party's status as supreme mother makes itself felt is through the process of solidarity, in embracing someone going through a similar trauma. The Party thus acts as a supreme deity, but one that also makes its presence known through various avatars, manifesting herself in the various revolutionary mother-surrogates that populate the novel. During Daojing's imprisonment, the older revolutionary, the "mother" figure, is executed. Daojing and the younger prisoner are bereft and rely on each other for comfort: "In the cold and dank cell only Daojing and Shuxiu were left. They groped for each, joining their emaciated fingers as one, just like two orphans who had just lost their mother lean on each other."[82] Similarly, in the last scene, when Daojing is about to collapse from exhaustion, she is propped up by a girl she does not know, and they hold onto each other as they march forward.

The figural realization of Daojing's dream at the end of the novel actualizes the liberation of her psyche from its individual confines and into a utopian, collective consciousness, of bringing her desires out from the night and into the daylight. Daojing's therapy from her childhood haunting consists of essentially giving herself up to the revolutionary wave and allowing her subjectivity to dissolve. However, in exchange for her forsaken individuality, one stained by petty-bourgeois habits of thought, she achieves the ecstasy of reunion, of becoming one with a sea of humanity. It is essentially a form of suicide, the destruction of her ego, but the reclamation of a greater, more ecstatic collective identity, one characterized by an everlasting embrace, at once anonymous and intimate. Two strands of history join as one: Daojing's own story of being an orphan and finding her lost mother, and the nation marching ever forward toward liberation, guided and aided by the maternal Party. In manifesting Daojing's dream, the revolution also helps bring it to an end. The "realization" of Daojing's dream, its restaging at the end of the novel, is simultaneously the "correct" interpretation of the dream content. It is only through the hermeneutic transformation of Daojing's dream into an allegory for socialist utopia that her dream can have any legitimate meaning. Moreover, it completes a successful transition from a flawed, individualist Freudian model of mind to the correct socialist model of spirit.

As breathtaking as the conclusion is, its prose nevertheless threatens to collapse under the weight of its own tropes. The text effects the collapse of dream and reality by heavily relying on the figural, to form people as "waves," lyricize the flowing of their blood, and employ rhythmic syntax and creative punctuation in order to heighten an artificial discursive flow. The prose becomes virtually tactile, studded with catachreses, and it is hard not to feel as if the words are themselves a wave crashing over the reader, drawing us into its depths. The use of figuration is inevitable, but its hyperbolic use suggests that what Yang Mo is writing is not so much a manifest reality as it is simply another dreamscape, this one far beyond the boundaries of a single heroine's mind. The conclusion at once promises apotheosis and courts its own unraveling, its own disillusionment as a mere fantasy, a play on words. The collective and universal embrace promised by the end of the novel risks revealing itself as merely the self-embrace of a daydreamer.

Yang Mo spent the better part of ten years at work on her novel, and her diary gives us insight as to how she felt about her creation. Much like her heroine, Yang Mo presented herself in an array of different emotions in her diary, giving voice to her own self-doubt, sometimes giving herself pep talks to persevere with her novel, and goading herself to become a more ideal socialist. She was often ill, suffered from terrible insomnia, and underwent hormone therapies and injections to allay her symptoms. A good night's sleep, apparently, was hard for her to come by, and when she was able to sleep well, she was haunted by a number of dreams.

Her relationship to the novel was intensely personal. In the second afterword written in 1959, Yang Mo notes that her relationship to her novel was akin to that between mother and child.[83] The novel's status as a reminder of her own revolutionary past was powerful and even affected her dreams, as shown by this entry written in August 1955: "These past few days I've been dreaming of my comrades-in-arms [*zhanyou*] who passed away, all of whom were people I wanted to see but could not see. Could it be that my novel is causing [these comrades] to linger in my heart?"[84] Writing the novel became an actualization of Yang Mo's nostalgia for a more heroic past, a melancholic desire to see the comrades who were irretrievably lost to history. The powerful nostalgic desire that fueled her creation is evidenced by the almost hallucinatory relationship she had to her own characters. Her creation of characters seems like an attempt to resurrect and touch the dead. In January 1956, while suffering from a liver ailment, Yang Mo wrote down this vision:

> I can almost see Lu Jiachuan standing tall in front of me, extending his hand to me and smiling softly; I can almost see Lin Daojing who is just like me, a body racked with illness, frail, with furrowed brow and a grimace on her face. . . . . . I want to hold their hands, to speak to them intimately—I will tell Lin Daojing: "You still have a number of faults [*maobing*], you must fix them!. . . . . . " She will nod her head and say yes, and I will happily smile in response. . . . . . but who will help her fix them? Perhaps I will have to perform surgery on her.[85]

Her intimate relationship to her own creation has a hint of the occult about it, and it is all the more bizarre when she seeks to hold hands with her characters, and even "perform surgery" to remove the lingering traces of Lin Daojing's petty-bourgeois consciousness (and, by extension, Yang Mo's own). In addition to the hallucinatory visual quality of Yang Mo's private fantasies, there is also the yearning to reach out and physically touch the past, to hold it and even cut it open with a scalpel. The need to touch something long gone and yet more substantial, more desirable, and more real than what presently surrounded her lends the story behind *The Song of Youth* a particular poignancy. Whereas her characters are searching for lost mothers, it seems that for Yang Mo herself, the revolutionary past of the 1930s was itself a nostalgic figure of desire for which she longed. Her attempt to correct and transform her fictive companion is in fact a form of therapeutic work upon herself; by molding Lin Daojing's consciousness, removing the petty-bourgeois, individualist flaws that tenaciously remained, she was in effect molding her own psyche to fit the right model.

In this sense, then, *The Song of Youth* is itself like a dream in two powerful ways. It is a fantastic visualization of a lost heroic past, the resurrection of a powerful revolutionary nostalgia. Yang Mo, through her hands and literary scalpel, wishes to both touch the past and reshape it according to her desire. The novel is also a token of a palpable loss of revolutionary spirit that Yang Mo, writing in the 1950s, a time plagued with anxieties, suspicion, and paranoia among intellectuals, perhaps felt. The revolutionary history before 1949 was a vast, great, and majestic flowing sea, and in her novel Yang Mo perhaps expressed a desire to return to its waters. The utopian moment at the end of the novel betrays an ironically literal referent: it can be read not merely as a premonition of an epic, timeless moment of socialist triumph but as a quite plain reference to that historic event of December 9, 1935.

The narrative return to pre-revolutionary times ostensibly attempts to paint a picture of heroic continuity, demonstrating how we in the post-revolutionary "present" inherit and carry forward the work of the comrades who came before us. It is part of a larger project in creating a coherent, lasting revolutionary tradition, an act of fictive historiography that reminds the readers of their place in the revolutionary temporal chain, as well as of their forebears and future scions. This narrative of history moving toward utopia is, of course, a state-sponsored ideological fantasy, and Yang Mo's novel is a contribution to this teleology. However, in addition to this ostensibly noble project of narrating an equally noble revolutionary moment, there also lurks the presence of past history not as a mere token of the past and portent of a redeemed future but as a fantastic one-way ticket into the past. The nostalgic fantasy for a more heroic and epic past is one that seems to promise far more sensual experience than post-revolutionary reality. This is a somewhat different sense of history from the figure of utopian History that propels us in our struggle for freedom from necessity; it is history as actual, literal, and literalized past events, stripped of their allegorical overtones, a fantastic chronicle through which one can somehow quite literally gain access and entry into the past and thus escape the present. The novel provides powerful moments of such sensationalized history, including the mind-numbing extremes of torture and the sensations of being wholly enveloped in a crowd of marching bodies while bullets volley above. This ecstasy, this *jouissance*, is part and parcel of the genre of historical fiction, the assumption of a profound limit of experience whose palpable, tangible actuality can be vouched for through historic markers. Yang Mo's own hallucinatory relationship to her novel suggests how the story is not merely a piece in the revolutionary chain but itself a pathological symptom of a profound desire to *feel* history itself, to be enveloped, and perhaps disappear, in its embrace. In this sense, then, Yang Mo's effort to rewrite and resurrect history is not so much an act of continuity as a radical disjunction, the collision of two different senses of history that results in an anachronistic folding of history upon itself.

This suggests the presence of a double-voiced utopian mode at work in *The Song of Youth*.[86] The return to the past can easily be read as a voice of assent to the statist utopian narrative of revolution. However, the author's obsessive attachment to the past is one that seems to resist any real movement toward the future and suggests an individual pathological fixation that runs against the current of the collective waves moving triumphantly beyond 1949. Reading against the novel's grain, one can detect within this celebratory text of revolution a dissonant minor chord of disavowal. In this vein, one can sense a certain anxiety about the revolution as realized. Through this anxiety's symptomatic manifestation as a fantasy of historic fixation on a heroic past, one detects the allegoric space for the possibility of another utopia, one that transcends the statist utopia the novel ostensibly validates.

The Chinese press of the early 1950s used the colonial 1930s as a way of showing how the dreams expressed in that era had now been achieved thanks to the revolution. Those dreams were the symptoms of the "sharp contradictions" of a darker time; with the advent of socialism such dreams were overtaken by a reality that was touted as more wonderful and spectacular than any fantasy. Ostensibly Yang Mo's *The Song of Youth* was doing the same thing, providing a narrative picture of the political struggle in the early 1930s that laid the groundwork for the liberation nearly two decades later. As she wrote in her preface to the English edition, she wanted to show "how the dream of so many who had laid down their lives came true."[87] And there is no reason to question Yang Mo's intention and sincerity in contributing to such a teleological narrative. However, while History is moving ever forward, the trajectory of utopian desire in the novel is one that seems to instead reach backward. Whereas those in the 1930s dreamed of the future, Yang Mo was dreaming of a past that she wanted so very much to touch again.

CHAPTER 5

Dream Fugue

Jiang Qing, the End of the Cultural Revolution, and Zong Pu's Fiction

After the death of Mao, how was it possible to reimagine politics in the wake of socialism's cruel and violent manifestations? How could a socialist future even be imaginable? As the late 1970s rolled into the burgeoning democracy movements and "Culture Fever" of the 1980s, socialism and Marxism were for the most part abandoned as genuine models for political futurity as intellectuals looked elsewhere for utopian possibilities; some sought authenticity in their cultural "roots," while others rediscovered the semicolonial Republican era as a model of an alternate "alternative" modernity (or, perhaps better, a modernity interrupted) or looked to Western liberal democracy for inspiration. In the moments directly after the end of the Cultural Revolution, socialism still remained a redeemable possibility to some intellectuals, even those who had just suffered the trials of the previous decade. Certainly, maintaining the possibility of socialism carried the burden of dealing with a recent past marked by suppression, violence, and death.

It was necessary for some writers, including the established socialist realist Zhou Libo, to sidestep the entire history of "New China" and start over in the Sino-Japanese War, when communism still seemed like a wistful promised land. In contrast to Mao-era writing, where rhetoric about dreams was kept to a bare minimum, post-Mao literature began to depict dreams once again. Zhou Libo's (1908–79) 1978 story "Night at Xiang River" (Xiangjiang yi ye) retrospectively leaps back to the 1940s and tells the story of Communist soldiers fighting the Japanese. On the eve of a major battle, the soldiers and their commanding officer discuss the value of dreams and ideals:

> "No, I like a bit of excitement in my sleep, too." As was expected, the enemy was focusing its attention on the eastern front. Dong Qian, the commanding officer, was content enough that he decided to take part in the younger soldiers' conversation. "I love having exciting dreams, socialist and Communist dreams. How about you, Xiao Zhang? Do you like to dream, too?"
>
> "I do," answered Xiao Zhang. "But all my dreams are about things to eat, like fish, or chicken, or meat buns, or some leftover corn—that's what slips into my dreams."
>
> "Dreams are ideals." The commanding officer continued to lay out his point of view. "If a man doesn't have ideals, he won't dream."[1]

The story proclaims the need to dream boldly once again, whether they are dreams of edible plenty or of communism itself. Zhou Libo's use of the dream trope is symptomatic of the desire for a socialist "redux," a counterfactual yearning for another shot at the Revolution, with the hopes of avoiding the terrible excesses that followed in its wake.

Dream discourse in the late 1970s constituted a way for writers and critics to articulate this painful historical juncture; as a trope it was employed to explain the extremes of the Cultural Revolution but also as a means to imagine a way out of this difficult political and moral impasse. In the immediate aftermath of the arrest of Jiang Qing and the Gang of Four, critics seized on Jiang Qing's rhetorical use of *Dream of the Red Chamber*, the most celebrated novel in the Chinese tradition, to reveal the hallucinatory nature of her claim to power. In a polemical tour de force, critics troped Jiang Qing as a hysterical dreamer who fell for her own novelistic conceits—in turn, these fictional illusions brought real catastrophe to the nation.[2] By exploring this critical discourse, one can observe the close affinities between fictional trope and political rhetoric, and how the cross-circuiting of these two modes revealed the tropological nature of Mao-era political practice. While the critics were vehement in dismantling Jiang Qing's hallucinatory fantasies, they were relying on similar modes of rhetoric that could also be easily unraveled. Nevertheless, while such rhetoric may, under circumstances such as the Cultural Revolution, have destructive effects, trope is indispensable to the working of any politics at all.

Zong Pu's 1978 story "A Dream for Strings" (Xianshang de meng) directly invokes the rhetoric that cast Jiang Qing as a hallucinatory dreamer. Zong Pu's work in the late 1970s is part of a larger genre of "Scar Literature," testaments of suffering under the Cultural Revolution. As a whole, this genre has been derided as overly sentimental and moralistic denunciations of the Gang of Four and as lacking in critical introspection to the inherent problems of socialism itself. However, one critic argues that such writers' reflections of past experience constitute the "aesthetic rehabilitation of experience." Such narrative experiments functioned as a form of spiritual recuperation through which broken subjects could reconcile their place within history.[3]

Focusing on a story about intellectual suffering risks obscuring the very complex social and class circumstances underlying the Cultural Revolution. Recent sociological work on the Cultural Revolution illuminates its social complexity and provides invaluable context over and above interpretations that read the Cultural Revolution only as demonic terror emanating from Mao. After Liberation, there were considerable power struggles between the old elite, the educated and landowning classes (who would also comprise most of the intellectuals), and the new political Communist elites who had seized power.[4] Even when intellectuals signed up for the project of nation-building, their elite status often marked them as a suspect class. The Cultural Revolution was unique in that Mao called upon the youth to rebel against both the old, intellectual elite and the new, political elite that was accused of bureaucratic revisionism. The shared victimization of old and new elites alike precipitated "inter-elite unity."[5] With the end of the Cultural Revolution and Deng Xiaoping's rise to power, class hierarchy was restored, and a new "technocratic class order," consisting of members from both elites, was forged and called upon to assume political and economic rule over China.[6]

The brief flourishing of Scar Literature at the end of the 1970s constituted a form of political conciliation to intellectuals who had been persecuted in the previous decade of turmoil and was an invitation to express their incredible suffering. It was also an invitation to rejoin the social elite and further the legitimacy of the post-Mao regime. The Cultural Revolution constituted the most sustained and traumatizing attack upon intellectuals and precipitated among them their greatest sense of alienation from the state. The regime's rush to co-opt intelligentsia disaffection bespoke the necessity of intellectual support for post-Mao Communist rule. Thus intellectuals unleashed a wave of emotional and critical literary production that bore witness to their suffering. There is no denying the genuine emotion of these texts and the authenticity of the pain these intellectuals underwent. But these testimonials also bore evidence of the intellectuals' problematic relationship with the masses. As intellectual accounts of suffering were the only kinds of memoirs allowed to be published in this period, it led to the presumption that intellectuals were not only speaking for the people but that they *were* the people.[7]

These texts have effectively claimed to narrate the whole of the Cultural Revolution experience, when in fact these testimonies are only part of a wider totality that offers divergent perceptions, memories, and understandings of the revolutionary experience. Western published memoirs that depict the horrors of the Cultural Revolution in grotesque detail do more to "enhance the nationalism of an America—and a West—whose hegemonic position was beginning to be challenged" after the end of the Cold War than illuminate the actual vicissitudes of those complex experiences.[8] Thus post–Cultural Revolution literature finds itself vulnerable to charges from two diametrically opposed sides. On one hand, those uncomfortable with the collusion of intellectuals with the post-Mao ruling elite see such literature as incomplete in their denunciation of the entirety of Communist horror. On the other hand, Scar Literature's singular attention on the sufferings borne by a fractional elite, however significant, work to repudiate and negate the entirety of egalitarian initiatives in the Mao era. By repudiating all of Mao and the Gang of Four, such writers deflected attention from the greater masses that were no longer the intellectuals' burden.

But Scar Literature is not one monolithic construct—writers differed from one another, and even within a single text we can see inner contradictions and vacillation between different viewpoints. By focusing on Zong Pu's emotional story about trauma and redemption, we can see how her affect-laden narrative can help complicate simple characterizations not only of her experience as a persecuted intellectual but of the literary genre of Scar Literature as well. While "A Dream for Strings" can easily be read as a state-sanctioned cooptation of intellectual alienation,[9] it also offers a renewal for socialist ideals, especially in the way the story invokes an homage to the pre-1949 revolutionary heroes who were swallowed by the Cultural Revolution's turmoil.

The issue of sentimentality is complicated in Zong Pu's fiction. Her texts outline what may be termed "politico-affective space"; this is a space in which affects circulate and exchange between persons, binding them into a politicized multitude. This "common space" of shared feelings can be both physical (for example, Tiananmen Square) and symbolic (for example, a common dream).[10] By "affect," as opposed to the oftentimes pejorative term "sentiment," emphasis is placed on a form of feeling that is mobile in space and intersubjective in nature. It seeks to avoid the "expressive hypothesis," or the claim that emotive expression emanates from and affirms the presence of a stable, autonomous subject.[11] Of course, subjects do exist in Zong Pu's work. But far more salient in her fiction is the ability of affect to circulate between subjects and eventually hold together multitudes. This mobile affect can thus evoke common political hopes and desires. Zong Pu's work shows how affects that seem confined to private spheres of intimacy can filter into larger dimensions of mass political experience.

By focusing on themes of trauma, dream, and emotion in Zong Pu's story, we can observe a politics of sentimentality that is far more intricate and self-aware than appears on the surface. One scholar has argued that emotions are inherently tropological in nature. They stand in for an uncertainty of a knowledge that is yet incapable of articulation and help "mitigate epistemological uncertainties."[12] When emotion is revealed to be allegorical and figural in nature, we can then recognize the important ideological work it does in helping circulate forms of affect necessary for the functioning of politics. Zong Pu's sentimentality is not, as some critics have argued, a shallow instance of a simplistic humanism[13] but a deft and affecting exercise of political imagination that motivates formal intricacies and figural conundrums in her narrative practice. Zong Pu's use of sentiment reveals an "economy of pathos"[14] to express how emotion inaugurates a complicated spatiality between individual and collective, old and young, private and public, and dream and reality, and how narrative sentiment is activated by traveling between these spaces.

Through a comparison of "A Dream for Strings" with Zong Pu's 1957 literary debut, "Red Beans" (Hong dou), an intricate love story that was later denounced in the Anti-Rightist campaign, an aesthetic basis becomes evident for this "economy of pathos." In this young work Zong Pu already mapped out an aesthetics of spatiality and emotion that could be compatible with socialist politics and that would reappear, in more somber and moving form, in her much later 1978 story. This spatialized articulation of sentiment requires a narrative complexity that preserves formalized, discrete spaces, not least of which is the realm of dreams. By arguing for the necessary relationship between mobile emotion and a complicated construction of fictional spaces, we find that sentimentality cannot be equated with an aesthetic bluntness or flattening; rather, it requires the kind of intricate formalist latticework that an unsentimental high modernism might arrogate for itself.

Zong Pu's sentimental tales constitute in fact a sophisticated form of affective politics, a mobilization of emotional tropes that not only do political work but also imagine a way out of the violent excesses so easily ascribed to socialism in toto. The attacks on Jiang Qing were in no small part motivated by a certain political misogyny; Jiang Qing's hysterical dreamwork could not substitute for the "rational" epistemology of the true socialist critic. In much the same way, Scar Literature's excessive sentimentality prevented these texts from being truly critical assessments of the socialist era.[15] Zong Pu's stories provide an insightful way to imagine an affective, women-centered politics that can point to the residual, if fast-fading, promises of the socialist heritage. The irony is that while Zong Pu rehearsed the standard attacks on Jiang Qing's rule, the sentimentality of her narrative seems to draw from conventions common to women's popular culture. This irony, in turn, thus suggests that the antidote to Maoist hysteria was not the re-masculinization of the public sphere but an affirmation of an "intimate public," a sphere constituted by survivors of the trauma and embedded within tropes common to women's culture.

When the Gang of Four unraveled after Mao Zedong's death in 1976, press and public opinion quickly turned against the Gang's ringleader, Jiang Qing, who was accused of instigating the Great Proletarian Cultural Revolution (1966–76). Cartoons depicted Jiang Qing as a witch, a rat, and a fanatical devotee of Wu Zetian, the infamous Tang Dynasty ruler who usurped political power and declared herself emperor.[16] Jiang Qing became the focus of intense anger and resentment felt by those who suffered the ravages of the Cultural Revolution, a tumult that threatened to destroy the very legitimacy of socialist rule from within. With few to defend her, and without her all-powerful husband to act as a buffer, Jiang Qing was a safe and easy target for those seeking to give vent to their suffering.

Liu Mengxi, then a young scholar of the novel *Dream of the Red Chamber*, published a tirade against Jiang Qing in the September 1976 issue of *People's Literature*. His timing seemed precarious, for Mao had died that very month, and Jiang Qing was not arrested until October. That Liu Mengxi and the editors decided to go ahead with publication attests to the impatience of many to express their displeasure and disgust with Jiang Qing and her ilk. The title was "Ripping Apart Jiang Qing's Facade of Being 'Half a Red-ologist,'" "Red-ologist" (*hongxuejia*) being an abbreviated term for scholars of *Dream of the Red Chamber.* Jiang Qing had cited the novel in her speeches and considered herself an amateur expert. Her public association with *Dream* went as far back as 1954, when she championed an article written by two Shandong University students attacking the eminent scholar Yu Pingbo's studies of the novel for being "bourgeois" and "idealist" and following in the footsteps of the long discredited scholar Hu Shi.[17] The article argued for a vigorous political reading of the novel as a "manual of class struggle."[18] As a result of this campaign Yu Pingbo would find his career resuscitated only after Jiang Qing had finally left the political stage thirty years later.

Drawing upon Jiang Qing's supposed public statements about the novel, Liu Mengxi attacked Jiang Qing's opportunistic and often crass interpretations of the power struggles among factions of the Jia household. For Liu Mengxi, Jiang Qing's single-minded focus on the machinations of domestic power in the novel was a reflection of her own obsession with advancing her political ambitions. Referring to the historical context of *Dream*, Jiang Qing spoke approvingly of the Qing dynasty Yongzheng Emperor's successful usurpation of power from Kangxi and remarked that Yongzheng was "really something."[19] Moreover, she criticized Yongzheng for not hiding his treachery well enough. Liu Mengxi pointed out the linguistic subterfuge by which Jiang Qing was admitting her own raw political ambitions: "Any perspicacious person will know in an instant that she was 'borrowing the past to speak of the present,' 'pointing to a mulberry tree and calling it a locust tree,' while in actuality she was using the story of Yongzheng's usurpation as a way of explaining her own [seizure of] Party power."[20]

Here Liu Mengxi was using a variation of the idiom "to point to the mulberry tree and scold the locust tree instead" (*zhi sang ma huai*): in his rendition it is "zhi sang shuo huai." The idiom first appears textually in the Ming novel *Plum in the Golden Vase* (Jin ping mei) and later appears in *Dream of the Red Chamber.* In *Dream*, Wang Xifeng, the unscrupulous manager of the Jia household, deploys the idiom to describe the prickly, verbal backbiting of the senior maids and the way they insinuate criticisms of certain people by mentioning others.

That Wang Xifeng employs this idiom in reference to her garrulous maids emphasizes its association with women's gossip. Liu Mengxi's use of this idiom emphasizes the effect of figurative substitution, how one word stands in for and veils another. To "point at the mulberry tree while scolding the locust tree" encapsulates the power of trope, the ability to unite powerful passions to seemingly unrelated concepts. Moreover, the deictic power of this idiom (for the pointing, *zhi*, is quite literally an index) brings to relief the concrete ways in which fiction indexes bodies and emotions.[21] Texts' "emotionality" is what directs them, like a pointing finger, to real bodies suddenly drawn into political struggle. These citations of *Dream* reveal how the essence of politics can be located within the workings of fiction; it becomes clearer why fiction was so important in the development of modern politics in China. Liu Mengxi himself did not reveal the intertextual circularity of his usage of the idiom *zhi sang shuo huai*; his use alluded to the very literary text that formed the basis of his polemic but that he himself does not admit (he may have been unconscious to the extent his polemical rhetoric, like that of Jiang Qing, was indebted to fiction itself). In that sense, he seemed to veil his own hysterical rhetoric while denouncing Jiang Qing's. This inherent tie between fictional discourse and political rhetoric helps explain why those who sought to conduct scholarly, disciplined studies of literature, like Yu Pingbo, suddenly found themselves at the mercy of political forces beyond their control, their livelihoods ruined. Politics was thus discursively figured as a brutal and violent form of dream making.

Liu Mengxi emphasized the role of gender as a trope for political struggle that linked *Dream* to Jiang Qing's own political machinations. According to him, Jiang Qing had ostensibly argued that the ultimate power struggle in the novel was between the "patriarchal faction" (here, the word for faction is *dang*; the same word also denotes a political party and "the Party") and the "matriarchal faction," a battle between those who had public duties and those who ran the household: "In the power struggle between the matriarchal and patriarchal factions in the *Dream of the Red Chamber*, it is the matriarchal faction that is victorious."[22] Following a long tradition in Chinese history of being wary and suspicious of court women, Liu Mengxi argued that Jiang Qing was in effect admitting her own feminine treachery in seizing control. When he argued that Jiang Qing harbored a "dream of being emperor" (*huangdi meng*), he was alluding to those court women, the most famous being Wu Zetian of the Tang dynasty, who seized the throne for themselves. Moreover, by pointing to Jiang Qing's conflation of the struggle within the Communist Party (*dang*) with *Dream*'s ostensible struggle between matriarchal and patriarchal factions (*dang*), he thus discursively casts the power play of the Cultural Revolution as a conflict between orderly men and hysterical women. He ridicules some of Jiang Qing's more fanciful readings of the novel, such as suggesting that the two maids of Jia Baoyu, the main protagonist, were spies for "left-" and "right-"wing forces in the household. Liu Mengxi pointed out, however, that one character remains notably absent from Jiang Qing's various remarks, and that was Wang Xifeng, the scheming mistress of the household who, in no small part, helps bring about the family's catastrophic downfall:

> Wang Xifeng's . . . role is so important, . . . so why does Jiang Qing not discuss her? The reason is because there are surprising similarities between Jiang Qing, whose ambitions went against the Party, and Wang Xifeng. They both represent a corrupt, sinking class, they are both scheming plotters, devils that kill without blinking an eye. Jiang Qing is today's Wang Xifeng, in fact she is even more like Wang Xifeng than Wang Xifeng herself.[23]

According to Liu Mengxi, Jiang Qing's obsession with *Dream* was evidence of her grander dream of eventually becoming an emperor, an illusory ambition that Jiang Qing temporarily realized. However, like a dream, her tyrannical rule suddenly collapsed, precipitating a pathetic fall back to reality. Jiang Qing had thus written herself as the treacherous Wang Xifeng but remained oblivious of that fact, and ignorant of the retribution that Wang Xifeng and, by figural extension, she herself, would suffer. While using the fictional logic of *Dream* to further her political goals, Liu Mengxi argued that Jiang Qing ultimately failed to follow this logic to its appropriate conclusion. Jiang Qing committed an inconsistent reading of the novel. As he points out, this misreading was itself a metonym for Jiang Qing's flagrant misreading of her own political situation.

Liu Mengxi demonstrated that, in contrast to the amateur Jiang Qing, he was a superior reader of *Dream* and as evidence of his interpretive authority ended his polemic by citing a few verses from the novel. These lines come from chapter 5, in which the protagonist, Jia Baoyu, dreams of entering a magical realm where he reads heavenly registers that reveal the fates of the women in the household.

Each dossier is centered on one woman and is illustrated by enigmatic rebus-drawings that allude to her tragic fate. Baoyu also hears songs containing perplexing, riddle-like lyrics that also foreshadow the women's demise. Liu Mengxi quotes a few lines from the dossier dedicated to Wang Xifeng: "And half a life-time's anxious schemes / Proved no more than the stuff of dreams."[24] Commenting on the lines, Liu Mengxi concluded, "This is written for Wang Xifeng. But if we use this as a portrait of Jiang Qing, whose ambitions went against the Party, is it not very fitting?"[25] In Liu Mengxi's words, Jiang Qing "outdid" Wang Xifeng in her ambition and outrageousness, and his rhetoric suggested how Jiang Qing essentially wrote herself as a novelistic character, one that could easily surpass the flagrant scandals of her fictional model. This crucial chapter itself allegorically encompasses the rest of the novel. Those who can interpret the riddles and songs found in this chapter will understand what happens in the end. By using lines devoted to Wang Xifeng from this pivotal chapter, Liu Mengxi concluded his polemic with an interpretive tour de force that demonstrated his hermeneutic superiority, a suggestively masculine takedown and patronizing correction of an errant, clumsy female student. At the same time, in the midst of this virtuosic reading, Liu Mengxi seemed to blithely ignore the hermeneutic mise en abîme into which he himself had fallen. His own interpretive leaps resembled in no small part the manic, hysterical force of Jiang Qing's exegesis.

Two months later an article in the *People's Daily*, "Smashing Jiang Qing's Dream of Being Emperor," recapitulated verbatim many of the same themes from Liu Mengxi's article, often with more vitriol. The author went by the pseudonym "Stone Words" (Shiyan), suggesting both through metaphor and through its pun (*shiyan* can also be taken to mean "true words") that he spoke words of material truth in contrast to Jiang Qing's fanciful ravings. The name also hints at the novel's original title, *The Story of the Stone* (Shitou ji). The article's similarity with the previous one suggests that the author was the same person. By November 1976 Jiang Qing had already been arrested, and the author was freer to be unrestrained in his denunciation, and even noted that Mao himself made note of Jiang Qing's ambition to become Party chairman. The Gang of Four "made their dreams truly sweet, but in the end they were nothing but pretty soap bubbles."[26] The article, like the one preceding it, openly mocked Jiang Qing's "hysterical" interpretations of *Dream*. However, this article stressed far more the topsy-turvy switch between "left" and "right" under Jiang Qing's regime. In the same way that Jiang Qing arbitrarily assigned political positions to Baoyu's maids, she denigrated the Party faithful by assigning them the label of "Rightist" while promoting herself as a true Leftist. The truth, claimed the author, was the opposite: "Jiang Qing is precisely a true, authentic Rightist, she is the typical intra-Party capitalist, an unrepentant follower of the bourgeoisie. As far as the professional 'special agent' that 'stole her way into the other group,' that was no other than [Jiang Qing] herself."[27] The author was remarking on Jiang Qing's explication of the name Xiren, Jia Baoyu's supposed "right-wing" maid. Xiren translates roughly as "to infiltrate a person/body," and in the novel Xiren was given this name because her pleasant fragrance supposedly lingered on the person who had just encountered her. However, Jiang Qing transformed the name into *tou xi bie ren* to imply that what her name really denoted was her role in infiltrating the more "progressive" ranks of the household.

The dizzying confusion over who was truly "left" or "right," progressive or reactionary, was analogous to the shifting polarities of dream and reality.[28] Liu Mengxi's articles and others like it from the time insisted that Jiang Qing and her clique represented an aberration from the correct socialist course, a "dream" that, like a soap bubble, effectively burst.[29] Moreover, what the Gang of Four also embodied was a perverted socialist epistemology, a corrupted political knowledge that reversed all proper socialist values and transformed reality into a brutal phantasmagoria. But what these critics implied, despite themselves, was how political reality itself depended on who happened to hold power. Political power and the correct interpretation of political allegory mutually constituted one another; those with power can create and direct the force of political tropes, while those who can decode those tropes arrogate political power to themselves. Critics pointed to Jiang Qing's treatment of *Dream* not merely to show her laughable infelicities as a literary critic but to demonstrate that her misrule was, in essence, a grand fiction and a faded dream. And yet by making reference to *Dream*, they invoked a novel that not only self-referentially reflects upon its own fictionality but also reveals the sumptuous material world of the Jia household as but a dream. Jiang Qing's ability to manipulate the signifiers of socialist rule to her own ends, to "point to a mulberry tree and call it a locust tree," is akin to the semiotic misdirection that also occurs in dreamwork and in fiction. The critics' opportunistic use of *Dream*, mirroring Jiang Qing's own, revealed the fictionality of politics itself. These post-1976 critics who claimed that "socialist reality" had been restored, and its false double dispelled, ignored the very totality of awakening that *Dream* ostensibly insists upon and overlooked the very contingency and frailty of any reality that could be established after Mao. Their misogynistic focus on Jiang Qing's hysterical and reckless rule was in some ways a form of misreading and misdirection similar to Jiang Qing's own opportunistic interpretation of *Dream*. By focusing on Jiang Qing's hysterics, the critics elided the more fundamental issue of the hysteria within the authoritarian state itself, one given to manic reversals and vicious cycles of political disenchantment and reenchantment. While these critics were alert to the irony of Jiang Qing's misreadings, they seemed conspicuously insensitive to the very irony of their use of *Dream* to attack Jiang Qing. In mercilessly cutting through Jiang Qing's rhetoric, these writers opened themselves to the very critique they employed.

Liu Mengxi's heated rhetoric surrounding Jiang Qing's own hot air can easily lead one to think that political rhetoric should be abandoned in favor of sober, rational analysis and that political rhetoric inevitably inaugurates a descent on a slippery slope to violence and terror. But without trope, there can be no politics at all; the absence of rhetoric creates a "depoliticized politics,"[30] a technocratic regime that has not only been evacuated of all utopian possibility but has also emptied the public sphere of affect. A depoliticized realm is ultimately one stuck in paralysis, following the dictates of the State and Market under the guise of rational development. Depoliticization takes the wind out of dreaming; as the commanding officer in Zhou Libo's story noted, to not hold ideals prevents dreaming from happening in the first place. Violence and excess are real risks inherent within politics themselves, but that does not suggest that all exercise of politics necessarily leads to mass murder and book burnings. To enter the realm of the political does not mean that one is completely unable to relate to one's own passionate political practice without some measure of ethical, ironic distance.

The work of Zong Pu (born Feng Zhongpu, 1928–) might suggest the ways in which fiction, politics, and emotion can be brought together to rekindle a dream of political possibility. Her father was Feng Youlan (1895–1990), a famous historian of Chinese philosophy who was educated in the United States, where he studied under John Dewey. Feng Youlan worked as a professor in the United States but returned to China after the 1949 revolution. Both father and daughter endured considerable hardship during the Cultural Revolution.[31] During the Reform era, Feng Youlan and Zong Pu were rehabilitated. Zong Pu went on to publish many more stories, essays, and novels in the coming decades. Her Scar Literature texts constituted an attempt to come to terms with the violent historic events she and her family endured.

"A Dream for Strings" offers a striking vision of collectivity: in this case, a dream vision of a cello concert whereby the Cultural Revolution's pain and trauma are transmuted into redemptive joy for the audience. The emotional reverberations that emanate from this musical communion lead to a vision of the Monument to the Heroes in Tiananmen Square, now inscribed with the names of the turmoil's many victims. This concluding tableau may seem overly sentimental, even maudlin. However, the dream of a collective bound together through both music and political purpose is the culmination of an emotional tutelage that occurs between the story's two protagonists: an older cello teacher and her pupil, a girl whose parents have perished as a result of sustained persecution. What begins as the difficult relationship between the teacher and her traumatized student in the mundane, awakened world transforms into a collective musical apotheosis in dream space. But the fact that this crowd is displaced away from mundane reality into a timeless dreamscape also betrays some hesitance in representing the collective so soon after the Cultural Revolution's devastation. Thus the narrative's shifting of political apotheosis into dream space reveals the real limits to the forms of collectivity actually possible. What the story reveals, instead, is but a tentative outline of politicized yearnings for a redeemed socialist futurity that still awaits realization in the present day.

Zong Pu's compelling articulation of collective affect did not emerge only after the Cultural Revolution. Her earlier work suggests a template for thinking about emotion and politics that will find dramatic expression in her Scar Literature texts. Zong Pu's 1957 literary debut, the short story "Red Beans," offers a preliminary attempt to think through the connections between emotions and politics. Derided in the anti-Rightist campaign as a "poisonous weed," this story reveals an early articulation of collective emotion that still preserves a crucial space for intimate relations between individuals. Zong Pu's collective aesthetics do not negate the role of individuals or private relationships; instead, a genuine sense of collective affect can only be born from the totality of one's interpersonal engagements, both private and public.

OVERDETERMINED PASSIONS: ZONG PU'S "RED BEANS"

"Red Beans" was first published in the magazine *People's Literature* (Renmin wenxue) in July 1957. The story takes place on the eve of the Communist victory over the Nationalists in the Civil War. The heroine, Jiang Mei, a university student, struggles to choose between a passionate romance with a wealthy bourgeois classmate, Qi Hong, and the revolutionary politics exemplified by her activist roommate, Xiao Su.[32] Jiang Mei vacillates between two compelling emotional worlds: the romantic and sensual realm of love enjoyed with Qi Hong, and the communal paradise of socialist activism embodied by Xiao Su. While Xiao Su exhorts Jiang Mei to immerse herself in the real world of political struggle, her relationship with Qi Hong is notable for its dreamy, detached quality. Xiao Su criticizes what she thinks of as Qi Hong's otherworldly narcissism: "That Qi Hong is always playing the piano and always seems like he's dreaming. He's truly a selfish person—nothing can make him care about anything."[33]

Jiang Mei's indecision is finally resolved when her mother reveals, belatedly, that Jiang Mei's late father had not actually died of sudden illness but had been dragged away and murdered by Nationalist agents.[34] As a result of this revelation, Jiang Mei's dead father takes Xiao Su's place in a love triangle that has turned oedipal; she must now weigh her love for her father against that for her boyfriend. In the end, Jiang Mei makes the unsurprising choice to stay in China and work for the new society.

Her volatile relationship with Qi Hong is exemplified by the eponymous "red beans" she keeps in a box, hidden in a hole in her dormitory room wall behind a crucifix. The tiny red beans, often used as jewelry, were part of a hair clip given to her by her mother.[35] During a passionate altercation with Qi Hong, the clip falls to the ground. In anger, Qi Hong stomps on the clip, dispersing the stones. By way of apology, he houses the two red beans in a box as a form of "commemoration"; he leaves unclear, however, exactly what the red beans commemorate.[36] These two red beans, the precipitate of blood, tears, and passion, are thus hidden in a hole in the wall behind the very icon of religious passion, Christ on the Cross. As is recorded in the New Testament, Jesus, on his way to the Cross, prays "in an agony," his sweat resembling "great drops of blood falling down to the ground."[37] "Red Beans" is also the title of a short quatrain by Tang poet Wang Wei. In the poem, the red beans are a symbol of deep romantic longing.

The romantic world Jiang Mei shares with Qi Hong may seem to be more imbued with passion and emotion than is the separate, political world she shares with her comrades, people who prefer revolutionary marches to Western classical music. But early on we realize that this is not so. Jiang Mei's political education is as much emotional as it is intellectual; together with Xiao Su, she reads a book titled *Between Life and Death* (Fang sheng wei si zhi jian) that "described the bitter hardship which the Chinese people endured, and how, amid blood and tears, they all struggled for a new life."[38] The book's title implies the liminal state "between life and death" that ostensibly characterizes the masses' desperate plight. The effect of reading this book with Xiao Su "transported her into another world" in which she realizes the necessity of struggling for "everyone" (*dajia*): "[Jiang Mei's] mother had on occasion, while weeping, said, 'Everyone should be able to live well; no one should die in vain.' Her mother's notion of 'everyone' finally became concrete through her reading of the book."[39] She also reads Ai Siqi's textbook *Philosophy for the Masses* (Dazhong zhe xue).[40] "The masses" (*dazhong*) in the title echoes the "everyone" for whom Jiang Mei learns to feel empathy; the tome implies how Jiang Mei is encouraged to learn not just for her own intellectual development but for everyone else as well. Xiao Su encourages Jiang Mei to think in terms of the broad collective and wants to wrest Jiang Mei from her narrow obsession for Qi Hong. Xiao Su thus attempts to foster a different emotional attachment: one for the masses. Jiang Mei's political education is sentimental insofar as she learns the affective power of imagining the masses and empathizing with them. Through experiencing a pain that is collectively shared, Jiang Mei develops a political sensitivity. The motif of "everyone" is further repeated and given a musical dimension when Jiang Mei joins a glee club named "Everyone Sings."[41] Jiang Mei thus discovers a link between the collective power of singing together and the need to win a better life for "everyone."

The aforementioned red beans, hidden away behind the crucifix, and rediscovered by an older Jiang Mei after 1949, may only seem to signify a hidden realm of private, romantic emotion. One scholar has noted that the motif of the red beans symbolizes the autonomy of a uniquely private, female consciousness, one linked to collective consciousness but separate from it as well.[42] However, when we recall that the hair clip was a gift from her mother, a loyal widow to Jiang Mei's revolutionary father, it is impossible to disconnect these red beans from their evocation of revolutionary pathos as well. The red beans at first blush serve as a token of the exclusive passion she shares with Qi Hong, someone who claims to "hate the whole human race" except for her.[43] But cleaved within these red beans are also the "blood and tears" of the Chinese masses bearing the brunt of oppression. The narrative motivates the red beans in an overdetermined fashion: *both* romantic and political passions are projected onto this symbolic object. The prominence of blood in symbolizing both private and collective affect is further borne out when Xiao Su and her activist classmates sell their blood and pool together the proceeds in order to help Jiang Mei's mother overcome a prolonged illness.[44]

If the red beans signify as much collective pathos as they do a private one, then what need is there to keep them hidden? Why does the narrative insist on a seemingly secret hole in the wall? In the beginning of the story, an older Jiang Mei revisits her old dorm, the location of an upcoming Party meeting for which she serves as a representative. She is surprised to discover that the crucifixes are still hanging on the walls. The caretaker explains that originally they were to be taken down because of their superstitious nature; however, they were left behind as works of art.[45] The space in the wall behind the crucifix that houses Jiang Mei's love for Qi Hong is not hidden in some paranoid fashion but left to remain even under a new "atheist" regime. Rather than simply dismissing her romantic past, Jiang Mei commemorates her former passion in the same way that Qi Hong sought to commemorate their passion by means of the red beans. By leaving behind the red beans in the wall, Jiang Mei recognizes the importance of her former love but is also able to move forward.

The hole in the wall that hides the red beans is thus hidden in plain view. This complex description of a wall that holds spaces within it is figurative of a narrative and affective terrain that features a multiplicity of spaces and memories, one that reflects the different frames in which we experience emotion. In that vein, the wall is allegorical of a formal desire to create far more intricate and expansive narrative spaces that would give room for private passion but also link them with public passions. The idea of "economy of pathos" can help articulate how, in both "Red Beans" and "A Dream for Strings," affect heralds a relational space that connects the individual with the collective, the old with the young, the private with the public, and dream with reality.[46] The narrative pathos of "Red Beans" always functions in an act of exchange, between lovers, between parents and children, and between romance and politics. In some cases, it takes place in the context of an actual blood transfusion. Jiang Mei's red beans thus symbolize this act of multidirectional affective exchange. Without such dynamic circulation, emotion stultifies and dies. But there must be a structure capable of facilitating such exchange. The motif of the dormitory wall is symbolic of a differentiated narrative space that can allow for this affective circulation.

The political ideology of "Red Beans" requires that Jiang Mei sacrifice her love for Qi Hong for the benefit of the greater good. But despite her momentous sacrifice, Jiang Mei neither disavows nor represses her romantic experience. The story suggests that Jiang Mei's volatile romance serves as a form of sentimental education, an experience that allows her to develop into a more mature activist. While she must ultimately forsake a love that she fully understands was doomed to end, she still preserves her memories of this love and finds value in them. Perhaps idealistically, "Red Beans" paints a tolerant picture of a socialist society that is mature enough to realize the necessity of a certain measure of private life and private belief in order to make politics effective. Unfortunately, while Zong Pu and those who praised her story were perhaps hopeful for an ideal society that could be tolerant of a spectrum of ideas, history suggests that those who thought otherwise had the upper hand: Zong Pu would suffer for decades under a regime that demanded nothing less than an unrealistic single-minded passion for the Party-state.

But despite the backlash to which "Red Beans" was subjected, the fact that a story such as Zong Pu's could have been written at all and was praised by early critics demonstrates a wider discussion of affective space within Chinese socialism. "Red Beans" is thus remarkable in describing how different realms of emotional space can intersect; by preserving a porous boundary between these spaces, the text demonstrated how a socialist affective space could emerge. In its narrative nod to dream worlds and hidden wall cavities, "Red Beans" presents a differentially spatialized narrative world through which emotion can constitute the socialist subject as a totality of multiple human affiliations in different times and spaces.

PLAYING THE PEOPLE'S HEARTSTRINGS: ZONG PU'S "A DREAM FOR STRINGS"

This discussion of "Red Beans" helps illuminate a running theme in Zong Pu's work: the articulation of a porous traversal between the individual and the collective whereby these two realms of experience are not viewed as mutually exclusive. In many socialist realist texts, we often find characters who unhesitatingly sacrifice personal fulfillment to achieve broader political goals, or who conveniently conflate personal satisfaction with political activity. Zong Pu's work is more nuanced in illustrating the complexities of squaring personal desire with political aspiration. This theme finds particularly poignant and transcendent expression in "A Dream for Strings," first published in *People's Literature* in December 1978.[47] If "Red Beans" portrays the collective political affects that helped lead to the success of the 1949 Communist revolution, "A Dream for Strings" tentatively imagines how such collective emotion might salvage the Communist era from its destructive extremes. Whereas "Red Beans" focused on Jiang Mei's contested relationships with her lover, Qi Hong, and friend Xiao Su, "A Dream for Strings" features an intergenerational relationship between Murong Yuejun, a cello teacher who came of age in the Yan'an period, and the young Liang Xia. Xia's father was a close friend of Yuejun's and perished in the Cultural Revolution's maelstrom. Xia's mother dies soon after. That the story focuses on the tentative but ultimately intimate relationship between two women bespeaks the importance of female solidarity as a crucial component to the story. Of course, "Red Beans," by featuring as its protagonist a female college student, also engages with issues of feminist political agency; Jiang Mei's struggle to choose between a life of comfortable, bourgeois domesticity in American exile and one of patriotic commitment in China zeroes in on issues particular to women's experience.

However, the issue of gender also takes on particular salience in "A Dream for Strings"; the story was published in the background of the widespread denunciation of the recently deposed Jiang Qing. Zong Pu's story recapitulates this anti–Jiang Qing rhetoric in its portrayal of the April 5, 1976, Tiananmen Incident, a protest against the Gang of Four that originally began as a collective mourning for the late premier Zhou Enlai. Xia declares Jiang Qing to be a "white boned demon" who is "having those damned pretty dreams of hers."[48] This story thus echoes the misogynistic post-Mao line that sought to blame Jiang Qing's court meddling for the Cultural Revolution's excesses.

While Zong Pu's story recapitulates this hysterical discourse about Jiang Qing's misrule, it nevertheless relies upon female relationships to foster feelings of solidarity and revolutionary continuity. Her work thus suggests that the antidote to Maoist hysteria was not the re-masculinization of the public sphere but the formation of an "intimate public," a space initially constituted by female survivors of the trauma. An "intimate public" denotes a confessional, emotive space occupied by women and mediated through acts of popular commodity and cultural consumption.[49] The "intimate public" relies upon the rise of consumer culture that allows women to partake of a common emotional experience and worldview; the mediation of commodities functions to both channel political yearnings and diffuse and refract them into private and domestic concerns. The capitalist "intimate public's" relation to politics is always tentative and ambivalent.

Applying the concept of "intimate public" to the socialist field requires some major reconsideration. Mao-era China was not primarily a market society; production, both material and cultural, did not seek to mystify the social processes that undergirded it as in commodity fetishism but instead sought to reveal the sociality of all productive endeavor. The "private sphere" occupied by women in socialism was not kept away from the larger political public; rather, it engaged with that public through a spectrum that linked the personal and the political. On the other hand, Zong Pu's work also reveals the persistence of melodramatic conventions in portraying women's emotional life. "Red Beans," in particular, is unique in its detailed depiction of the conventional tale of frustrated love in the background of the Civil War. Zong Pu draws a prominent line of mediation between Jiang Mei's private emotional experience and her collective affective commitments. "A Dream for Strings" does not feature a melodramatic love plot, but its sympathetic portrayal of women's confessional space serves as a powerful counterpoint to the strongly misogynistic denunciations of Jiang Qing. While the two heroines are themselves victimized by Jiang Qing's political machinations, they find a measure of healing precisely through their intimate homosocial bond. Zong Pu's description of a feminine confessional space is marked by an intense emotional intimacy. But this intimacy is not permanently confined to private, gendered space: it eventually opens itself up into a common political space in which the masses can engage in politico-affective attunement. In this vein, Zong Pu's portrayal of an "intimate public" ultimately transcends gender and takes on universal significance.

In associating melodrama here with gender, there lies the strong risk of reifying a kind of affective expressivity as exclusively feminine. But it is not merely accidental that the two protagonists of this story are women. The problem of how Yuejun and Xia achieve a kind of emotive solidarity revolves around the question of how they forge a "women's space" in which they can confide in each other their private suffering. Moreover, the relationship between them reminds us of Jiang Mei and Xiao Su's own close bond in "Red Beans." Again, what is notable in both stories is how the intimate relationship between women is then mediated with universal political aspirations.

Zong Pu's deployment of melodrama also underscores the frequent presence of music that heightens her stories' emotionality. Whether it is Beethoven and Chopin in "Red Beans" or a cello piece that induces tears in "A Dream for Strings," Zong Pu's fiction features a sentimental soundtrack that reminds one of Hollywood and pre-1949 Chinese melodrama. Music plays a dual role in Zong Pu's stories that recapitulates her description of private and public affect. It fills the emotional space between private individuals, whether it is Jiang Mei and Qi Hong's love for Massenet or Xia's cello lessons with Yuejun. But music can and does assume a far broader, far more collective dimension in the revolutionary songs Xiao Su and her friends sing and in the sublime cello concert that brings together the lost souls of the Cultural Revolution.

Zong Pu's work seems to bear strong remnants of women's culture popular in Republican China, and in particular the oft-derided "Mandarin Duck and Butterfly" style of popular literature.[50] There are throwbacks to earlier forms of melodramatic convention that caused her work to be deemed far too "bourgeois" according to the standards of socialist realism.[51] "Red Beans" was published during the relaxed period of the Hundred Flowers campaign when writers had more latitude in expression; "A Dream for Strings" was published right after the end of the Cultural Revolution, a far more liberal period for aesthetic creation. The historic circumstances under which these stories were published help explain their considerable novelty. She mediates between the otherwise private "intimate public" of women's popular and middlebrow culture and collective activism. What begins in her stories as the concerns of women undergoing emotional struggle changes into a far broader collective experience that transcends gender.

The concept of "affective mapping" can designate a way in which emotion can be deployed to forge a collective sense of solidarity even when such emotions seem to be inherently private in character.[52] "Affective mapping" thus allows us to imagine emotions in contours that are at once spatialized and socialized, suggesting a terrain in which a collective can both share an emotional experience and reflect critically upon the common historical and political conditions that underpin this experience. While the concluding dream in "A Dream for Strings" emanates from within the depths of Yuejun's being, it nevertheless sets its coordinates in a space that is both public and vulnerable. Yuejun's most personal and private reveries transform into a collective experience, a public square that feels as intimate as a private embrace.

Prior to this apotheosis of collective harmony, the relationship between Yuejun and Xia initially gets off to a rocky start. Yuejun receives a visit from a recently orphaned Xia after she has relocated to Beijing to live with a relative. Xia requests cello lessons from Yuejun. The Cultural Revolution's horrors have left deep scars on Xia, who has learned to cope with the losses of her life with sarcasm and detachment. Moreover, because of her father's downgraded status as a counterrevolutionary, she has been barred from continuing her education and occupational training. As a result she becomes a wild child, rootless, with neither a sense of tact nor direction. The trauma of witnessing her parents' persecution and her own trials has resulted in nights filled with haunting dreams: "Alas, those days, those heavy, somber [*chenzhong*] days! Liang Xia, moreover, was just a child! During that time she had frequent dreams, and in those dreams she always saw a large rock pressing against her body, and no matter what she did she could not dislodge it. She would cry out, cry herself awake, and even then she still felt this heavy weight [*chenzhong*] upon her."[53] With time, however, the terrible dreams cease, and like the stone that presses down upon her in her dreams, Xia becomes stone-like herself, numb to the world. The large stone weighing down upon Xia is the sublime feeling of history in a terrible form. Whereas the Russian Formalist Viktor Shklovsky once famously used the example of a stone's "stoniness" as that which can renew poetic sensibility,[54] the deadening pressure exerted by the stone of history flattens any ability to feel anything else. As a suffocating mass within Xia's psyche, it blocks the passage of emotion, as evidenced by Xia's inability to cry. The sensorial overload of the stone manifests itself with time not as a heightened sensitivity to the world but instead as a traumatized numbness. She grows unable to indulge in any sincere emotion and instead develops a tough, cynical edge, a hardened skepticism against the political lies that surround her. This deeply worries Yuejun, who wishes that Xia would allow herself to confess her pent-up suffering in the form of tears: "[Yuejun] only hoped that she and Xia could weep together. More important was for Xia to allow herself to weep . . . only tears could wash away that cynical smile and melt the frost that enveloped her heart."[55] Yuejun's desire to draw tears out of Xia so they can have a good cry together is emblematic of the surfeit of emotion that saturates this melodramatic text.

Xia's status as an orphan and societal outcast only deepens as the story progresses. Her uncle, recently promoted in the Party, finds the presence of his niece in the household politically compromising. Eager to leave a home in which she is no longer welcome, Xia persuades Yuejun to take her in. While their cohabitation is for the most part agreeable, Yuejun remains perturbed by Xia's behavior, a discomfort compounded by the frequent male visitors who call upon her. However, as 1976 rolls by, Xia grows more somber, and Yuejun begins to suspect that Xia is up to something. The story's climax is the death of Premier Zhou Enlai and the April 5 Tiananmen Incident. Yuejun discovers that during this period of mass mourning, Xia has been distributing leaflets protesting against the Gang of Four in buses and parks, including one that explicitly names the object of her ire: "Down with the white-boned demon that has brought catastrophe to the nation and disaster to the people: Jiang Qing!"[56] The day after Yuejun finds out about Xia's acts of rebellion, Xia disappears, never to return home again.

The narrative thus hangs, in the end, on the expectation of the return of the "prodigal" daughter. Will she be reunited with her adoptive guardian, Yuejun? Will she find her rightful place in socialist society and redeem the tragic deaths of her loyal parents? But rather than give us an answer one way or another, the story completely shifts register and plunges us into Yuejun's dream:

> That night, Yuejun had a dream. She dreamed of a concert in which she was performing, her cello emitting the sounds of glory and victory, and in the middle of the audience there was a pair of dark black eyes, following the movements of the cello's bow. It was Xia!
>
> Suddenly, the person playing the cello on the stage was not her, but Xia. With deft, skillful movements Xia produced an august tune

> that went straight into people's spirits. She let flow tears of joy and victory. The bright lights that filled the stage shone brightly on the silver sequins on her white gauze dress, as well as on her pearly tears that flowed drop by drop in that silver light. The notes of the cello resounded, filling the hall, piercing the air. It was august, heroic, victorious music! This was music that all men and women produced on their heartstrings, it was the music produced by the people's heartstrings! "Father! My father!" Xia cried suddenly. Her clear, crisp voice pierced through the glorious music, and floated up to the very clouds. On that great, high Monument to the Heroes of the People in Tiananmen Square, inscribed by Chairman Mao and Premier Zhou Enlai, appeared the name of Liang Feng [Xia's father] as well as many, many other names. . . . They sacrificed themselves along the ever progressing road of our dear socialist fatherland. Although their ways of sacrificing themselves were not the same as previous heroes, they have every right to live on in the hearts of our people, and to remain everlasting from now on!
>
> The dreams of people will certainly be realized; the dreams of demons will certainly be destroyed. That is the inevitable course of history.[57]

The story might have concluded with a reunion between Yuejun and her protégé; after all, it was published in 1978, by which time Jiang Qing was already in prison, and a measure of political stability had come to China. Even though the last line tells us that the dreams of people, as opposed to those of demons (such as Jiang Qing), will inevitably come true, for the diegetic present the dream remains unfulfilled. Zong Pu's text demurs from forcing utopian desire to manifest itself. It seems to patiently wait for the truly right moment (if ever) to announce itself as narrative reality. Although the text in the end declares that dreams will come true, the narrative itself formally hedges.[58]

The story's ending suggests how dream can be a narrative mode for expressing both an alternative historic narrative and an alternate mode of corporeal experience. The dream expresses a simultaneous metamorphosis of body, history, and narrative form. The intersubjective nature of dream experience, whereby one person can suddenly transmute into another, heightens the sense of collective purpose voiced by the dream. There are two notable bodily transformations: the first is Yuejun's, who first performs on the stage and then transmutes into Xia. The second is the change in Xia's own body: she changes from a dark, somber girl of stone into a graceful, goddess-like figure draped in a flowing white dress. This profound transfiguration in corporeal experience is echoed by the overwhelming presence of mass sentimentality. In many ways it is the inverse of the rage and frenzy of the Cultural Revolution and the opposite of the emotional vacuum that occurred in the wake of that revolution's trauma. Xia, a forlorn, lost orphan in the beginning, transforms into an iconic figure; not only does she represent a redeemed, healed socialist subject, but she is also given elevated figural status in the dreamscape: Xia serves as metaphor for all the souls gathered. Tiananmen itself becomes transfigured from a political space where chaos and terror reign into a magical dream space where recuperation can occur.

Such a dream does not merely offer another historic narrative; it also suggests another way in which historicity can be embodied by the senses. How does such a dream propose a new way of experiencing history that does not seem as if one is being crushed by a heavy stone? Soaring music takes the place of mad denunciations; melody emphasizes a kind of bodily communion that defies the overt propaganda of the Cultural Revolution. Yuejun's dream acts as a salve for history's wounds and suggests not only the communion between generations but also Xia's recovery from her own spiritual and physical victimization. The dream thus suggests a renewed integration of the subject within history.

The story's concluding dream splits the narrative into formally separate modes of representation; however, it is not as if there is a realist narrative that is devoid of pathos and a dream narrative that is saturated with it. Both parts are imbued with pathos, even if it seems that Xia is conspicuously devoid of it as a result of her trauma. While Xia seems stone-like and numb, it is precisely this lack of emotion that elicits such sympathy in Yuejun. What the two narrative sections stage, then, is the process by which Yuejun is able to spark and elicit Xia's own emotional flame and thereupon transfer a store of affect gained from decades of experience. Revolutionary subjectivity can thus be secured by being saturated with pathos transmitted from another. However, whereas in the first narrative section pathos seems to operate by a logic of transfer, in the dream, pathos operates by a different logic of effusive abundance. The dream space is an echo chamber in which the slivers of emotion Yuejun tried to elicit from Xia become amplified into a rousing chorus. This is the truly "communist" vision of pathos, marked by a large surplus shared equally by all. And it is no wonder that this only happens in a dream, not in the "wakened narrative." This dream remains distinct from historic actuality, so as not to usurp its place.

The ways in which emotions transfer between women, among multitudes, and across distinct partitions of the text constitute an "economy of pathos" that structures the subjective conflicts and differences between characters, ideologies, and realms of private and public experience. It can be all too easy to think of emotion as if it were an on-and-off switch; we have either sentimental melodrama or dry, dispassionate realism. In considering Zong Pu's fiction, it may be helpful to see how pathos infuses the entire text in different degrees of intensity, qualities, and vectors. This multifaceted view can hopefully avoid the kind of binary reductions that label certain political ideologies as either being coldly devoid of emotion (hence the need for "socialism with a human face") or being vulgarly saturated with cheap sentiment (hence revolutionary "kitsch").

What began as a melody that Yuejun sought to transmit to Xia becomes, in Yuejun's dream, a song able to elicit sympathetic resonance in the "people's heartstrings." Music is essential in helping demarcate the spatial parameters of collective attunement because of its unique ability to echo through the confines of the subject and induce a sense of sublime commonality. It serves as a reservoir of populist, or even democratic, affects. This sense of common rapture that music induces tells us something about what might be politically possible through collective endeavor. But what "A Dream for Strings" reminds us is that these collective uprisings of popular feelings do not happen spontaneously, without warning. They germinate in the intimate contacts between individuals struggling to achieve connection.

We witness the process of emotional transfer on a number of different scales. First of all, the cello lessons Yuejun gives Xia constitute a form of emotive tutelage. Through music, Yuejun is literally passing on her accumulated affective experience to Xia with the hope that she will gain emotive recovery. Literary theorist Rei Terada has described a "law of emotive thermodynamics" by which a perceived lack of feeling in one person may elicit the arousal of feeling in another person.[59] What constitutes this "law of emotive thermodynamics" in Xia's cello lessons follows a different economy entirely in the dream; Yuejun, who was performing on the stage, suddenly switches places with Xia. In turn, Xia collects Yuejun's emotive substance and transforms it into redemptive music for all of the listeners in the spectral audience gathered at Tiananmen. Music itself, in its resonant echoes, flows into and fills empty spaces, displacing deadening silence. The law of conservation transmutes into echoed infinity. Zong Pu's answer to the destructive mass passions of the Cultural Revolution does not consist in negating collectivities or defusing emotions; it instead seeks to heal the wounds of that frenzy through a shared experience of music.

We can also see this emotional transfer at a formal level; the last line of the story is a rhetorical gesture toward disenchantment: human dreams will become reality, while demonic dreams will be smashed. Such a declaration serves the purposes of political knowledge, informing us how we can convert dreams into their proper political valence. But it can also be read as a kind of obligatory narrative justification for the author's indulgence in dream. However, the fact that the dream does not come true and thus conform to an ideologically forced narrative realization, and that the story refuses such diegetic resolution, enhances the emotive power of the dream that substitutes for a proper ending. The melodic pathos that the dream engenders jumps over the law of history as encapsulated by the textual fence that is the last line of the story, and its unresolved echoes linger on and on, just like a resounding sonata. The dream thus becomes the vehicle through which the emotion engendered as a response to the Cultural Revolution's violence can linger as a figure of hope. But this hope ultimately thrives on the dream's lack of realization; its manifestation into reality would seem to diminish its affective power.

As opposed to the mere ephemerality of Jiang Qing's dream, the text suggests the importance of discursive materiality that Yuejun's dream in the end insists upon. The dream features a transfigured bodily experience that coincides with a history that has been redeemed. It draws upon the virtual "realness" of a dream as we experience it and affirms the dream as a real phenomenological mode of being. However, precisely because it exists in the form of the dream, this mode of being thus lies in a paradoxical state; it always indexes the "waking reality" that exists beside it. Dream here functions in an ironic fashion, suggesting both the solidity and totality of material transfiguration, as well as such transfiguration's tangential acknowledgment of another material reality beside it. Irony is employed here not to mock or parody reality but to convey a sense of both the fragmentation of historical experience and the attempt to mentally grasp it. By suggesting an ironic counterpoint between dream and reality, the text inaugurates not cynicism but rather a powerful affective charge of yearning that both pulls dream and reality together and maintains a crucial critical distance.

That Zong Pu decided to end the story in the mode of dream when she could have emplotted Xia's release and reunion with Yuejun speaks to how she insists upon a certain representational irony. While the last line insists that the dreams of men "will come true," the story does not manifest this future tense; it remains in this waiting room of an anticipatory reality. In what ways, then, does this text thus express a wariness of the official rhetoric of the dream "made real" under socialism, the constant insistence that communism was either arriving or had already arrived? Socialist rhetoric's insistence on the absolute immanence of Communist futurity always already proleptically inscribed in the present left no room for a rhetoric of dream that, while possessing its own sense of phenomenological, material possibility, preserved its sense of irony and refused to dissolve itself into historic actuality.

For Jiang Qing's critics, then, "dream" was a mode of politicized negation that allowed them to render unintelligible and illegible Jiang Qing's political discourse. It also allowed them to declare Jiang Qing's political activity non-knowledge, while elevating their stance as constituting the truth. What this critical dream discourse did not feature was any sense of self-aware irony; Jiang Qing was caught up in a dream, while her critics were grounded in reality. If Zong Pu's story had simply rehearsed this critical discourse, it would rightly be accused of falling into the fallacy of this simplistic binary thinking. However, the dream scene in the end introduces a representational irony, for how can Zong Pu claim that Jiang Qing is simply dreaming while her heroine also dreams? Zong Pu thus recasts the critics' use of dream with a twist: "dream" here points to the tenuousness of all historic experience and how it can travel between the different modalities of "reality" and "dream," history and fiction. While the critics insisted that Jiang Qing's political error was nothing but an empty fiction, Zong Pu insists on the value of fiction, precisely with its dreamlike artifice, as a way of thinking and feeling through a difficult historic impasse.

Jiang Qing and her critics' engagement with *Dream* revealed the uncannily fictional nature of political discursive struggle and how fiction became a privileged intellectual resource for tropes that could be employed as political weapons. The effects could be tragic. But it is difficult to imagine any effective politics that is devoid of rhetoric.[60]

Politics is not always a matter of sober townhouse discourse; it is often conducted within the fuzzy logic of rhetorical and affective persuasion. Politics is to a large degree experienced corporeally in inchoate fashion and proves difficult to clearly articulate with technical precision. Perhaps Zong Pu cannot offer more specific terms than "human" or "dream" to speak of what she yearns. But what need to be excavated are the deep affective investments that lie behind such seemingly hollow words; what needs to be conveyed is a sense of political redemption that can at the moment only be encapsulated in the tremulous notes of a cello. What Zong Pu's fiction reminds us is that politics is not just about ideological statements; it is also about the emotionally textured yearnings that give politics its vital energy.

Furthermore, Zong Pu offers a political vision that mitigates against the highly misogynistic critique of Jiang Qing's supposedly hysterical rule. Critics like Liu Mengxi who engaged in critiques of Jiang Qing pursued what might be termed a "de-feminization" of the political realm, a reconsolidation of political masculinity that had happened countless times in Chinese court history. In the place of hysterical firebrands like the Gang of Four, sober, pragmatic technocrats like Deng Xiaoping would rule. In this new restoration, no woman could ever pretend to be emperor again.

Zong Pu imagines a possible solution to the impasse that refrains from displacing women from the political arena. Rather than rejecting sentimentality as too feminine, she openly embraces its place in political discourse. And when examined carefully, it reveals a deeper political intelligence. In the end, sentimentality transcends gender altogether: the dream audience in Tiananmen is composed of men and women. In its place is the synthesis that a term "intimate public" implies: an expression of civic solidarity as expressed through binding, personalized pathos.

Zong Pu's story makes use of the dream discourse employed by Jiang Qing's critics. She rehearses the strident denunciations of the reviled leader of the Gang of Four. But the story also transcends mere binary polemic. Her use of dream as rhetoric and trope in her story suggests how fiction reveals the ironic fragmentation of historic experience and thus implies the tenuousness of claims that "this" time and space are either reality or dream. Thus the "dreams" of Jiang Qing and the story's protagonist should not be viewed so much as dueling rivals but as mutually defining ideological elaborations of the Cultural Revolution's historical paradox. Like many revolutions, there will never be a singular experience that can be claimed by all or a singular narrative that everyone can tell, no matter how much regimes and historians attempt to do so. Zong Pu's fiction illuminates the Cultural Revolution as a counterpoint of tragedy and hope featured in equal measure.

Conclusion

Lu Xun and the Dreams of Politics and Literature

This book was first conceived and written well before the PRC government, under the leadership of President Xi Jinping, began to promulgate the idea of the "Chinese Dream" (Zhongguo meng) in 2012 as a slogan for national development and rejuvenation. Since the term started to appear in official speeches and publications, there has been much debate surrounding its meaning. Western critics have pondered whether the "Chinese Dream" is an imitation of the "American Dream." Xi Jinping's public speeches given between 2012 and 2014 shed light on some recurring features of what he terms "the Chinese Dream of the rejuvenation of the Chinese nation" (*Zhonghua minzu weida fuxing de Zhongguo meng*).[1] They include the recovery of a "5000-year-old" culture and civilization, the promotion of patriotism and hard work, the creation of a "moderately prosperous" society (*xiaokang shehui*),[2] harmonious foreign relations, and assiduous study among young people.

There is neither enough space nor enough time to discuss the "Chinese Dream" at length; this is better left to other scholars. But the analysis offered in this book should make clear that the linkage between dream and political economy is not a recent phenomenon but instead another instance in a chain of ideas linking dreaming, China, and the travails of modernity. What is unique here is that the rhetoric of dreaming has become such a central part of governing rhetoric in ways that are unprecedented in modern Chinese history. If Chinese imperial courts once used dreams to divine heavenly messages about the realm, now the modern Chinese state is using the rhetoric of dreams to give the population a vision of the way forward.

After decades of technocratic reform and widespread "depoliticization," the sudden enthusiasm for national dreams seems to attest to the PRC government's tacit acknowledgment of the need for a new language of political possibility. People desire to speak in a way that transcends purely economistic and developmental discourse, one that gives voice to personal and collective yearnings. As Xi Jinping notes, "individual dreams should be closely integrated with the Chinese Dream."[3] The Chinese Dream, in its integration of personal wishes with collective desires, thus figures a "shared soul" (*gong tong de hun*) that unites not just the citizens of the PRC but all people of Chinese descent.[4] The Chinese Dream attests to a "spirit" that seems analogous to Georg Hegel's concept of *Geist*: an idealist conception of collective will that moves through history. The Chinese Dream as trope effectively conflates individual consciousness with a collective entity, the Chinese nation; such rhetoric naturalizes the fabricated existence of abstract conceits.

However, as Lu Xun revealed in his essay about *Eastern Miscellany*'s 1933 issue on dreams, dreams themselves are special forms of political speech that can be controlled, managed, and repressed.[5] Just as it was in the past, it seems the Chinese Dream also seeks to contain, control, and bind all political rhetoric within its own narrow confines. The leadership thus provides an outlet for its citizens to participate in a sanctioned language-game, but they must follow certain rules. Visions of a harmonious society held together by the complementary pairing of an authoritarian state and capitalist economy are heralded as expressions of the Chinese Dream; however, the clamor for free speech and greater democracy in places like the Special Administrative Region of Hong Kong are seen as expressions of sedition. Why cannot the voices of protest for a more democratic and equal society also be seen as unique iterations of a Chinese Dream? And who gets to decide which expressions of futurity are dreams and which are treason?

If the American Dream and the Chinese Dream have something in common, it perhaps lies in the risk of promoting a naively optimistic rhetoric of future prosperity and abundance without reflecting critically on the historical and social conditions that move people to dream in the first place. When dreaming transforms from a dialectical process of reflection into the rubber-stamping of clichéd ideology (of whatever persuasion), it may veer from radical hope to tragic hubris. As Chapter 3's discussion of Mao Dun's *Midnight* demonstrated, the reckless ambitions of national prosperity can all too easily become a dream from which one awakes, not the portent of a transfigured future. Reports from the summer of 2015 about the precipitous tumbling of the Chinese stock market revealed the cracks in this

Chinese Dream. As the Chinese banking system sought to shield the economy from the fallout of the global financial crisis that broke out in 2008, they encouraged a speculative bubble in property and stocks that only temporarily allayed the hardships borne by people the world over. While not very large in comparison to the overall population, a substantial number of citizens invested their savings in stocks, only to find their wealth, and their dreams, depleted. As one anonymous blogger noted on an Internet BBS forum, "the Chinese Dream . . . was really just a dream."[6] While Xi Jinping offered an idealistic rhetoric about a dream of national rejuvenation, in actual practice national dreams were tied to faith in economic mirages that could no longer be sustained.[7] Political futurity was recklessly tied to economic futures.

It may very well be instructive to look back at a century of writers who pondered on dreams about China and their own lives. In his frequently cited 1922 preface to the collection of stories *Call to Arms*, Lu Xun makes explicit mention of dreams:

> When I was young, I too had many dreams, most of which I later forgot—and without the slightest regret. Although remembering the past can bring happiness, it can also bring a feeling of solitude; and where is the pleasure in clinging on to the memory of lonely times passed? My trouble is, though, that I find myself unable to forget, or at least unable to forget entirely. And it is this failure of amnesia that has brought [*Call to Arms*] into existence.[8]

Lu Xun sees his own maturation into adulthood as a sequential chain of dreams, each dream falling apart and giving rise to a new one that also fails. Lu Xun first dreamed of saving his father through traditional Chinese medicine and knowledge, only to have his father die and his family ground into bankruptcy. He then dreams of Western science and medicine as that which will save the nation, only to become disillusioned as a student in Japan. Then he turns to the dream of literature as that which can save souls, and begins a journal; the journal is aborted before it can come to fruition. After flailing in a prolonged period of utter despondency he is somehow persuaded to pick up his pen again and write for futurity, unsure at all of the results.

Dreaming is something that Lu Xun tries to abandon once and for all, only to discover that to live is to dream, no matter how many times such dreams will inevitably dissolve. What he realizes is his own mistake in believing there is some kind of magical blueprint, whether it be tradition, science, or literature, that can be an effective, complete panacea for all of the social ills that plague his nation. His disappointment leads, in his own narration, to paralysis and hopelessness. But he learns that political change is not about having the right answer in front of one's eyes; politics entails the process of beginning again, starting anew, and allowing oneself to fail.

It has been argued that the project of mass industrial modernity in the twentieth century constituted a "dreamworld" that has now passed on, leaving us to deal with its substantial consequences and struggling to find a new solution to present crises that do not recapitulate the considerable mistakes of the past.[9] For China, literature as an institution of modernity was undeniably a part of this dreamworld and has remained, although much diminished, as a focal point for national and cultural pride. Literature as mass, state-sponsored institution also left in its wake memories of suppression, censorship, and occasional mind-numbing banality. The Chinese state's continual clamor for a Nobel Prize in Literature by an author they approved (which they finally achieved with Mo Yan's win in 2012) seemed more of an outdated whimper for cultural respectability in a world that has long ceased to care.

In an aesthetic field increasingly crowded by film, television, and Internet-driven new media, it is hard to see how literature can continue to be accorded aesthetic primacy. The greatest challenger to literature's hegemony over mass culture has been the rise of technologically sophisticated, well-marketed popular forms. Technological innovation has also changed the way we read literature itself; the rise of electronic readers will irrevocably change the material culture of the book. One cannot help walking into a community bookstore without a palpable feeling of advance melancholy that this physical space, where readers rub elbows while perusing books they will probably not buy, is in the very process of vanishing, perhaps to be replaced by an electronics store.

Literature can no longer promise a direct, strategic vision of political change. No one seriously thinks that re-creating a literary-institutional model in the style of communism in the contemporary moment is a good idea or even feasible. Literature has long ceased to be the exclusive platform for political and affective inculcation that late Qing political reformer Liang Qichao hoped it would be over a century ago. But it can still suggest the intuitive beginnings of political thought and provide emergent contours of a possible utopia. This limitation is, in fact, a great strength of aesthetic literature. What literature can do is provide the emergent forms of thought, empathy, and intuition that may spur readers into imagining that other worlds are possible. It is precisely because of literature's intense engagement with imagination and emotion, one facilitated by its formal and symbolic intricacy, that it can catalyze an affective and intellectual ferment through which a politics of solidarity may be possible. For those of us who do believe that there is a relation between the arts and hope for a more just world, the best thing we can do to develop this relation is to emphasize ever more strenuously what Cyril Birch once called the "particle of art."[10] It is precisely by paying due attention to the affective materiality of literary text that we discover the aesthetic resources for articulating hope. In our insistence that students do not just read, but read closely, slowly, and reflectively, we model for them a practice of temporality that resists its efficient instrumentalization for economic production but yet offers an experience of time that is rich in meaning.

The lingering thread of dreams that haunted Lu Xun into middle age did not constitute a failure to put the past behind and live firmly in "reality"; rather, attending to this thread, and seeing where it goes in unexpected and serendipitous fashion, constitutes the very narrative trajectory of life itself. To attach oneself to this ever tenuous thread of dreams is to have faith in hope, to be accepting of disappointment, and to be completely and forever open to the future. From the vantage point of these fragile dreams, we learn that the social, political, and economic configurations that constitute "reality" itself are themselves ever changing, and so must our response also be protean and fluid in nature. It is precisely in the lingering traces of past, failed dreams that a road to a more just future may come into view. This study concludes not by offering a sense of closure or end but by encouraging all of us to start dreaming again.

GLOSSARY OF CHINESE CHARACTERS

Ai Siqi 艾思奇
Axuan 阿萱

Ba Jin 巴金
baihua 白話
Baosu 抱素
Beiming 焙茗
bei yayi 被壓抑
buduan tuibian 不斷蛻變

Cao Xueqin 曹雪芹
Changshi congshu 嘗試叢書
Chen Duxiu 陳獨秀
Chen Shiyuan 陳士元
chenzhong 沉重
chi ren shuo meng 癡人說夢
chizha 叱咤

dai 呔
dailei 帶累
dajia 大家
dang 黨
Dao 道
Daoerdun zhi jianshuo 道爾頓制淺說
daoqing 道情
"Daoyan" 導言
Daozai 道載
Dazhong zhexue 大眾哲學
dazibao 大字報
Deng Xiaoping 鄧小平
dianxing 典型
Dong Qian 董千
Dongfang zazhi 東方雜誌
Dongyao 動搖
Du Liniang 杜麗娘
Du Yuanzai 杜元載

emeng 噩夢 and 惡夢

Fan Bowen 範博文
Fan Yanqiao 範煙橋
Fang Luolan 方羅蘭
Fang sheng wei si zhi jian 方生未死之間
Feng Youlan 馮友蘭
Feng Zhongpu 馮鐘璞
"Fengxue zhi ye" 風雪之夜
Fu Lianzhang傅連暲

gei Dao zaile yixia 給道載了一下
geming xianshizhuyi yu geming langmanzhuyi 革命現實主義與革命浪漫主義
gongtong de hun 共同的魂
"Gou de bojie" 狗的駁詰

guahao 掛號
Guo Moruo 郭沫若
guoyu meng meng le 過於夢夢了
Gushi xinbian 故事新編

hai bu zhidao fenbie 還不知道分別
haiyao dailei le wo 還要帶累了我
haiyao dailei tamen li 還要帶累他們哩
haohao dangdang 浩浩蕩蕩
haowu yiyi 毫無意義
He Qifang 何其芳
Hong deng ji 紅燈記
"Hong dou" 紅豆
Hong lou meng 紅樓夢
hongxuejia 紅學家
Hu Feng 胡風
Hu Shi 胡適
huangdi meng 皇帝夢
huangmiu 荒謬
Huanmie 幻滅
huanxin 歡欣
Hui 慧
Huifang 蕙芳

Jia 家
Jia Baoyu 賈寶玉
jiang 將
Jiang Mei 江玫
Jiang Qing 江青
ji'e 飢餓
Jin ping mei 金瓶梅
Jing 靜
jingshen 精神
jingyi 驚異
Juehui 覺慧
Juemin 覺民
Juexin 覺新

Kaiming Shudian 開明書店
Kangxi 康熙
kuang 狂
"Kuangren riji" 狂人日記

Lao Can youji 老殘遊記
Lao She 老舍
"Li Shuangshuang xiaozhuan" 李雙雙小傳
Li Zhun 李准
Liang Feng 梁鋒
Liang Xia 梁遐
Lin Daojing 林道靜
Lin Peiyao 林佩瑶
Lin Shu 林紓
Liu E 劉鶚
Liu Mengxi 劉夢溪
Liu Shaoqi 劉少奇
Liu Xiaobo 劉曉波
Liu Yuying 劉玉英
Lu Jiachuan 盧嘉川
Lu Xun 魯迅
Lun yu 論語

mamu 麻木
Mao Dun 茅盾
Mao Zedong 毛澤東
maobing 毛病
meng夢
Meng 夢
Meng zhan yi zhi 夢占逸旨
menghuan 夢幻
mengjian 夢見
mengjing夢境
mengyouzhe 夢遊者
mu 畝
Mudan ting 牡丹亭
Murong Yuejun 慕容樂珺

Nahan 吶喊
nei 內
Nülan wu hao 女籃5號

paishan daohai de renqun 排山倒海 的人群

Qi Hong 齊虹
"Qi wu lun" 齊物論
Qiang Meng 強猛
Qiang Weili 強唯力
qing 情
Qingchun zhi ge 青春之歌
qingle ge jiaqi de jia 請了個假期的假
"Qiuqizhe" 求乞者
"Qiuye" 秋夜
Qu Qiubai 瞿秋白
Qu Yuan 屈原

ren 人
Renmin ribao 人民日報
Renmin wenxue 人民文學

sanluan man chuang de ribao 散亂滿床的日報
sanwen shi 散文詩
shehui diaocha 社會調查
shehuizhuyi lai de zheme kuai 社會主義來得這麼快
Shen Dehong 沈德鴻
Shenbao 申報
shenme 什麼
shewang 奢望
Shi 蝕
shiji diaocha 實際調查
"Shijian kaishi le!" 時間開始了
shili 勢利
shixian 實現
Shiyan 石言 (stone words)
shiyan 實言 (true words)
Shu Xincheng 舒新城
Shuhong 樹紅
Shuxiu 淑秀
Sun Wuyang 孫舞陽

Taishang ganying pian 太上感應篇
Tang Xianzu 湯顯祖
Tao'an mengyi 陶庵夢憶
taochu mengjing 逃出夢境
Tiananmen 天安門
"Ting shuo meng" 聽說夢
Tong yi ge shijie, Tong yi ge mengxiang 同一個世界，同一個夢想
tongku 痛苦
tou xi bie ren 偷襲別人
tuanti 團體
"Tuibaixian de chandong" 頹敗線的顫動

Wang Hefu 王和甫
Wang Ruoshui 王若水
Wang Shitao 王詩陶
Wang Wei 王維
Wang Wenshi 王汶石
Wang Xifeng 王熙鳳
Wang Zhenjia 王振家
wen yi zai Dao 文以載道
Wo he jiaoyu 我和教育
wo mengjian ziji zai zuomeng 我夢見自己在做夢
"Wo shi shei?" 我是誰
wo yuanyi zai wuxing wuse de xianxue linli de cubaoshang jiewen 我願意在無形無色的鮮血淋漓的粗暴上接吻
Wu Jianren 吳趼人
Wu Sunfu 吳蓀甫
Wu Zetian 武則天

Xi Jinping 習近平
"Xia ye" 夏夜
"Xianshang de meng" 弦上的夢
xianshi 現實
xianshizhuyi 現實主義

Xiao Zhang 小張
Xiao Su 蕭素
xiaokang shehui 小康社會
Xie Jin 謝晉
xieshi 寫實
xieshi pai 寫實派
xieshizhuyi 寫實主義
xiesidili dafazuo 歇斯底里大發作
Xihu mengxun 西湖夢尋
Xin shitou ji 新石頭記
Xinli zazhi 心理雜誌
Xinlixue da yi 心理學大意
Xinlixue mingci 心理學名詞
Xiren 襲人
xiuru 羞辱
Xiwang 喜旺
Xu Manli 徐曼麗

Yan Keqin 嚴克勤
"Yan shuangxia de meng" 嚴霜下的夢
yan zhi 言志
Yan'an 延安
yang 陽
Yang Mingyuan 楊明遠
Yang Mo 楊沫
yeban 夜班
Yecao 野草
yi hanghang, yi duidui 一行行，一隊隊
"Yijue" 一覺
yin 陰
"Ying de gaobie" 影的告別
Yongzheng 雍正
Yu Pingbo 俞平伯
Yu Yongze 余永澤
yuanmeng 圓夢
Yunyun 芸芸
Yusi 語絲

zawen 雜文
Zhang Dai 張岱
Zhang Yaoxiang張燿翔
Zhang Yimou 張藝謀
zhanyou 戰友
Zhao Botao 趙伯韜
Zhaohua xishi 朝花夕拾
zhen 真
Zheng Zhenduo 鄭振鐸
zhengzong 正宗
zhenshi 真實
zhi sang ma huai 指桑罵槐
zhi sang shuo huai指桑說槐
zhiji 知己
Zhongguo meng 中國夢
Zhonghua minzu weida fuxing de Zhongguo meng 中華民族偉大復興的中國夢
Zhonghua Shuju 中華書局
Zhou Enlai 周恩來
Zhou Libo 周立波
Zhou Shuren 周樹人
Zhou Yang 周揚
Zhou Zhongwei 周仲偉
Zhou Zuoren 周作人
Zhuangzi 莊子
zhuanshu 篆書
zhukou 住口
Ziye 子夜
Zong Pu 宗璞
zuguo 祖國
zuomeng 做夢

NOTES

INTRODUCTION

1. Wu Jianren, *Xin shitou ji*, 6.

2. Ibid., 7.

3. Liu E, *Lao Can youji*, 5–10. Harold Shadick's translation is titled *The Travels of Lao Ts'an.*

4. Confucius and Slingerland, *Analects*, 65.

5. Zhuangzi and Watson, *Zhuangzi*, 44.

6. Foucault, "Dream, Imagination, and Existence," 51.

7. For a wonderfully uncanny representation of this fear, see Eric Cartman's nightmare about the Opening Ceremonies in the episode "The China Problem," from the twelfth season of the animated comedy *South Park*.

8. In December 2008 a Chinese online petition, known as Charter 08 and signed by many intellectuals, called for greater political liberalization as well as even more neoliberal economic "reforms" and was modeled somewhat on the famous Czechoslovakian Charter 77. Its chief proponent, Liu Xiaobo, was promptly arrested and convicted of subversion. He was subsequently awarded the Nobel Peace Prize in 2010. In the last sentence the writers echo the Olympic slogan by stating that they hope to "realize the people's unflagging wish and dream [*mengxiang*] of the last hundred years." See Charter 08.

9. In the last few years, the central government has done precisely that: I will briefly remark on the recent "China Dream" in the conclusion.

CHAPTER 1: SLEEPING THROUGH CATASTROPHE

1. Wagner, "China 'Asleep' and 'Awakening,'" 48–58. His exhaustive study features an informative graph that shows the number of references to the "nation asleep/awake" metaphor in the Chinese press from 1884 to 1920. The graph shows a quite high peak between the years 1896 and 1907, the heyday of late Qing nationalism.

2. Wolfgang Schivelbusch's *Disenchanted Night*, Eluned Summers-Bremner's *Insomnia: A Cultural History*, Craig Koslofsky's *Evening's Empire*, and Roger Ekirch's *At Day's Close* are wonderful books that explore modern understandings of nighttime. Simon Williams's *The Politics of Sleep*

and Jonathan Crary's *24/7* explore the diminution of night and sleep under conditions of contemporary capitalism.

3. Koslofsky, *Evening's Empire*, 2.

4. Ibid., 174–75.

5. Summers-Bremner, *Insomnia*, 66.

6. Marx, *Capital*, 1:389–411.

7. Summers-Bremner, *Insomnia*, 84.

8. Benjamin, *The Arcades Project*, 389.

9. Tong Lam, in his history of the role of facts and social surveys in late-Qing and Republican China, argues that Chinese intellectuals' sense of epistemic belatedness "traumatized" them with "this perceived national humiliation." Lam's insistence on collective trauma and humiliation is well taken, but there should also be acknowledgment of a robust sense of curiosity, wonder, and even pleasure involved in the search for new knowledge. See Lam, *A Passion for Facts*, 4–12, 38–41. Fa-ti Fan has summarized the European view of China's purported lackadaisical attitude toward science and "facts" in the decades following the Opium War. See Fan, *British Nationalists in Qing China*, 87.

10. Strassberg, introduction, 1.

11. Ong, *The Interpretation of Dreams in Ancient China*, 174.

12. Foucault, "Dream, Imagination, and Existence," 42.

13. Ibid., 59. Foucault's assertion of the dream as modulated world coincides well with Daniel Tiffany's argument that toys are modular illustrations for materiality that cannot otherwise be made intelligible or visible. See Tiffany, *Toy Medium*, 52.

14. Brigitte Teboul-Wang notes that the dates mentioned in *Dream Reminiscences* span from 1612 to 1657, but the complete collection was probably not compiled until near the end of his life. See Teboul-Wang, introduction, 10. She has produced a full, annotated French translation. Philip Kafalas has published a fine monograph on Zhang Dai's literary writings. See Kafalas, *In Limpid Dream*.

15. Freud famously made note of the palimpsest-like nature of the mind in his 1925 essay "A Note on the 'Mystic Writing-Pad.'"

16. Wang Hui, "Scientific Worldview," 127.

17. Ibid., 136.

18. Science as critique and science as social praxis came together in important ways for the sake of nation-building, a process in which public, civic emotions constituted a key component. Discussing the French revolutionary terror, Sophie Wahnich argues that the championship of "reason" as the arbiter of political deliberation was coupled from the very beginning with a strong, civic passion for the nation that was birthed from the revolution and that upheld the rule of reason: "The notion of reason is not opposed to the register of the emotions, but rather echoes it. Love of the *patrie* is the foundation of reason." See Wahnich, *In Defence of the Terror*, 72.

19. Jingyuan Zhang, *Psychoanalysis in China*, 34–35.

20. Ibid., 86.

21. Ibid.

22. Shu, *Wo he jiaoyu*, 388.

23. Shu, *Meng*, 82.
24. Ibid., 1–2.
25. Ibid., 4.
26. Freud, *The Interpretation of Dreams*, 651.
27. Ibid., 658–59.
28. Zhang Yaoxiang, "Bianjizhe yan," 3. I did not locate the original run but came across a compendium of the most important articles, organized by subject and published in 1931 and republished the year after. By 1931 the journal had been out of print, and in all only fourteen issues were produced. While the articles bear the name of their authors, they do not have dates attached, so the articles mentioned hereafter can only be dated sometime in the 1920s. Zhang Yaoxiang, the compiler, wrote that the impetus for publishing the anthology was to make up for previous journals that had been lost, as well as to provide a ready reference for seminal native research on psychology. See Zhang Yaoxiang, "Bianjizhe yan," 1.
29. Ibid., 1.
30. Du, "Meng," 377.
31. This was, of course, directly related to the vogue for the "social survey" (*shehui diaocha*). The form and epistemic modality of these social surveys helped "produce legible and calculable empirical facts that were associated with the representation, imagining, and governing of the Chinese nation." Lam, *A Passion for Facts*, 2.
32. Du, "Meng," 382.
33. Ibid., 380.
34. Ibid., 382.
35. See Richard Strassberg's recent translation of and introduction to Chen Shiyuan's *Lofty Principles of Dream Interpretation* (Meng zhan yi zhi) in his *Wandering Spirits: Chen Shiyuan's Encyclopedia of Dreams*. His introduction provides an instructive survey into the variety of dream culture in premodern China.
36. Lam, *A Passion for Facts*, 2–6.
37. Huters, "Mirages of Representation," 13.
38. Wang Hui, "Scientific Worldview," 133.
39. Lukács, *The Historical Novel*, 24.
40. Chen Duxiu, "On Literary Revolution," 141.
41. Terry Eagleton has usefully deployed Wittgenstein's concept to think about categories of literature. See Eagleton, *The Event of Literature*, 19–23.
42. Here I am expressing a different opinion from that of Roman Jakobson, who argues that realism as a historical literary movement of the nineteenth century is but one of several competing definitions. See Jakobson, "On Realism in Art," 39. I am arguing that realism's historic origins are more a condition for its existence than a definition.
43. Button, *Configurations of the Real*, 3, 54–60.
44. Ross Wetzsteon recounts this episode in a tribute to his former teacher. See Wetzsteon, "Nabokov as Teacher," 245.
45. Andrew F. Jones's book *Developmental Fairy Tales*, on the role of evolutionary thinking in Chinese intellectual and aesthetic discourse, lays

out the pervasive influence of biological sciences in thinking through Chinese modernity.

46. Žižek, introduction, 24.

47. However, it is important to note that the terms *xieshizhuyi* (realism [literally, "write reality-ism"]) and *xieshi pai* (realist school) predated the use and later dominance of *xianshizhuyi*. Marston Anderson traces *xieshi*'s arrival from Japan (J: *shajitsu*) and points to Liang Qichao's work as the "first significant Chinese use of the term." See Anderson, *The Limits of Realism*, 28. Lydia Liu categorizes *xianshi* as a "Sino-Japanese-European loanword in modern Chinese." See Lydia Liu, *Translingual Practice*, 294. The literary term "realism" (Ch: *xianshizhuyi*; J: *genjitsushugi*) is an example of a suffixed compound from modern Japanese. See Lydia Liu, *Translingual Practice*, 345.

48. Jakobson, "On Realism in Art," 42.

49. Ibid., 41.

50. Ibid., 39–43.

51. Ibid., 40.

52. Indeed, seven years later Jakobson, in partnership with Yurii Tynianov, would attempt such a mediation between historical and formal approaches with their programmatic essay "Problems in the Study of Language and Literature."

53. Vera Schwarcz has pointed out that early May Fourth interest in science was not the dogmatic "scientism" it is often accused of being. Rather, the May Fourth intellectuals were very much invested in the epistemological stakes and issues that science foregrounded. See Schwarcz, *The Chinese Enlightenment*, 100.

54. Anderson, *The Limits of Realism*, 17.

55. Ba Jin, *Family*, 188.

56. Belinsky, "Thoughts and Notes on Russian Literature," 3.

57. Vissarion Belinsky to Vasily Botkin, September 8, 1841, in Belinsky, *Sobranie sochinenii*, 9:482.

58. As Tolstoy concluded in his second Sebastopol Sketch of 1855, "the hero of my story, whom I love with all my heart and soul . . . is truth." See Tolstoy, *Sebastopol Sketches*, 109.

59. Kliger, *The Narrative Shape of Truth*, 5–34.

60. My desire to place crisis as a constitutive component in understanding realism is inspired by Marxian analyses of capitalism as a political economic system that is in perpetual crisis. However, crisis in itself does not spell immediate catastrophic disaster; if anything, crisis often serves to drive further capitalist expansion.

61. Button, *Configurations of the Real*, 54, 67–69.

62. Ibid., 69.

63. Indeed a lot of my approach is loosely inspired by Irina Paperno's analysis of the "semiotics of behavior" among the nineteenth-century Russian realists and, most crucially, the life and work of Nikolai Chernyshevsky in her book *Chernyshevsky and the Age of Realism*. Her work is exemplary in adapting structuralism and semiotics to realist literature. and ideology despite realism's professed claims to unmediated representation and transparency.

64. Jingyuan Zhang, *Psychoanalysis in China*, 85.

65. Irina Paperno notes how Lev Tolstoy often used the "transcendental potential of dreams" to "open a hidden recess of linear time." See Paperno, "*Who, What Am I?*" 24.

66. It was Zheng Zhenduo, as well as Mao Dun, who issued a call for a "literature of blood and tears." See Anderson, *The Limits of Realism*, 44.

67. Here I draw inspiration from Bill Brown's distinction between "objects" and "things." Objects are those bodies, entities, and concepts made intelligible to the subject, those things that can be "read." "Things," on the other hand, straddle the limit between intelligibility and opacity; they are usually made palpable through disruption in our modes of behavior and knowledge. See Bill Brown, "Thing Theory," 4–5.

68. This is Peter Button's term. See Button, *Configurations of the Real*, 54.

69. Here I am inspired by David Harvey's notion of a "spatial fix" whereby dominant capitalist powers seek to defer their own crises of accumulation to subjugated parts of the world. See Harvey, *Limits to Capital*, 415, 431–38. In that sense, I argue we need to regard third-world realisms not as pale imitations of their first-world models but as a dynamic interaction and engagement with both the globalized and uneven circulation of literary forms and institutions and the (not unconnected) demands of domestic national development.

CHAPTER 2: DREAMING AS REPRESENTATION

1. Anderson, *The Limits of Realism*, 91.

2. Lu Xun, *Lu Xun quanji*, 1:438–39. Unless otherwise noted, all Chinese citations of Lu Xun's work are from the 2005 edition of his collected works. Julia Lovell has produced the most recent complete translation of Lu Xun's fiction. See Lu Xun, *The Real Story of Ah-Q and Other Tales of China*.

3. Lee, *Voices from the Iron House*, 91.

4. Ban Wang, *The Sublime Figure of History*, 79.

5. Ibid., 87.

6. Xiaobing Tang, "Lu Xun's 'Diary of a Madman' and a Chinese Modernism," 1225–28.

7. Ming Dong Gu, "Lu Xun and Modernism/Postmodernism," 37.

8. Alastair Fowler's classic treatment of genre and mode (*Kinds of Literature*) exemplifies this far more dynamic and open approach to questions of literary categories. Slavic literary studies, substantially influenced by the contributions of the Russian Formalists and structuralism, have long engaged in such sophisticated formal analysis and interpretation.

9. Li Rong, "Wuci de yuyan," 218.

10. Carolyn T. Brown has a fine essay that argues how Lu Xun's use of the dream form in *Wild Grass* is his attempt to "heal" the "Chinese body" and "spirit" analogous to the way a psychoanalyst may heal a patient by bringing the unconscious "into awareness and to be integrated with the conscious." Her approach engages far more with Freudian psychoanalysis than mine. See Carolyn T. Brown, "Lu Xun's Interpretation of Dreams," 77.

11. As Brown notes, in more psychoanalytic fashion, "[The] dream provides the means for splitting the dreamer's mind and allowing . . . two parts of the psyche, to directly address one another." See Carolyn T. Brown, "Lu Xun's Interpretation of Dreams," 71.

12. Lu Xun, *Lu Xun quanji*, 2:166.

13. Ibid., 2:169.

14. Ibid., 2:229.

15. Feuerwerker, *Ideology, Power, Text*, 61.

16. Urban, "The 'I' of Discourse," 36–37.

17. Hamburger, *The Logic of Literature*, 286.

18. Hamburger does concede that first-person narrated fiction appears to be, like lyric, a reality statement emanating from a speaking "I." However, she maintains that such fiction merely "feigns" a real situation of a speaking "I." See ibid., 311–14.

19. Culler, *Theory of the Lyric*, 105.

20. Hamburger, *The Logic of Literature*, 276. Perhaps a way of understanding this seemingly counterintuitive difference between the lyric-I and a real "I" is to think about how U.S. courts have granted corporations legal personhood even though we would not conventionally think of corporations as being "persons."

21. Žižek, *The Sublime Object of Ideology*, 13.

22. Lu Xun, *Lu Xun quanji*, 10:290. In the original text, the English term is placed alongside the Chinese term *mengyouzhe*, or "dream-traveler."

23. Lu Xun, *Lu Xun quanji*, 4:481.

24. Ibid., 4:483. Nicholas Kaldis has remarked perceptively about this parallel. See Kaldis, "The Prose Poem and Aesthetic Insight," 157.

25. Lu Xun, *Lu Xun quanji*, 4:481.

26. Wittgenstein, *Philosophical Investigations*, 193e.

27. Lu Xun, *Lu Xun quanji*, 4:483.

28. Ibid., 4:482.

29. Sun Yushi, *Yecao yanjiu*, 142.

30. Lu Xun, *Wild Grass*, 46. I make use of the English translation produced by the Foreign Languages Press; however, for other passages where I think the translation may have obscured moments in the original text I wish to highlight, I have substituted my own.

31. Ibid.

32. Ibid., 47.

33. Lu Xun, *Lu Xun quanji*, 4:483.

34. Ibid., 2:210.

35. Ibid.

36. Ibid.

37. Ibid., 2:210–11.

38. Lu Xun, *Wild Grass*, 49.

39. Lu Xun, *Lu Xun quanji*, 2:169.

40. Ibid., 2:171.

41. Kaldis, "The Prose Poem and Aesthetic Insight," 68.

42. Lu Xun, *Lu Xun quanji*, 2:171.

43. Pun Ngai, "Opening a Minor Genre of Resistance in Reform China," 535.

44. Lu Xun, *Lu Xun quanji*, 2:203.

45. Nicholas Kaldis remains unconvinced that this piece has much merit or efficacy as social critique. He declares "The Dog's Retort" to be "an unimpressive attempt at ironical critical commentary on the foolishness of social customs and hierarchical distinctions." See Kaldis, *Chinese Prose Poem*, 218.

46. Kaldis notes that the social critique would be better served by the *zawen* essay and not in a prose poem—the "complex introspective philosophical and psychological ideas" of the prose poem genre do not lend themselves to didactic social critique. See Kaldis, *Chinese Prose Poem*, 220.

47. As Nicholas Kaldis perceptively notes in his monograph on *Wild Grass*, the way the historical description employs metaphor blurs the line between the "real" and the aesthetic, although I would not go so far as to say that this figuration "robs the image of its historical objectivity." See Kaldis, *Chinese Prose Poem*, 261. Certainly Lu Xun was aware of the problems that narrative technique, representational considerations, and ideology pose in presenting history, something he demonstrated to full effect in *Old Stories Retold*, but I do not think his awareness of the formal constructedness of history led him to discount the importance of historical objectivity tout court.

48. Lu Xun, *Lu Xun quanji*, 2:228.

49. Ibid.

50. Ibid.

51. Ibid., 2:229.

52. Andrew F. Jones has written extensively on Lu Xun's intellectual and aesthetic engagement with evolutionary and developmental thinking. See Jones, *Developmental Fairy Tales*, 63–98.

53. Lu Xun, *Wild Grass*, 68.

54. Lu Xun, *Lu Xun quanji*, 2:229–30.

55. Sun Yushi, *Yecao yanjiu*, 190–91.

56. Ibid., 195.

57. Kaldis, "The Prose Poem and Aesthetic Insight," 63. His recent monograph offers a chapter-length study on the issue of genre in the prose poem. See Kaldis, *Chinese Prose Poem*, 95–124.

58. Monroe, *A Poverty of Objects*, 37.

59. To be sure, beyond the poem/prose dichotomy, *Wild Grass* flaunts a heterogeneity in form and structure, one to be seen in his later literary works, including *Old Tales Retold* (Gushi xinbian) and the more autobiographical *Dawn Flowers Plucked at Dusk* (Zhaohua xishi). One piece is not a prose poem at all but a poem in verse that parodies both the classical love poetry of Zhang Heng (Han dynasty) and the ribald, satiric verse of Zhang Dayou. "The Passerby" is a dramatic sketch featuring three characters. The complexities of hybridity are not simply confined to the shifting polarity between poetry and prose.

60. Eikhenbaum, *Literatura*, 125–26.

61. Shklovsky, *O teorii prozy*, 13.

62. A recent monograph (*A Common Strangeness*) seeks to employ ideas about Formalist estrangement in the discussion of contemporary Chinese, Russian, and American poetry. Jacob Edmond asks how the disorienting processes of globalization leave their considerable imprint in avant-garde poetic meditation on strangeness in these three countries. His book is an admirable demonstration of the enduring relevance of what might seem to be outdated questions.

CHAPTER 3: REALISM'S HYSTERICAL BODIES

1. The abridged version was published by Kaiming Shudian. Mao Dun's preface was written in 1934. I consulted a Hong Kong reprint from the 1960s. See Cao Xueqin, *Hong lou meng jie ben*. I thank David Rolston for pointing me to this volume in spite of my initial hesitation.
2. Mao Dun, "Dao yan," 1.
3. Ibid., 4.
4. Ibid., 5.
5. Ibid., 4.
6. Ibid., 6.
7. Ibid., 7.
8. Jing Tsu discusses this issue briefly, mostly in order to discuss Lu Xun's critique of this issue in his essay "Ting shuo meng." See Tsu, *Failure*, 212–15.
9. "Xinnian de mengxiang," 79.
10. Ibid., 81.
11. Ibid., 4.
12. Ibid., 7.
13. Ibid., 30.
14. Ibid., 73.
15. Cao Wansheng, *Mao Dun yishu meixue*, 46.
16. White, *The Content of the Form*, 157.
17. David Wang, *Fictional Realism*, 101.
18. David Wang, in his recounting of Mao Dun's struggles with Communist leadership and the Sun Society, as well as his torturous relationships with his wife, Kong Dezhi, and mistress Qin Dejun, points to more biographical reasons for Mao Dun's pain. See David Wang, *The Monster That Is History*, 99–106.
19. White, *The Content of the Form*, 157.
20. Fredric Jameson has argued that a proper "social hermeneutic" will mediate between both the figure of the body and that of the social community. See Jameson, *The Political Unconscious*, 74.
21. Mao Dun, *Wo zouguo de daolu*, 1:396.
22. Ibid.
23. Mao Dun, *Mao Dun xuanji*, 3:8.
24. Ibid., 3:9.
25. Ibid., 3:11.
26. Ibid., 3:13.
27. Mao Dun, *Mao Dun quanji*, 1:37.

28. Anderson, *The Limits of Realism*, 131.

29. Ibid., 11.

30. Mao Dun, *Mao Dun quanji*, 1:10.

31. Ibid., 1:99.

32. Žižek, *The Sublime Object of Ideology*, 48.

33. J. Hillis Miller tries to unravel the concept of the "narrative line" as a "catachresis," a fundamental misnomer of what actually occurs. See Miller, *Ariadne's Thread*, 21.

34. Mao Dun, *Mao Dun quanji*, 1:47.

35. Ibid., 1:48.

36. Ibid., 1:47.

37. Ibid., 1:49.

38. Yu-shih Chen, in her monograph on Mao Dun, has a far more negative evaluation of the author's narrative skills: "I have never felt that any one of his novels is particularly well-written. Quite the contrary, I have always felt that his novels and stories, especially the early ones, do not hang together well: there are too many desultory episodes in them, too much unexplained violence, and too many eccentric characters encountering mystifying fates." See Yu-shih Chen, *Realism and Allegory in the Early Fiction of Mao Tun*, 3.

39. Anderson, *The Limits of Realism*, 134.

40. Mao Dun, *Mao Dun quanji*, 1:93.

41. Ibid., 1:92.

42. Ibid., 1:96.

43. Ibid., 1:98–99.

44. Anderson, *The Limits of Realism*, 135.

45. Chow, *Woman and Chinese Modernity*, 104–5.

46. Ibid., 107.

47. Feng, *The New Woman in Early Twentieth-Century Chinese Fiction*, 105.

48. This queer reading of narrative and authorial hysteria is inspired by Daniel Boyarin's fantastic essay about Freud's own homosexual desire and hysteria. See Boyarin, *Unheroic Conduct*, 205–10.

49. David Hull has produced a full translation of this second novella. See Mao Dun, *Waverings*.

50. Mao Dun, *Mao Dun quanji*, 1:258.

51. Hsu Meng-hsiung and A. C. Barnes have produced a full English translation. See Mao Dun, *Midnight*.

52. Mao Dun, *Wo zouguo de daolu*, 1:488.

53. Cao Wansheng, *Mao Dun yishu meixue*, 104.

54. Quoted in Mao Dun, *Wo zouguo de daolu*, 1:509.

55. Ibid., 1:506–7.

56. Ibid., 1:489.

57. Vernon, *Money and Fiction*, 18–19.

58. Mao Dun, *Mao Dun quanji*, 3:147.

59. Ibid., 3:157.

60. In the scene with Axuan, Fan Bowen questions Wu Sunfu's desire to stay in the silk trade as a form of national development, pointing out that

garments made from Chinese silk, but woven outside and then sold on Chinese soil, cannot be considered a wholly Chinese product. See ibid., 3:149.

61. Ibid., 3:88.

62. Ibid.

63. Ibid., 3:89.

64. Ibid.

65. "Brother" and "sister" are common terms of affection among friends and unwed lovers.

66. Mao Dun, *Mao Dun quanji*, 3: 92.

67. This character, Xu Manli, dances on tables to the delight of her industrialist admirers and patrons. David Wang argues that Mao Dun's salacious treatment of this modern courtesan betrayed the author's hidden misogyny: "[Mao Dun's] feminine style, at its best, is but a costume drama. Take away his profeminist mask, and he shows a misogynist face." See David Wang, *Fictional Realism*, 89.

68. I am indebted to the translation of this title used by Catherine Bell. She provides a discussion of the popularity of this text in China. See Bell, "A Precious Raft to Save the World."

69. Mao Dun, *Mao Dun quanji*, 3:515–16.

70. Tang Xianzu, *Peony Pavilion*, ix. For the original, see Tang Xianzu, *Mudan ting*, "Zuozhe tici" (author's preface).

71. For more on externalized belief, see Žižek, *The Sublime Object of Ideology*, 33–35.

72. Mao Dun, *Mao Dun quanji*, 3:516.

73. Ibid., 3:527.

74. Ibid., 3:523.

75. Ibid., 3:540.

76. Ibid., 3:506.

77. Ibid., 3:507.

78. Ibid., 3:541.

79. Yeh, *Shanghai Splendor*, 79.

80. Mao Dun, *Mao Dun quanji*, 3:478–79.

81. Ibid., 3:480.

82. Ibid., 3:481.

83. Anderson, *The Limits of Realism*, 150.

84. Ibid., 147.

85. David Harvey deploys the concept of "spatial fix" to explain how capitalism manages crises by displacing them to peripheral spaces. See Harvey, *Limits to Capital*, 439–42. Mao Dun's imputation of hysteria to his female characters seems to function as a kind of narrative "spatial fix."

CHAPTER 4: SLEEPLESS NIGHTS IN FAST SOCIALISM

1. I thank Dai Jinhua for pointing this poem out during a talk at Harvard University in 2012.

2. Hu Feng, "Shijian kaishi le!"

3. Wang Ruoshui, "Mengxiang yu xianshi."

4. Ibid.

5. In the 1980s Wang Ruoshui would become one of the leading Marxist humanist dissidents who criticized the regime, and he was forced from his post as deputy editor of the paper in 1983, although he was later reinstated in a position of little consequence. See Kelly, "The Emergence of Humanism," 159; Kelly, "Editor's Introduction," 3. His unabashed idealism in the promise of the socialist state, as expressed in the article discussed above, perhaps precipitated his later criticism of the regime's abuses. He died in 2002 in the United States where his wife was pursuing a fellowship at Harvard University.

6. Paperno, *Chernyshevsky and the Age of Realism*, 4.

7. For more detailed discussion about the radical intelligentsia of the 1860s and how they distinguished themselves from their more romantic, moderate predecessors, see Paperno, *Chernyshevksy and the Age of Realism*, 4–12; and Katz and Wagner, introduction, 2–7.

8. Chernyshevsky, "The Aesthetic Relation of Art to Reality," 287.

9. Ibid., 317.

10. Ibid.

11. Ibid., 318.

12. Ibid., 287.

13. Wang Ruoshui, "Mengxiang yu xianshi."

14. Ibid.

15. Ibid.

16. Writing about the Stalinist experience, Evgeny Dobrenko notes that the new "reality" as created by Socialist Realism soon overtook the place of dreaming: "By painting 'dreaming' into the picture of 'realism,' the Socialist Realist aesthetic removed the 'romantic' gap between them . . . up to the point that it seemed that reality was more beautiful than a dream." See Dobrenko, *The Political Economy of Socialist Realism*, 63.

17. Ming Li, "Psychology in China," 281; Higgins and Zheng, "An Introduction to Chinese Psychology," 230. Pavlov's influence was dominant on the Chinese psychological scene from Liberation through the 1950s. A Chinese edition of his complete works was published in 1958. Following the political estrangement between the Soviet Union and China at the end of the 1950s, Pavlov's influence began to wane. See L. B. Brown, *Psychology in Contemporary China*, 34.

18. Ming Li, "Psychology in China," 280.

19. Despite the opprobrium Freud earns in the socialist period, his name and various Freudian terms nevertheless appear in the *Lexicon of Psychology* (Xinlixue mingci) produced by the Chinese Academy of Sciences in 1954. This work was part of a whole series of "Vocabularies" across the sciences meant to produce a common Chinese nomenclature for English technical terms, with Guo Moruo serving as general editor. Terms such as "Freudianism," "dream," "hysteria," "repression," and "unconscious" appear, but more specialized terms, like "primary process" and "secondary process," do not. In the Soviet context, attacks on Freudianism in the early 1930s, culminated in its "demise" in 1936. See Halfin, *Terror in My Soul*, 236, 241.

20. "Sulian baokan lunwen zhaiyao."

21. "Ren weishenme yao zuomeng?"

22. Fu Lianzhang, "Shuo meng."

23. Wendy Larson has provided an account of how spirit differs from the unconscious. See Larson, *From Ah-Q to Lei Feng*, 91–94.

24. Simon Williams argues that contemporary society has entered a period of what he terms "fast capitalism" marked by a "compression of time and quickening pace of everyday life" and "erosion of boundaries" between public and private lives. See Williams, *The Politics of Sleep*, 3.

25. Bakhtin, *The Dialogic Imagination*, 84–85.

26. In his posthumously published diary, communist icon Lei Feng (1940–1962) records several dreams. All of them feature visions of Mao Zedong. See Lei Feng, *Lei Feng riji*, 5, 29, 53.

27. When Vladimir Lenin wrote of cogs and screws fourteen years before the Bolshevik Revolution he was referring to party literature, not aesthetic literature. See Eagleton, *Marxism and Literary Criticism*, 40–41.

28. Mao Zedong, "Talks at the Yan'an Forum on Literature and Art," 470.

29. Clark, *The Soviet Novel*, 37.

30. Lan Yang, "'Socialist Realism' versus 'Revolutionary Realism Plus Revolutionary Romanticism,'" 96.

31. Wang Wenshi, *Fengxue zhi ye*, 250.

32. Yomi Braester discusses the semiotics of the "lantern and Mao" in his chapter on the revolutionary play *Red Lantern* (Hong deng ji). The trope of the lantern does not symbolize illumination and transparent communication "but rather a structure that upholds the Party's arbitrary interpretation of all signs." See Braester, *Witness Against History*, 127.

33. Qing Bo, "Denglong ji," 96.

34. Nighttime lighting, once a symbol of utopian modernity and illumination in nineteenth-century Europe, degenerated into an ominous symbol of totalitarian control in the twentieth century: "The Utopian dream of nights lit up as bright as day was transformed into the nightmare of a light from which there was no escape." See Schivelbusch, *Disenchanted Night*, 134.

35. "Dulesi de meng."

36. A day after the *People's Daily* published their denunciation of Dulles, the *Los Angeles Times* reiterated China's position by quoting the *People's Daily* article. See "Red China Hits Dulles' Dream."

37. Sha, "Dulesi de mengyi."

38. The formula of "I know very well, but all the same" has been elucidated the most by Octave Mannoni. See Mannoni, *Clefs pour L'imaginaire*, 9–14. See also Žižek, *The Sublime Object of Ideology*, 23–33.

39. Fan Yanqiao was a prodigious writer of popular fiction, literary critic, and overall polymath. In the 1920s and 1930s he was a leading writer of "Saturday School" fiction. In 1927, he published a history of Chinese fiction. He perished in the Cultural Revolution.

40. Fan Yanqiao, "Deng," 76.

41. Ibid., 77.

42. Ibid.
43. Ibid.
44. An English translation of Wang Wenshi's stories (but excluding "Summer Night") was produced by Foreign Languages Press. See Wang Wenshi, *Night of the Snowstorm.*
45. Wang Wenshi, *Fengxue zhi ye*, 6.
46. Ibid., 9.
47. Ibid., 7.
48. Ibid., 11.
49. Ibid., 12.
50. Ibid., 13.
51. An English translation, based on the *Renmin wenxue* version of the story, is available. See Li Zhun, "A Brief Biography of Li Shuangshuang."
52. For an insightful analysis of the genesis and narrative of Li Shuangshuang, see King, *Milestones on a Golden Road*, 71–92.
53. Li Zhun, "Li Shuangshuang xiao zhuan," 341.
54. Ibid., 332.
55. Wang Wenshi, "Xia ye," 16–17.
56. Ibid.
57. Freud, "Fetishism," 205–6.
58. Nan Ying has translated this novel into English. See Yang Mo, *The Song of Youth.*
59. As Cyril Birch, just five years after *The Song of Youth*'s publication, notes, "The tendency . . . to go back to the 1930s for material may well represent a means of escape into a 'margin of creativity.'" He goes on to describe the more nuanced, layered descriptions of protagonists in the novel: "The Communists . . . are depicted in heroic terms, but in shadow, as figures mysterious and brooding, almost one would say as Byronic heroes." Birch, "The Particle of Art," 8.
60. Yue Meng, "Female Images and National Myth," 127.
61. Yang Mo, *Qingchun zhi ge*, 162.
62. Ibid.
63. This former province, known in Standard Chinese as Rehe, was invaded and occupied by Japan in 1933. After the defeat of the Japanese, Jehol was governed successively by the Nationalists and Communists. In 1955, the province was dissolved and divided among Hebei, Liaoning, and the Inner Mongolia Autonomous Region.
64. Yang Mo, *Qingchun zhi ge*, 30.
65. Lingzhen Wang, *Personal Matters*, 137.
66. Yang Mo, *Qingchun zhi ge*, 37.
67. Freud, "Civilization and Its Discontents," 64.
68. Ibid., 65.
69. Ibid., 72.
70. Ibid., 67.
71. Yang Mo, *Qingchun zhi ge*, 362–63.
72. Lingzhen Wang, *Personal Matters*, 136.
73. Yang Mo, *Qingchun zhi ge*, 383.

74. See Lingzhen Wang, *Personal Matters*, 125–39. Moreover, the novel references Maxim Gorky's novel *Mother* a number of times.

75. Yang Mo, *Qingchun zhi ge*, 229.

76. Clark, *The Soviet Novel*, 15.

77. Yang Mo, *Qingchun zhi ge*, 612.

78. Lingzhen Wang argues that there is no climax, whether emotional or libidinal. Instead, the heroine simply collapses in exhaustion in a form of "self-sacrifice." See Lingzhen Wang, *Personal Matters*, 134. But is not the striving for exhaustion, even oblivion, the very enactment of *jouissance*, the collapse of the self in its rush to be embraced wholly, completely, by the other?

79. Button, "Aesthetics, Dialectics and Desire," 198–99.

80. However, imprisonment, including torture, is seen positively by the characters as a form of revolutionary training. As Daojing tells her younger cellmate, "We're not in a prison, we're in the University of Marxism-Leninism." Yang Mo, *Qingchun zhi ge*, 391.

81. As Freud himself notes: "[The infant] must be very strongly impressed by the fact that some sources of excitation . . . can provide him with sensations at any moment, whereas other sources evade him from time to time—among them what he desires most of all, his mother's breast—and only reappear as a result of his screaming for help." Freud, "Civilization and Its Discontents," 67.

82. Yang Mo, *Qingchun zhi ge*, 397.

83. Ibid., 615.

84. Yang Mo, *Zibai*, 243.

85. Ibid., 256–57.

86. "Double-voicing" derives from Mikhail Bakhtin's discussion of "double-voiced discourse" in Dostoevsky's fiction. Bakhtin argued that there is a special class of discursive utterance that is not just directed to the addressee but also directed to another interlocutor outside the immediate referential context. Bakhtin, *Problems of Dostoevsky's Poetics*, 185–87.

87. Yang Mo, *The Song of Youth*, author's preface.

CHAPTER 5: DREAM FUGUE

1. Zhou, "Xiangjiang yi ye," 27.

2. A search for the word "hysteria" in the online archive of the *People's Daily* dating from 1949 uncovered 1,230 instances of the term. "Hysteria" was often brandished against domestic and foreign enemies, including Soviet Revisionists, Vietnam, capitalist roaders, and both the Gang of Four and its detractors. At least twelve articles from the late 1970s described Jiang Qing as "hysterical." A narrower search for the phrase "hysterical fit" (*xiesidili dafazuo*) culled 58 entries, and the vast majority of them, 39, dated from the first four years of the Cultural Revolution. It is clear from this rudimentary search that those who derided Jiang Qing as "hysterical" were playing off what had become a familiar Cultural Revolution trope.

3. Ban Wang, *Illuminations from the Past*, 107.

4. Andreas, *Rise of the Red Engineers*, 11.

5. Ibid.

6. Ibid., 213–14. Yiching Wu's recent monograph, *The Cultural Revolution at the Margins*, admirably portrays the debates about socialism among those who took active part in the movement.

7. Mobo Gao points to the difficulty of figuring out who are the Chinese and who speaks for the Chinese, especially when it comes to characterizations of the Cultural Revolution as "ten years of calamity" See Gao, *The Battle for China's Past*, 1, 13–17.

8. Xiaomei Chen, "Growing Up with Posters," 103.

9. This story and Zhou Libo's "Night on Xiang River" were among the awardees of the nationwide Outstanding Short Story Prize for 1978.

10. David Harvey's notion of "relational space" is helpful in elucidating the porous form of space, at once physical and symbolic, that I am outlining. Relational space, for Harvey, is an always provisional and shifting space that emerges from the myriad intersections of history, politics, and culture, and is shaped by people's different yearnings, experiences, and memories. See Harvey, *Cosmopolitanism and the Geographies of Freedom*, 136–38.

11. Terada, *Feeling in Theory*, 11.

12. Ibid., 49.

13. Jing Wang, *High Culture Fever*, 35.

14. This term is borrowed from Rei Terada and will be elaborated upon later.

15. Richard King has noted how literary production of the immediate post-Mao era is "awash in tears of grief, anger, and self-pity." See King, *Milestones on a Golden Road*, 165.

16. Terrill, *Madame Mao*, 372–73.

17. He, *Dictionary of the Political Thought of the People's Republic of China*, 298; Terrill, *Madame Mao*, 219–20.

18. Terrill, *Madame Mao*, 219.

19. Liu Mengxi, "Sixia Jiang Qing 'Ban ge hongxuejia' de huapi," 86.

20. Ibid.

21. As Sara Ahmed has pointed out, "'figures of speech' are crucial to the emotionality of texts." See Ahmed, *The Cultural Politics of Emotion*, 12.

22. Quoted in Liu Mengxi, "Sixia Jiang Qing 'Ban ge hongxuejia' de huapi," 87.

23. Ibid.

24. Cao Xueqin, *The Story of the Stone*, 1:143.

25. Liu Mengxi, "Sixia Jiang Qing 'Ban ge hongxuejia' de huapi," 87.

26. Shiyan, "Fensui Jiang Qing de huangdi meng."

27. Ibid.

28. As Yiching Wu writes, "the concepts 'proletarian' and 'bourgeois' became hopelessly twisted terms used (and misused) to signify political loyalty, ideological correctness, and moral purity." See Yiching Wu, *Cultural Revolution at the Margins*, 235.

29. This was not the last time that the press spoke about Jiang Qing's dalliance with *Dream*. Through 1977 there was a whole slate of articles, in smaller organs, referring to Jiang Qing's "Red" obsession.

30. Wang Hui, *The End of the Revolution*, 5.

31. Zong Pu offers an account, written in 1989, of witnessing firsthand the struggle sessions involving eminent scholars, including He Qifang and Yu Pingbo. In turn, she herself was persecuted for being Feng Youlan's daughter. See Zong, "Yi jiu liu liu nian xia qiu zhi jiao de mou yi tian," 101–7.

32. Geremie Barmé has produced an excellent translation of this story. See Zong, "Red Beans."

33. Zong Pu, "Hong dou," 16. I thank former student Allison Tse for helping me better understand Qi Hong's personality.

34. Ibid., 23.

35. Ibid., 15.

36. Ibid., 19.

37. Luke 22:44.

38. Zong Pu, "Hong dou," 15.

39. Ibid., 15–16.

40. Ibid., 17.

41. Ibid., 16.

42. Jianmei Liu, *Revolution Plus Love*, 191.

43. Zong Pu, "Hong dou," 17.

44. Ibid., 20.

45. Ibid., 14.

46. Terada, *Feeling in Theory*, 13.

47. Aimée Lykes has translated this story as "A Dream on Strings." See Zong Pu, "A Dream on Strings."

48. Zong Pu, "Xianshang de meng," 33.

49. Berlant, *The Female Complaint*, viii.

50. Moreover, we should not overlook the strong influence of Hollywood-style melodrama even in post-1949 Chinese film. *Woman Basketball Player No. 5* (Nülan wu hao, dir. Xie Jin, 1957) is notable for its sympathetic portrayal of women's private lives and even private space in the midst of patriotic politics. Joan Judge notes a flourishing print culture dating from the early Republic that focused on women's themes but was often derided as trivial by New Culture Movement ideologues. See Judge, *Republican Lens*, 4–5. Rey Chow has discussed the various historical and contemporary debates over Mandarin Duck and Butterfly literature. See Chow, *Woman and Chinese Modernity*, 34–83.

51. As Jianmei Liu notes, "Red Beans" was criticized for "the writer's nostalgia for the bourgeois love relationship." See Jianmei Liu, *Revolution Plus Love*, 189.

52. Flatley, *Affective Mapping*, 4.

53. Zong, "Xianshang de meng," 31–32.

54. Shklovsky, *O teorii prozy*, 13.

55. Zong, "Xianshang de meng," 38.

56. Ibid., 43.

57. Ibid., 44.

58. Interestingly enough, the last line about dreams does not appear in Zong Pu's collected works from 1996, thus suggesting a permanent deferral

of people's dreams in an era of neoliberal capitalism (it does appear in the 1987 edition). Nor do the references to Chairman Mao and Premier Zhou as having inscribed the monument appear in later versions.

59. "Kant implies that when emotion drains away from a noble mind, this very circumstance excites emotion in another. . . . Under the generally economic law of emotive thermodynamics, the total amount of feeling is not diminished by the affectlessness of a noble mind." Terada, *Feeling in Theory*, 84.

60. Xiaomei Chen's work on post-Mao theater echoes the need to critically reassess aesthetic production after the Cultural Revolution in more sympathetic terms. She argues that the early years of the post-Mao era was a watershed moment in cultural production, reflecting a "naïve but singularly sincere surge of democracy. . . . All these developments required extraordinary daring from members of literary and artistic circles." See Xiaomei Chen, *Acting the Right Part*, 24.

CONCLUSION

1. Xi, *Governance of China*, 41; Xi, *Tan zhiguo lizheng*, 39.

2. Xi, *Governance of China*, 38; Xi, *Tan zhiguo lizheng*, 36

3. Xi, *Tan zhiguo lizheng*, 45. The English translation differs from the original, so I have provided my own.

4. Xi, *The Governance of China*, 69; Xi, *Tan zhiguo lizheng*, 63.

5. Recent commentators on the Chinese Dream have referred to the 1933 *Eastern Miscellany* issue. See Ren Zhongping, "Zhujiu minzu fuxing de 'Zhongguo meng.'"

6. "Rongzi pingcang quan jilu." I thank Luke Habberstad for bringing this to my attention.

7. News outlets reported that soon-to-be graduates from Tsinghua University's School of Economics and Management were instructed to chant the slogan "Revive A Shares! Benefit the People!" during their commencement ceremony. After much online criticism, the slogan was abandoned. Tsinghua's president, Qiu Yong, did instruct all graduates to "dream big and take responsibility." See Cecilia Li, "Tsinghua Business Graduates Scrap Market-Oriented Slogan."

8. Lu Xun, *The Real Story of Ah-Q and Other Tales of China*, 15.

9. Buck-Morss, *Dreamworld and Catastrophe*, ix.

10. Birch, "Particle of Art," 4.

REFERENCES

Ahmed, Sara. *The Cultural Politics of Emotion*. New York: Routledge, 2004.

Anderson, Marston. *The Limits of Realism: Chinese Fiction in the Revolutionary Period*. Berkeley: University of California Press, 1990.

Andreas, Joel. *Rise of the Red Engineers: The Cultural Revolution and the Origins of China's New Class*. Stanford, CA: Stanford University Press, 2009.

Ba Jin (Pa Chin). *Family*. Trans. Sidney Shapiro. Long Grove, IL: Waveland, 1989.

Bakhtin, Mikhail. *The Dialogic Imagination: Four Essays*. Trans. Caryl Emerson and Michael Holquist. Austin: University of Texas Press, 1981.

———. *Problems of Dostoevsky's Poetics*. Trans. Caryl Emerson. Minneapolis: University of Minnesota Press, 1984.

Belinsky, Vissarion. *Sobranie sochinenii v deviati tomakh* (Collected Works in Nine Volumes). Moscow: Khudozhestvennaia Literatura (Aesthetic Literature), 1976–82.

———. "Thoughts and Notes on Russian Literature." In *Belinsky, Chernyshevsky, and Dobrulyubov: Selected Criticism*, ed. Ralph E. Matlaw, 3–32. New York: Dutton, 1962.

Bell, Catherine. "'A Precious Raft to Save the World': The Interaction of Scriptural Traditions and Printing in a Chinese Morality Book." *Late Imperial China* 17, no. 1 (1996): 158–200.

Benjamin, Walter. *The Arcades Project*. Trans. Howard Eiland and Kevin McLaughlin. Cambridge, MA: Belknap, 1999.

Berlant, Lauren. *The Female Complaint: The Unfinished Business of Sentimentality in American Culture*. Durham, NC: Duke University Press, 2008.

Birch, Cyril. "The Particle of Art." In *Chinese Communist Literature*, ed. Cyril Birch, 3–14. New York: Praeger, 1963.

Boyarin, Daniel. *Unheroic Conduct: The Rise of Heterosexuality and the*

Invention of the Jewish Man. Berkeley: University of California Press, 1997.

Braester, Yomi. *Witness Against History: Literature, Film, and Public Discourse in Twentieth-Century China*. Stanford, CA: Stanford University Press, 2003.

Brown, Bill. "Thing Theory." *Critical Inquiry* 28, no. 1 (2001): 1–22.

Brown, Carolyn T. "Lu Xun's Interpretation of Dreams." In *Psycho-Sinology: The Universe of Dreams in Chinese Culture*, ed. Carolyn T. Brown, 67–77. Washington, DC: Woodrow Wilson International Center for Scholars, 1988.

Brown, L. B. *Psychology in Contemporary China*. Oxford: Pergamon Press, 1981.

Buck-Morss, Susan. *Dreamworld and Catastrophe: The Passing of Mass Utopia in East and West*. Cambridge, MA: MIT Press, 2000.

Button, Peter. "Aesthetics, Dialectics and Desire in Yang Mo's *Song of Youth*." *positions* 14, no. 1 (2006): 193–217.

———. *Configurations of the Real in Chinese Literary and Aesthetic Modernity*. Leiden: Brill, 2009.

Cao Wansheng. *Mao Dun yishu meixue* (Mao Dun's Aesthetics). Beijing: Zhongguo Shehui Kexueyuan Chubanshe (Chinese Academy of Social Sciences Press), 2004.

Cao Xueqin. *Hong lou meng* (Dream of the Red Chamber). 2 vols. Beijing: Renmin Wenxue Chubanshe (People's Literature Press), 2003.

———. *Hong lou meng jie ben* (Abridged Edition of Dream of the Red Chamber). Ed. Mao Dun. Hong Kong: Xianggang Xuelin Shudian (Hong Kong Scholars Bookstore), 196[?].

———. *The Story of the Stone*. Trans. David Hawkes and John Minford. 5 vols. London: Penguin, 1973–86.

Charter 08. May 21, 2009. http://www.inmediahk.net/node/1001730.

Chen Duxiu. "On Literary Revolution." Trans. Timothy Wong. In *Modern Chinese Literary Thought: Writings on Literature*, ed. Kirk A. Denton, 140–45. Stanford, CA: Stanford University Press, 1996.

Chen, Xiaomei. *Acting the Right Part: Political Theater and Popular Drama in Contemporary China*. Honolulu: University of Hawaii Press, 2002.

———. "Growing Up with Posters in the Maoist Era." In *Picturing Power in the People's Republic of China: Posters of the Cultural Revolution*, ed. Harriet Evans and Stephanie Donald, 101–22. Lanham, MD: Rowman and Littlefield, 1999.

Chen, Yu-shih. *Realism and Allegory in the Early Fiction of Mao Tun*. Bloomington: Indiana University Press, 1986.

Chernyshevsky, Nikolai. "The Aesthetic Relation of Art to Reality." In *Selected Philosophical Essays*, 281–381. Moscow: Foreign Language Publishing House, 1953.

———. "Esteticheskoe otnoshenie iskusstva k deistvitel'nosti" (The Aesthetic Relation of Art to Reality). In *Sochineniia v dvukh tomakh* (Works in Two Volumes), 1:71–173. Moscow: Izd-vo "Mysl" (Thought Press), 1986–87.

———. *Shenghuo yu meixue* (Life and Aesthetics). Trans. Zhou Yang. Beiping: Xin Zhongguo Shuju (New China Bookstore), 1948.

———. *What Is to Be Done?* Trans. Michael R. Katz. Ithaca, NY: Cornell University Press, 1989.

Chow, Rey. *Woman and Chinese Modernity: The Politics of Reading Between East and West*. Minneapolis: University of Minnesota Press, 1991.

Clark, Katerina. *The Soviet Novel: History as Ritual*. Bloomington: Indiana University Press, 2000.

Confucius, and Edward Slingerland. *Analects: With Selections from Traditional Commentaries*. Indianapolis: Hackett, 2003.

Crary, Jonathan. *24/7: Late Capitalism and the Ends of Sleep*. London: Verso, 2014. Kindle Edition.

Culler, Jonathan. *Theory of the Lyric*. Cambridge, MA: Harvard University Press, 2015.

Dobrenko, Evgeny. *The Political Economy of Socialist Realism*. Trans. Jesse M. Savage. New Haven, CT: Yale University Press, 2007.

Du Yuanzai. "Meng" (Dream). In *Xinli zazhi xuancun* (Selections from the Journal of Psychoanalysis), ed. Zhang Yaoxiang, 366–82. Shanghai: Zhonghua Shuju (Zhonghua Bookstore), 1933.

"Dulesi de meng" (Dulles' Dream). *Renmin ribao* (People's Daily), July 3, 1957, 7.

Eagleton, Terry. *The Event of Literature*. New Haven, CT: Yale University Press, 2012.

———. *Ideology: An Introduction*. London: Verso, 1991.

———. *Marxism and Literary Criticism*. Berkeley: University of California Press, 1976.

Edmond, Jacob. *A Common Strangeness: Contemporary Poetry, Cross-Cultural Encounter, Comparative Literature*. New York: Fordham University Press, 2012.

Eikhenbaum, Boris. *Literatura: Teoria, Kritika, Polemika* (Literature: Theory, Critique, Polemic). Leningrad: Priboi, 1927.

Ekirch, A. Roger. *At Day's Close: Night in Times Past*. New York: Norton, 2005.

Fan, Fa-ti. *British Nationalists in Qing China: Science, Empire, and Cultural Encounter.* Cambridge, MA: Harvard University Press, 2004.

Fan Yanqiao. "Deng" (Lamp). *Renmin wenxue* (People's Literature) 151 (1962): 76–77.

Feng, Jin. *The New Woman in Early Twentieth-Century Chinese Fiction.* West Lafayette, IN: Purdue University Press, 2004.

Feuerwerker, Yi-Tsi Mei. *Ideology, Power, Text: Self-representation and the Peasant "Other" in Modern Chinese Literature.* Stanford, CA: Stanford University Press, 1998.

Flatley, Jonathan. *Affective Mapping: Melancholia and the Politics of Modernism.* Cambridge, MA: Harvard University Press, 2008.

Foucault, Michel. "Dream, Imagination, and Existence." Trans. Forrest Williams. In *Dream and Existence*, by Michel Foucault and Ludwig Binswanger, ed. Keith Hoeller, 31–78. Atlantic Highlands, NJ: Humanities Press, 1985.

Fowler, Alastair. *Kinds of Literature: An Introduction to the Theory of Genres and Modes.* Cambridge, MA: Harvard University Press, 1982.

Freud, Sigmund. "Civilization and Its Discontents." In *The Standard Edition of the Complete Psychological Works of Sigmund Freud*, trans. James Strachey, 21:57–145. London: Hogarth, 1953–74.

———. "Fetishism." In *Sexuality and the Psychology of Love*, ed. Philip Rieff, 204–9. New York: Touchstone, 1997.

———. *The Interpretation of Dreams.* Trans. James Strachey. New York: Avon, 1965.

———. "A Note on the 'Mystic Writing-Pad.'" In *The Standard Edition of the Complete Psychological Works of Sigmund Freud*, trans. James Strachey, 19:225–32. London: Hogarth, 1953–74.

Fu Lianzhang. "Shuo meng" (On Dreams). *Renmin ribao* (People's Daily), December 13, 1959, 8.

Gao, Mobo. *The Battle for China's Past: Mao and the Cultural Revolution.* London: Pluto Press, 2008.

Gu, Ming Dong. "Lu Xun and Modernism/Postmodernism." *Modern Language Quarterly* 69, no. 1 (2008): 29–44.

Halfin, Igal. *Terror in My Soul: Communist Autobiographies on Trial.* Cambridge, MA: Harvard University Press, 2003.

Hamburger, Käte. *The Logic of Literature.* 2nd rev. ed. Trans. Marilynn J. Rose. Bloomington: Indiana University Press, 1973.

Harvey, David. *Cosmopolitanism and the Geographies of Freedom.* New York: Columbia University Press, 2009.

———. *Limits to Capital.* London: Verso, 2006.

He, Henry Yuhuai. *Dictionary of the Political Thought of the People's Republic of China*. Armonk, NY: M. E. Sharpe, 2001.

Higgins, Louise T., and Mo Zheng. "An Introduction to Chinese Psychology: Its Historical Roots Until the Present Day." *Journal of Psychology* 136, no. 2 (2002): 225–39.

Hu Feng. "Shijian kaishi le!" (Time Has Begun) *Renmin ribao* (People's Daily), November 20, 1949, 7.

Huters, Theodore. "Mirages of Representation: May Fourth and the Anxiety of the Real." In *Working Papers in Asian/Pacific Studies 91–01 (Chinese Literature and the West: The Trauma of Realism; The Challenge of the (Post)modern)*, ed. Arif Dirlik and Edward Fowler, 1–23. Durham, NC: Duke University Asia/Pacific Studies Institute, 1991.

Jakobson, Roman. "O khudozhestvennom realizme" (On Realism in Art). In *Raboty po poetike* (Works on Poetics), ed. M. Gasparov, 387–93. Moscow: Progress, 1987.

———. "On Realism in Art." In *Readings in Russian Poetics*, ed. Ladislav Matejka and Krystyna Pomorska, 38–46. Ann Arbor: Michigan Slavic Publications, 1978.

Jakobson, Roman, and Yurii Tynianov. "Problems in the Study of Language and Literature." Trans. H. Eagle. *Poetics Today* 2, no. 1 (1980): 29–31.

Jameson, Fredric. *The Political Unconscious: Narrative as a Socially Symbolic Act*. Ithaca, NY: Cornell University Press, 1981.

Jones, Andrew F. *Developmental Fairy Tales: Evolutionary Thinking and Modern Chinese Culture*. Cambridge, MA: Harvard University Press, 2011.

Judge, Joan. *Republican Lens: Gender, Visuality, and Experience in the Early Chinese Periodical Press*. Berkeley: University of California Press, 2015.

Kafalas, Philip A. *In Limpid Dream: Nostalgia and Zhang Dai's Reminiscences of the Ming*. Norwalk, CT: Eastbridge, 2007.

Kaldis, Nicholas. *The Chinese Prose Poem: A Study of Lu Xun's "Wild Grass" (Yecao)*. Amherst, NY: Cambria, 2014.

———. "The Prose Poem and Aesthetic Insight: Lu Xun's Yecao." PhD diss., Ohio State University, 1998.

———. "The Prose Poem as Aesthetic Cognition: Lu Xun's Yecao." *Journal of Modern Literature in Chinese* 3, no. 2 (2000): 43–82.

Katz, Michael R., and William G. Wagner. Introduction to *What Is to Be Done?* by Nikolai Chernyshevsky, trans. Michael R. Katz, 1–36. Ithaca, NY: Cornell University Press, 1989.

Kelly, David A. "Editor's Introduction." *Chinese Studies in Philosophy* 16, no. 3 (1985): 3–7.

———. "The Emergence of Humanism: Wang Ruoshui and the Critique of Socialist Alienation." In *China's Intellectuals and the State: In Search of a New Relationship*, ed. Merle Goldman with Timothy Cheek and Carol Lee Hamrin, 159–82. Cambridge, MA: Council on East Asian Studies, 1987.

King, Richard. *Milestones on a Golden Road: Writing for Chinese Socialism*. Vancouver: University of British Columbia Press, 2013.

Kliger, Ilya. *The Narrative Shape of Truth: Veridiction in Modern European Literature*. University Park: Pennsylvania State University Press, 2011.

Koslofsky, Craig. *Evening's Empire: A History of Night in Early Modern Europe*. Cambridge: Cambridge University Press, 2011.

Lam, Tong. *A Passion for Facts: Social Surveys and the Construction of the Chinese Nation-State, 1900–1949*. Berkeley: University of California Press, 2011.

Larson, Wendy. *From Ah-Q to Lei Feng: Freud and Revolutionary Spirit in 20th Century China*. Stanford, CA: Stanford University Press, 2009.

Lee, Leo. *Voices from the Iron House: A Study of Lu Xun*. Bloomington: Indiana University Press, 1987.

Lei Feng. *Lei Feng riji* (Diary of Lei Feng). Beijing: Jiefang Jun Wenyi Chubanshe (Liberation Army Literary Press), 1964.

Li, Cecilia. "Tsinghua Business Graduates Scrap Market-Oriented Slogan." *New York Times*, July 14, 2015. http://cn.nytimes.com/china/20150714/c14sino-tsinghua/en-us/.

Li, Ming. "Psychology in China: A Brief Historical Review." *Journal of Psychology* 128, no. 3 (1994): 281–87.

Li Rong. "Wuci de yuyan: Lun 'Yecao' de shenti yanshuo" (Wordless Language: The Discourse of the Body in Wild Grass). *Zhongguo xiandai wenxue yanjiu* (Modern Chinese Literature Research) 3 (2007): 201–21.

Li Zhun. "A Brief Biography of Li Shuangshuang." Trans. Johanna Hood and Robert Mackie with Richard King. In *Heroes of China's Great Leap Forward: Two Stories*, ed. Richard King, 15–61. Honolulu: University of Hawaii Press, 2010.

———. "Li Shuangshuang xiao zhuan" (The Story of Li Shuangshuang). In *Li Shuangshuang xiao zhuan* (The Story of Li Shuangshuang), 332–66. Beijing: Renmin Wenxue Chubanshe (People's Literature Press), 1977.

Liu E. *Lao Can youji* (The Travels of Lao Can). Beijing: Renmin Wenxue Chubanshe (People's Literature Press), 2001.

———. *The Travels of Lao Ts'an*. Trans. Harold Shadick. New York: Columbia University Press, 1990.

Liu, Jianmei. *Revolution Plus Love: Literary Histories, Women's Bodies, and Thematic Repetition in Twentieth-Century Fiction*. Honolulu: University of Hawaii Press, 2003.

Liu, Lydia. *Translingual Practice: Literature, National Culture, and Translated Modernity—China, 1900–1937*. Stanford, CA: Stanford University Press, 1995.

Liu Mengxi. "Sixia Jiang Qing 'Ban ge hongxuejia' de huapi" [Tearing down Jiang Qing's "Half a Red-ologist" Veil]. *Renmin wenxue* (People's Literature) September (1976): 86–87.

Lu Xun. *Lu Xun quanji* (Complete Works of Lu Xun). 18 vols. Beijing: Renmin Wenxue Chubanshe (People's Literature Press), 2005.

———. *The Real Story of Ah-Q and Other Tales of China: The Complete Fiction of Lu Xun*. Trans. Julia Lovell. London: Penguin, 2009.

———. *Wild Grass*. Trans. Yang Xianyi and Gladys Yang. Beijing: Foreign Languages Press, 1985.

Lukács, Georg. *The Historical Novel*. Trans. Hannah and Stanley Mitchell. London: Merlin, 1962.

Mannoni, Octave. *Clefs pour l'imaginaire, ou, L'autre scène* (Keys of the Imaginary, or, The Other Scene). Paris: Editions Seuil, 1969.

Mao Dun. "Dao yan" (Foreword). *Hong lou meng jie ben* (Abridged Dream of the Red Chamber), ed. Mao Dun, 1–7. Hong Kong: Xianggang Xuelin Shudian (Hong Kong Scholars Bookstore), 196[?].

———. *Mao Dun quanji* (Complete Works of Mao Dun). 40 vols. Beijing: Remin Wenxue Chubanshe (People's Literature Press), 1984.

———. *Mao Dun xuanji* (Selected Works of Mao Dun). 3 vols. Beijing: Renmin Wenxue Chubanshe (People's Literature Press), 1997.

———. *Midnight*. Trans. Hsu Meng-hsiung and A. C. Barnes. Peking: Foreign Languages Press, 1979.

———. *Waverings*. Trans. David Hull. Hong Kong: Chinese University of Hong Kong Press, 2014.

———. *Wo zouguo de daolu* (The Road I Have Traveled). 2 vols. Beijing: Renmin Wenxue Chubanshe (People's Literature Press), 1997.

Mao Zedong. "Talks at the Yan'an Forum on Literature and Art." In *Modern Chinese Literary Thought: Writings on Literature, 1893–1945*, ed. Kirk A. Denton, 458–84. Stanford, CA: Stanford University Press, 1996.

Marx, Karl. *Capital*. Vol. 1. Trans. Ben Fowkes. London: Penguin, 1990.

Meng, Yue. "Female Images and National Myth." In *Gender Politics in Modern China*, ed. Tani E. Barlow, 118–36. Durham, NC: Duke University Press, 1993.

Miller, J. Hillis. *Ariadne's Thread: Story Lines*. New Haven, CT: Yale University Press, 1992.

Monroe, Jonathan. *A Poverty of Objects: The Prose Poem and the Politics of Genre*. Ithaca, NY: Cornell University Press, 1987.

Ngai, Pun. “Opening a Minor Genre of Resistance in Reform China: Scream, Dream, and Transgression in a Workplace.” *positions* 8, no. 2 (2000): 531–55.

Ong, Roberto K. *The Interpretation of Dreams in Ancient China*. Bochum: Studienverlag Brockmeyer, 1985.

Paperno, Irina. *Chernyshevsky and the Age of Realism: A Study in the Semiotics of Behavior*. Stanford, CA: Stanford University Press, 1988.

———. *“Who, What Am I?”: Tolstoy Struggles to Narrate the Self*. Ithaca, NY: Cornell University Press, 2014.

Qing Bo. “Denglong ji” (The Lantern). *Renmin wenxue* (People’s Literature) 92 (1957): 95–96.

“Red China Hits Dulles’ Dream.” *Los Angeles Times*, June 4, 1957.

“Ren weishenme yao zuomeng?” (Why Do People Dream?). *Renmin ribao* (People’s Daily), February 21, 1949, 4.

Ren Zhongping. “Zhujiu minzu fuxing de ‘Zhongguo meng’” (Building up the Chinese Dream of Rejuvenating the Nation). *Renmin ribao* (People’s Daily), April 1, 2013, 1.

“Rongzi pingcang quan jilu” (Complete Record of Financial Close Positions). July 8, 2015. *Chuansong men*, http://chuansong.me/n/1522607.

Schivelbusch, Wolfgang. *Disenchanted Night: The Industrialization of Light in the Nineteenth Century*. Trans. Angela Davies. Berkeley: University of California Press, 1988.

Schwarcz, Vera. *The Chinese Enlightenment: Intellectuals and the Legacy of the May Fourth Movement of 1919*. Berkeley: University of California Press, 1986.

Sha Ou. “Dulesi de mengyi” (Dulles’s Dream Ravings). *Renmin wenxue* (People’s Literature) 112 (1959): 56.

Shiyan. “Fensui Jiang Qing de huangdi meng” (Smashing Jiang Qing’s Dream of Being an Emperor). *Renmin ribao* (People’s Daily), November 14, 1976, 5.

Shklovsky, Viktor. *O teorii prozy* (The Theory of Prose). Moscow: Federatsiia, 1929.

Shu Xincheng. *Meng* (Dream). Shanghai: Zhonghua Shuju (Zhonghua Bookstore), 1927.

———. *Wo he jiaoyu: Sanshi wu nian jiaoyu shenghuo shi* (1893–1928) (Education and Me: Thirty-Five Years in a Life of Education). Shanghai: Zhonghua Shuju (Zhonghua Bookstore), 1945.

Strassberg, Richard. Introduction to *Wandering Spirits: Chen Shiyuan’s*

Encyclopedia of Dreams, by Chen Shiyuan, trans. Richard Strassberg, 1–47. Berkeley: University of California Press, 2008.

"Sulian baokan lunwen zhaiyao" (Summary of Soviet Discussions in the Press). *Renmin ribao* (People's Daily), January 3, 1953, 3.

Summers-Bremner, Eluned. *Insomnia: A Cultural History.* London: Reaktion Books, 2008.

Sun Yushi. *Yecao yanjiu* (Research on Wild Grass). Beijing: Zhongguo Shehui Kexue Chubanshe (Chinese Academy of Social Sciences Press), 1982.

Tang Xianzu. *Mudan ting* (Peony Pavilion). Ed. Xu Shuofang and Yang Xiaomei. Beijing: Renmin Wenxue Chubanshe (People's Literature Press), 2005.

———. *Peony Pavilion.* Trans. Cyril Birch. Boston: Cheng and Tsui, 1999.

Tang, Xiaobing. "Lu Xun's 'Diary of a Madman' and a Chinese Modernism." *PMLA* 107, no. 5 (1992): 1222–34.

Teboul-Wang, Brigitte. Introduction to *Souvenirs rêvés de Tao'an* (Dream Reminiscences of Tao'an), by Zhang Dai, trans. Brigitte Teboul-Wang, 7–13. Paris: Gallimard, 1995.

Terada, Rei. *Feeling in Theory: Emotion After the "Death of the Subject."* Cambridge, MA: Harvard University Press, 2001.

Terrill, Ross. *Madame Mao, The White Boned Demon: A Biography of Madame Mao Zedong.* New York: Simon and Schuster, 1992.

Tiffany, Daniel. *Toy Medium: Materialism and Modern Lyric.* Berkeley: University of California Press, 2000.

Tolstoy, Lev. *Sebastopol Sketches.* Trans. David McDuff. Harmondsworth: Penguin, 1986.

Tsu, Jing. *Failure, Nationalism and Literature: The Making of Modern Chinese Identity, 1895–1937.* Stanford, CA: Stanford University Press, 2005.

Urban, Greg. "The 'I' of Discourse." In *Semiotics, Self, and Society*, ed. Benjamin Lee and Greg Urban, 27–51. Berlin: Mouton de Gruyter, 1989.

Vernon, John. *Money and Fiction: Literary Realism in the Nineteenth and Early Twentieth Centuries.* Ithaca, NY: Cornell University Press, 1984.

Wagner, Rudolf. "China 'Asleep' and 'Awakening': A Study in Conceptualizing Asymmetry and Coping with It." *Transcultural Studies* 1 (2011): 3–139.

Wahnich, Sophie. *In Defence of the Terror: Liberty or Death in the French Revolution.* Trans. David Fernbach. London: Verso, 2012.

Wang, Ban. *Illuminations from the Past: Trauma, Memory, and History in Modern China.* Stanford, CA: Stanford University Press, 2004.

———. *The Sublime Figure of History: Aesthetics and Politics in Twentieth-Century China.* Stanford, CA: Stanford University Press, 1997.

Wang, David. *Fictional Realism in 20th-Century China: Mao Dun, Lao She, Shen Congwen*. New York: Columbia University Press, 1992.

———. *The Monster That Is History: History, Violence and Fictional Writing in Twentieth-Century China*. Berkeley: University of California Press, 2004.

Wang Hui. *The End of the Revolution: China and the Limits of Modernity*. London: Verso, 2009.

———. "Scientific Worldview, Culture Debates, and the Reclassification of Knowledge in Twentieth-Century China." Trans. Hongmei Yu. *Boundary 2* 35, no. 2 (2008): 125–55.

Wang, Jing. *High Culture Fever: Politics, Aesthetics, and Ideology in Deng's China*. Berkeley: University of California Press, 1996.

Wang, Lingzhen. *Personal Matters: Women's Autobiographical Practice in Twentieth-Century China*. Stanford, CA: Stanford University Press, 2004.

Wang Ruoshui. "Mengxiang yu xianshi" (Dreams and Reality). *Renmin ribao* (People's Daily), January 6, 1953, 3.

Wang Wenshi. *Fengxue zhi ye* (Night of the Snowstorm). Beijing: Zhongguo Qingnian Chubanshe (China Youth Press), 1962.

———. *Night of the Snowstorm*. Beijing: Foreign Languages Press, 1961.

———. "Xia ye" (Summer Night). *Renmin wenxue* (People's Literature) 122 (1960): 13–23.

Wetzsteon, Ross. "Nabokov as Teacher." In *Nabokov: Criticism, Reminiscences, and Tributes*, ed. Alfred Appel Jr. and Charles Newman, 240–46. Evanston, IL: Northwestern University Press, 1970.

White, Hayden. *The Content of the Form: Narrative Discourse and Historical Representation*. Baltimore: Johns Hopkins University Press, 1987.

———. *Figural Realism: Studies in the Mimesis Effect*. Baltimore: Johns Hopkins University Press, 1999.

Williams, Simon. *The Politics of Sleep: Governing (Un)consciousness in the Late Modern Age*. New York: Palgrave Macmillan, 2011.

Wittgenstein, Ludwig. *The Philosophical Investigations: The German Text, with a Revised English Translation*. Trans. G. E. M. Anscombe. Oxford: Blackwell, 2001.

Wu Jianren. *Xin shitou ji* (The New Story of the Stone). Zhengzhou: Zhongzhou Guji Chubanshe (Zhongzhou Antiquities Press), 1986.

Wu, Yiching. *The Cultural Revolution at the Margins: Chinese Socialism in Crisis*. Cambridge, MA: Harvard University Press, 2014.

Xi Jinping. *The Governance of China*. Beijing: Foreign Languages Press, 2014.

———. *Tan zhiguo lizheng* (The Governance of China). Beijing: Waiwen Chubanshe (Foreign Languages Press), 2014.

Xinlixue mingci (A Lexicon of Psychology). Beijing: Zhongguo Kexueyuan Chubanshe (Chinese Academy of Sciences Press), 1954.

"Xinnian de mengxiang" (Dreams of the New Year). Special supplement of *Dongfang zazhi* (Eastern Miscellany) (January 1933): 1–83.

Yang, Lan. "'Socialist Realism' versus 'Revolutionary Realism Plus Revolutionary Romanticism.'" In *In the Party Spirit: Socialist Realism and Literary Practice in the Soviet Union, East Germany and China*, ed. Hilary Chung. Special issue of *Critical Studies* 6 (1996): 88–105.

Yang Mo. *Qingchun zhi ge* (The Song of Youth). Beijing: Beijing Shiyue Wenyi Chubanshe (Beijing October Literature Press), 1992.

———. *The Song of Youth*. Trans. Nan Ying. Beijing: Foreign Languages Press, 1978.

———. *Zibai: Wo de riji* (Confession: My Diary). Guangzhou: Huangcheng Chubanshe (Huangcheng Press), 1985.

Yeh, Wen-hsin. *Shanghai Splendor: Economic Sentiments and the Making of Modern China, 1843–1949*. Berkeley: University of California Press, 2007.

Zhang Dai. *Souvenirs rêvés de Tao'an* (Dream Reminiscences of Tao'an). Trans. Brigitte Teboul-Wang. Paris: Gallimard, 1995.

———. *Xihu mengxun; Tao'an mengyi* (Searching for West Lake in Dream; Dream Reminiscences of Tao'an). Ed. Xia Xianchun and Cheng Weirong. Shanghai: Shanghai Guji Chubanshe (Shanghai Antiquities Press), 2001.

Zhang, Jingyuan. *Psychoanalysis in China: Literary Transformations, 1919–1949*. Ithaca, NY: Cornell East Asia Series, 1992.

Zhang Yaoxiang. "Bianjizhe yan" (Editor's Note). In *Xinli zazhi xuancun* (Selected Articles of the Journal of Psychology), 1–3. Shanghai: Zhonghua Shuju (Zhonghua Bookstore), 1933.

Zhou Libo. "Xiangjiang yi ye" (Night on Xiang River). *Renmin wenxue* (People's Literature) 226 (1978): 22–33, 47.

Zhuangzi, and Burton Watson. *Zhuangzi: Basic Writings*. New York: Columbia University Press, 2003.

Žižek, Slavoj. Introduction to *On Practice and Contradiction*, by Mao Zedong, 1–28. London: Verso, 2007.

———. *The Sublime Object of Ideology*. London: Verso, 1989.

Zong Pu. "A Dream on Strings." Trans. Aimée Lykes. In *Perspectives in Contemporary Chinese Literature*, ed. Mason Y. H. Wang, 229–72. University Center, MI: Green River Press, 1983.

———. "Hong dou" (Red Beans). *Renmin wenxue* (People's Literature) 7 (1957): 14–25.

———. "Red Beans." Trans. Geremie Barmé. In *Fragrant Weeds—Chinese Stories Once Labeled as "Poisonous Weeds,"* ed. W. J. F. Jenner, 195–228. Hong Kong: Cheng and Tsui, 1983.

———. "Xianshang de meng" (A Dream for Strings). *Renmin wenxue* (People's Literature) 12 (1978): 29–44.

———. "Yi jiu liu liu nian xia qiu zhi jiao de mou yi tian" (A Certain Day Between Summer and Autumn of 1966). In *Zong Pu juan* (Writings of Zong Pu), 101–7. Beijing: Renmin Wenxue Chubanshe (People's Literature Press), 2000.

———. *Zong Pu daibiao zuo* (Selected Works of Zong Pu). Ed. Lang Baodong. Zhengzhou: Huanghe Wenyi Chubanshe (Huanghe Literature Press), 1987.

———. *Zong Pu wenji* (Collected Works of Zong Pu). Vol. 2. Beijing: Huayi Chubanshe: (Huayi Press), 1996.

INDEX

CPSIA information can be obtained
at www.ICGtesting.com
Printed in the USA
BVHW071934070920
587865BV00003B/17

9 780295 748115